For Sharon. And for Lauren and Abby.

Cake

SHANE CURRAN

with Tommy Conlon

PENGUIN
IRELAND

PENGUIN IRELAND

Published by the Penguin Group
Penguin Ireland, 25 St Stephen's Green, Dublin 2, Ireland (a division of Penguin Books Ltd)
Penguin Books Ltd, 80 Strand, London WC2R 0RL, England
Penguin Group (USA) Inc., 375 Hudson Street, New York, New York 10014, USA
Penguin Group (Canada), 90 Eglinton Avenue East, Suite 700, Toronto, Ontario, Canada M4P 2Y3
(a division of Pearson Penguin Canada Inc.)
Penguin Group (Australia), 707 Collins Street, Melbourne, Victoria 3008, Australia
(a division of Pearson Australia Group Pty Ltd)
Penguin Books India Pvt Ltd, 11 Community Centre, Panchsheel Park, New Delhi – 110 017, India
Penguin Group (NZ), 67 Apollo Drive, Rosedale, Auckland 0632, New Zealand
(a division of Pearson New Zealand Ltd)
Penguin Books (South Africa) (Pty) Ltd, Block D, Rosebank Office Park,
181 Jan Smuts Avenue, Parktown North, Gauteng 2193, South Africa

Penguin Books Ltd, Registered Offices: 80 Strand, London WC2R 0RL, England

www.penguin.com

First published 2014
001

Copyright © Shane Curran, 2014

The moral right of the author has been asserted

Set in 12/14.75 pt Bembo Book MT Std
Typeset by Jouve (UK), Milton Keynes
Printed in Great Britain by Clays Ltd, St Ives plc

A CIP catalogue record for this book is available from the British Library

ISBN: 978–1–844–88353–0

www.greenpenguin.co.uk

Penguin Books is committed to a sustainable
future for our business, our readers and our planet.
This book is made from Forest Stewardship
Council™ certified paper.

MIX
Paper from
responsible sources
FSC
www.fsc.org   FSC™ C018179

Contents

Prologue: The Dressing Room

A dressing room is a bit like a jail. And it's a bit like a zoo too, I can tell you. It's also a haven, a sanctuary, a retreat; an escape from the outside world. But if you spend too long inside it you'll want to escape back to the outside world fairly lively.

For starters, it's not built with luxury in mind, not designed for creature comfort. It's usually a concrete box with a low ceiling and the walls bleeding with sweat. The windows are small, and often there's iron bars protecting them from flying footballs or from people breaking and entering.

But sometimes I think the iron bars are there to prevent players from getting out. Anyway, in my mind they always add to the impression of a prison. You and your colleagues are the inmates, incarcerated until someone opens the door and lets you run free on to the field.

It's a cage where twenty-five or thirty men are stripped down to their bare bollocks while rattling inside with fear and anxiety and insecurity. The stress comes out of their mouths in rivers of foul language. It comes out through the pores on their skin. It comes out in the stink of fellas farting and shitting and pissing. Fellas walking round, scratching their balls and pulling their tools and spitting and shouting and puking and swearing.

The closer it gets to kick-off, or throw-in, the higher the anxiety rises. Everyone's togged by now in the team jersey, the prison uniform. All you're missing really is a guard at the door with a baton, who decides when he's going to let you out.

Fellas start kicking the door. Or a fella will start pucking himself in the chest with his fists, like an ape. Then another fella will start at the same crack. And suddenly you've a dozen fellas beating themselves like fuckn apes. Or you'll have two fellas pucking each other and jawing at each other, and the eyes bulging out of their heads.

There's dirt on the floor, wads of dried mud kicked into corners, filthy socks, abandoned water-bottles, discarded medical tape, buckled coat hangers, ragged towels, empty deodorant cans.

The heat off the bodies, the testosterone, the adrenalin, the nerves: it's too hot in here now, the atmosphere is tropical, the stench everywhere. The walls are sweating, you are sweating, everyone is sweating. Come on! Let us the fuck out of here before we turn into complete and total animals.

The door opens, daylight comes rushing in, you go pouring out of the black hole and on to the green sward. And instantly you relax a bit. You remember your instructions, the pre-prepared strategies and plans. You take your position, the whistle blows and you get down to work.

If it's a good day and the result goes your way, you return to the jail with a pep in your step and a smile on your face. It's not a jail at all now. It's a comedy store, a hive of chatter and laughter and good vibes and fresh anecdotes from the game just played. You strip the uniform, hit the showers, put on a fresh shirt and return to the civilian world of family, friends and work.

On Tuesday night you're back for training, and the mood changes again. Some fellas arrive in good form, other fellas arrive with a cloud on their face and throw the gear bag on the floor. Some of these fellas are permanently cranky and snippy and snarky. There's shit going on at home, or shit going on at work, or shit going on with the girlfriend, and they hate the fuckn hardship of the training anyway.

And God help anyone, usually a young fella, who innocently walks in and sits down in the wrong place. We're all very territorial about our spot in the dressing room. Some animals leave a piss mark on their territory to warn off rivals. We'd do the same if we could. Your own space is sacrosanct, and if someone else decides to claim it he'll be told where to go in no uncertain terms.

There are rules among the inmates, and claiming your own space is one of them. It's the only way that thirty different beasts are going to get along. We might look like a fairly homogeneous bunch when we're lined up together in the same socks, shorts and shirts. But we're all individuals with different temperaments and humours and manners and levels of IQ. And sometimes you have to tread carefully when you're trying to navigate your way through this fine collection of specimens, this charming group of thick and ignorant, smart and witty, hairy, smelly, ugly bastards that make up your average Irish team.

The way you tread carefully is not to tread carefully at all. Everyone is fair game for a joke, a prank, a bit of messing or piss-taking of some description. There are boundaries, I suppose, but usually it's hard to find them or remember them. We're grown men, with jobs and responsibilities, some of us with families of our own. But we're a bunch of schoolboys too. Everyone has his weak spot, including the fat fellas with their big fuckn bellies on them, struggling with their weight, struggling with their self-esteem, while the fit, ripped and handsome lads hog the mirrors and strut around like they're catwalk models. Those fellas are ridiculous altogether.

I used to be thin, skinny as a rake. But now I'm in a permanent battle with the middle-aged spread. As of this year, 2014, I reckon I have spent thirty-three years in dressing rooms, man and boy. That's a fair old innings. I figure I've pretty much seen it all in there, and heard it all. I've said a fair amount in there too. I must be institutionalized by now, a dressing-room lag who has served a full life sentence, with no remission for good behaviour. I have done my time, I have slopped out with the best of them and the worst of them. I've had my rows and arguments and friendships and jokes and one-liners and slagging matches. I've revelled in the comedy and wallowed in the sadness, felt the joy and swallowed the despair. I've seen generations of players go and come and go while I've still turned up, addicted to the energy, the culture, the permanent sense of possibility and renewal.

That's the real attraction. The dressing room is a place where you can live a different life, a heightened life; a place that lifts you out of your mundane world; a place that amplifies your emotions, charges up your life force, enables you to strive for greater things beyond the humdrum reality of your station. It's a place where you feel you are living closer to the edge, inhabiting a world of excitement and hope and fear, always looking forward to the next game, the next drama. Above all, always looking forward. It's a place where you feel more alive and where, on the best days, your dreams come alive too.

It's the place where a bunch of people come together and vow to each other to make history together. And if you're really, really lucky, it's the place to which you return after you've carved out that slice of history, not a prison any more but a dirty, stinking small corner of paradise.

It's a hole in the ground, a dressing room; a kip, a slum and a hovel. But it's heaven too, on the great days and, the rest of the time, a home away from home. I've been a citizen of that room longer than most people. My time there is almost up. I am ready to take my leave. And it's time, I feel, to share my story as a willing prisoner, a happy inmate of that concrete box with its bleeding walls.

1. The Penalty

Connacht minor football final, 1989
Roscommon v. Galway, MacHale Park, Castlebar
We were a point down with seconds to go when the referee awarded us a penalty.

It was the second penalty John Cosgrove had given us that day. I was the centre forward and designated penalty-taker, and I had fluffed the first one, in the first half: hit the post. Now there was a decision to be made: take the point and settle for a draw or go for a goal, and winner takes all? Cosgrove informed us that this would be the last kick of the game.

I dashed over to the sideline for a quick confab with our manager, Jimmy Finnegan. But Jimmy already had his mind made up: we were going for a point – and Peadar Glennon, the designated free-taker, was going to take it.

I wasn't happy. In fact I had the hump good and proper. At this stage most of the crowd was in for the senior final, between Roscommon and Mayo – 30,000 or more. Anyway the message was relayed to Peadar, so he got the ball and marched up to the penalty spot with it. Backs and forwards gathered in a line behind the penalty-taker, as they usually do, and I took my position along with them. But I made sure I was standing directly behind Peadar because I had a different idea. Walking back in from the sideline I'd made my mind up. It just came to me in a flash: I would take the penalty, and I would go for a goal, not a point. When Peadar backed away from the ball to begin his run-up, I would jump out of the line and smash it.

I happened to be standing beside Seán Óg de Paor, the Galway defender who would go on to win two All-Irelands in a great career with their seniors. As Peadar placed the ball, de Paor said, 'It's going over the bar.' He'd presumed correctly that because the free-taker was hitting it, we had opted for the point. It was the percentage play, the safe option: take the point and live to fight another day.

But I said back to him, 'It's not going over the fuckn bar.'

He said, 'What?'

I said, 'Watch this.'

By now Peadar had stepped back from the ball. He took two or three steps to the left and settled himself. He was just about to begin his run-up when I flashed past him and walloped the ball to the roof of the net. It went straight over the goalkeeper's head, under the black spot on the crossbar. The crowd erupted and I wheeled away, arms in the air, running off on a mazy celebration.

Because I was off on our victory lap, I didn't see what happened next. According to the late Seán Kilfeather's report in the *Irish Times*, 'The referee recovered the ball from the net, placed it on the penalty line and crossed his arms in a gesture which nobody understood. He then took the ball and ran from the field, hotly pursued by several Galway players who obviously believed that he allowed the score. This view was shared by Roscommon and the officials in charge of the match arrangements.

Our captain, Seán Staunton, was presented with the cup and we all took turns lifting it up and waving to the crowd. We were Connacht champions. Back in the dressing room there was an unbelievable buzz. The place was crowded with players and subs and officials. A few journalists arrived in, and questions were being asked about who had won it. But there was no doubt in our minds. We had the bloody cup, after all. Eventually we togged in and went back out to watch the senior game, which ended in a draw. Afterwards we went to the Travellers' Friend Hotel in Castlebar for a team meal. The mood was still great, everyone high with the victory.

Anyway we're sitting down for the dinner and the cup is on the table when next thing, two delegates from Connacht Council come marching into the function room – blazers and good bellies and red faces on them. And without so much as a by-your-leave they announce that the match has been given to Galway and they take the cup off the table and walk out with it. Just like that! Typical GAA ignorance. We were all looking at them, looking at each other, not knowing what to think. Like, what the hell's going on here? Marched in, took the cup, and marched out again. Are they serious? Who are these fuckers?

We found out later that the referee had handed in his match report to Connacht Council officials just an hour or two after the game. This was pretty much unheard of at the time. Referees normally had several days to do up their match report and send it off to the relevant committee. But in this case he'd drafted it more or less straight away. Apparently he'd been besieged by various Galway heads outside his own dressing-room door. Kilfeather described it in his article as 'the fastest referee's report in the history of the game'. Cosgrove's report said that my goal had been disallowed because another player, Glennon, was standing within thirteen metres of the ball when I struck it, and we were therefore in breach of the rule regarding penalty kicks. The final official scoreline was Galway 2-8, Roscommon 0-13. No sign of my goal at all. It had been wiped from the record, as if it never existed.

But we didn't know any of this at the time. We were all in the dark about what was going on. You didn't have mobile phones or Twitter in those days. We headed back to Castlerea that evening, glued to the car radio, hoping to hear some word on the situation. We stopped in Gerry Fitzmaurice's pub in Ballinlough on the way back. Someone bought me a pint, and it was one of the first pints I ever had because I didn't really drink at the time. This was July; I had turned eighteen in April. Anyway, the evening news came on in the pub – and there it was: the controversial penalty, the protests, the confusion and the speculation. It had become a news story as well as a sports story.

I got home that night, to be told by my parents that reporters had been phoning all evening looking for comments and wondering where I was. Someone in the county board had rung to tell me I was to say nothing at all to the press. The next morning there were a few reporters hanging around outside the house. My poor mother didn't know what to do or what to make of it all.

Later that day, word came through that there was going to be a rally in Hyde Park a few nights later. The Roscommon GAA community wasn't going to take this lying down! And let me say, when the Rossies get thick about something, they fairly get thick about something. Hundreds of supporters turned up on the night. The minor team was there, and the senior team also turned up in a show of solidarity. Speeches were made and a warning was issued to Connacht Council that if they didn't rescind their decision, the Roscommon seniors might well back out of their replay match with Mayo too.

Connacht Council and the Galway county board were both in a bit of a corner on this one. Technically, we had infringed the rules all right. It wasn't Glennon's fault – how was he to know that I was going to appear out of the blue and hit the penalty? The poor old referee had been caught totally off guard as well. I mean, it was a hundred years of established practice and tradition that the fella who places the ball on the spot is the fella who takes the penalty. If the ref had been thinking straight, he should have disallowed the goal and ordered the penalty be retaken. I'd have been taken away in a straitjacket and Peadar would've chipped it over the bar and everyone would've settled for a draw. Or were Galway entitled to a free out for this technical infringement? No one seemed to know what the correct course of action should have been. There was no precedent for this situation, as far as I knew. It was all a complete hames.

John Cosgrove, a Crossmolina man, was just overwhelmed by events. I don't think he even had time to think for himself or to work out what to do. He had positioned himself on the endline to watch the penalty been taken, and suddenly it all got out of control. We went berserk, celebrating, and the Galway players started hounding him straight away. There was an exit through the fence that separated the supporters from the field behind the goals. John was trying to stay one step ahead of the protesting players and a few officials suddenly materialized beside him and escorted him off the field and out through the gate in the fence.

Roscommon might have infringed in the rule book, but the reality was that in normal circumstances Glennon would've taken his point and Galway would've been facing a replay anyway. I don't think they wanted it said of them that they'd won a Connacht title in the committee room. They were coming under a lot of public pressure to offer a replay and, in fairness to them, that's exactly what they did. A few days after our public meeting in the Hyde, they issued a statement offering the replay. It would be played in Castlebar the following Wednesday evening as a stand-alone fixture. That killed the controversy stone dead. Everyone was relieved; it was a fair compromise.

So we all rocked up to MacHale Park the following week, and a huge crowd turned up as well. The controversy had generated massive amounts of media coverage and it caught the public imagination. This was still only a minor match after all, with no senior match afterwards to draw the masses, but something like 7,000 people turned up to see the sequel.

In those days the referee who'd done a drawn game always got the replay. I'd say it was a bit of a poisoned chalice for John Cosgrove, but it was his gig and he had to get on with it. And wouldn't you believe it, just a few minutes into the replay didn't he award us a penalty – another one! This time there was no discussion with the sideline. I grabbed the ball and took charge. I hadn't a doubt in the world that I was going to bury it. I had my superstitions at the time and one of them was to bless myself any time I stood up to take a penalty. From a young age up I'd always taken them for club, school and county. The gas thing is that, just as I blessed myself, didn't Mr Cosgrove bless himself too. I know this because I have a brilliant photograph at home of the two of us blessing ourselves at the same time. I had my reasons, John had his.

I stuck the penalty right in the top corner. The drama didn't end there: the match ended in a draw and went to extra time. Once again we were trailing as it went into injury time, except this time we were two points down, not one. It was desperation stuff at this stage, and we did what any team desperate for a goal usually does in these circumstances: we launched the ball high and long towards their goalmouth. And unbelievably, the smallest man on the field did the rest. Eddie Ennis was about five foot six. He'd come in off the bench and wasn't long on the field. The ball dropped, Eddie rose majestically and flicked it to the back of the net. Suddenly there was bedlam all over again. The Rossies went berserk, on the field, on the terraces and in the stand. And this time there was no denying us. After all the

twists and turns we'd won the bloody thing. It was a fantastic feeling
and a fantastic night too. We headed back to Castlerea with the cup
that night, the whole squad, and ended up in the Casino nightclub,
celebrating till the wee small hours. We had beaten Sligo handily in
the semi-final; we had played Galway in the final and played them
again in a replay that went to extra time. You couldn't say it was a
massive campaign, but it felt like a great odyssey all the same, after all
the drama and ups and downs.

We were hammered in the All-Ireland semi-final by an outstanding Derry team that included the likes of Anthony Tohill and Gary
Coleman, who would go on to win Derry's first senior All-Ireland
title four years later. There was no shame in that, they were just a
brilliant team.

It is twenty-five years ago now and I haven't met Eddie Ennis since.
I haven't come across John Cosgrove either. There's a lot of water
gone under the bridge since, but I have plenty of sympathy for John
because he probably suffered a lot at the time. It was a big controversy and the referee had been central to it. But listen, there was no
harm done, nobody got shot, and everyone was in uncharted territory. The Connacht Council didn't know how to handle it. And of
course, like a lot of things that seem terribly serious at the time, it's
looked back on now as a sort of comedy of errors.

To this day people still come up to me and talk about it. And usually they break into a laugh when they start talking about it. I guess
it put me on the map. Your name comes to national attention overnight when a controversy like that blows up. The incident gets
magnified over a very short period of time. Your face is on television,
your name is in the headlines, your photo is in the newspapers.

And I suppose you could say it became the start of the narrative on
my life and times in sport as well. In the two and a half decades
since, I've acquired a reputation as an extrovert, a madcap eccentric,
a maverick – pick your cliché. I don't mind; a lot of it is true. The
thing is, though, any time I do try something a bit different, I'm just
following my own instincts. It always feels natural to me. I'm not
trying to force anything or contrive a situation just for the sake of it.

I've always followed my own star because I trust myself, I trust my intuition, I trust my gut feelings.

But that's not to say that I don't engage my brain when I'm going off on one of my solo runs, literal or otherwise. The ideas in my head are usually synchronized with the feeling in my gut. Some things that I do mightn't make sense to others, but they make sense to me.

And what I did that day in Castlebar made sense to me. The reason it made sense to me was that one of our star players had got sent off in the second half. Lorcan Dowd was a brilliant forward and, if the match went to a replay, we were going to be missing him. He would be suspended. Galway and ourselves were very evenly matched – we knew that before the first game, and the ebb and flow of the two games bore that out. At the time when we were awarded that injury-time penalty, I worked out in my head very quickly that missing Dowd for the replay might scupper our chances. That's why I didn't agree with Jimmy Finnegan. I felt in my bones that this was going to be the best opportunity we'd get of winning that Connacht title. What's more, on the law of averages, a team is not going to miss two penalties in the one game. All of this went through my head in a flash. I was calculating the odds, and I reckoned the odds would be stacked against us the next day.

The point here is that there was method to my madness, if people want to call it madness. I didn't think it was mad at all; I thought it was the logical thing to do. I'd had a brainstorm, but my brain was working. And I've had many more brainstorms over the years since. Sometimes they didn't work out, but more often than not they did.

I'm not afraid to take risks, and never have been. I believe that teams sometimes need a bit of inspiration to give them a jolt of energy, a shot of electricity. And I'll repeat the point: just because I come up with something off-the-cuff doesn't mean I haven't thought it through. Usually I have. I can process a whole series of thoughts in a second and, before I know it, I'm reacting, I'm doing the thing that's come into my head.

In the GAA, maybe in Ireland as a whole, people are afraid to stand out. I don't know if it's part of our culture or what, but there's a sort of unspoken pressure on people to keep the head down: don't be different, don't stand out, it's better to conform. I think there's a failure of courage here. You've got to be able to stand up to that sort of attitude and show some courage. Show some leadership, do something different, take a risk. It was said at the time that what I'd done in that minor match was 'irresponsible'. And since then it's been said over the years by various begrudgers after I've done something unorthodox or unconventional. But I think the opposite: I think I'm actually taking responsibility; I'm trying to show a bit of leadership or a bit of defiance or even a bit of bravado. I think a bit of bravado is good, especially if you play for teams that have inherited an inferiority complex that's been built up over generations. In doing what I've done over the years, I've tried to change that sort of mindset. I've never lacked for confidence, I've never been afraid to stand out from the crowd, and I've tried to spread that confidence among teammates and even the supporters watching in the stands. It's my way of taking a stand; and sometimes you have to take risks to take a stand. People who don't like to see a streak of individualism in a player, or in anyone in general, will call you an 'exhibitionist', or a showman or an attention-seeker.

I don't do it for that reason. And when I do mess up, I don't stick my head in the sand and blame someone else or pretend it never happened. I'm not bullheaded like that. I do question myself, I do reflect on what I did and why I did it. You won't develop as a person if you don't criticize yourself or if you don't accept criticism from other people. And looking back on that penalty controversy with the benefit of twenty-five years' hindsight, I could make a case to myself that it wasn't the right thing to do. I'm aware of that argument. It wasn't the right thing to do because (a) it was illegal and (b) it showed a certain lack of respect for authority. Our manager had given an order and I had disobeyed it.

On the other hand, you could say I did it because I could. I did it because I knew how to do it. I knew how to hit penalties. I had the technique and I had the bottle. I knew in my heart and soul that I was going to score it. I didn't forget my technique as I raced up to that ball: I kept my eye on it, my body shape was correct, I kept my head over the ball and put my foot through it. It was a clinical strike, it was a proper penalty, if I may say so. And, as it happened, we also got Lorcan Dowd back for the replay. The first game was declared null and void — typical official GAA bureaucracy — so any suspensions arising from it were also null and void. So Lorcan played, we all played, and we went home with the cup.

That penalty controversy is part of folklore now, certainly in Roscommon, and it's part of my story too. I'm glad that it is, I look back on it with a lot of affection, and I also know that it has made a lot of people smile over the years. If it hadn't worked out, I know I'd have been in the doghouse for a long time afterwards. I'd have let down my teammates, our management and our supporters, and that's a horrible thought to contemplate. But I've never had to contemplate it, because it all worked out. And I'll say this one more time: I was never going to miss.

It was a controversy then, it's a story now. And sport, among other things, is all about writing new stories.

2.   Homage to Castlerea

This day anyway, our teacher was late for the science class. I was about fourteen at the time and a student at the Vocational School in Castlerea. Now, 'student' might be overstating it a bit because I found it physically and mentally impossible to actually study any book for any duration. Not even five minutes. I couldn't retain any information out of a book and had no aptitude for studying. I'm sure it had something to do with my dyslexia.

I should say as well that we never called it the Vocational School, we called it 'The Tech'. And I was in a class in the Tech with about eight or nine other so-called students. We got on famously because, to a man, they had no interest in books either; not a screed of a notion that ever was earthly. Obviously we weren't the brightest, academically. Classes were streamed in those days, the As, Bs and Cs, and we were in B, parked in the middle, neither full brainboxes nor complete dopes. It wouldn't have made any difference if I'd been in A or C, because the likes of Irish, English, history, geography, maths and whatever else was on the menu – it was all in one ear and out the other.

But there were two things we were interested in. The first was sport of all kinds. The second was crack. We were stone mad about crack: having it, making it, talking it, whichever way possible. We could have had PhDs in the crack and all its manifestations, if it was on the curriculum. Every day was one long laugh. I mean to say, every single day was a howl.

So this day our teacher was late for our science class, and we decided to conduct a few experiments of our own. Naturally enough, we got the Bunsen burners going on the gas rings and started pouring stuff out of bottles into them. And there was a lot of stuff in the physics and chemistry room, various compounds in powder form, and sulphuric acid too – I seem to remember the sulphuric acid for some reason. Anyway, we were mixing it all into these beakers with water and the sulphuric acid and then pouring it goodo into the Bunsen burners. Every single strange-looking substance that could be thrown into the mix was added for divilment. You couldn't say it was a controlled experiment. It was a fuckn out-of-control experiment.

All of these chemicals and beakers and various apparatuses were stored in a series of glass cabinets along one wall. And next thing didn't a crack appear in the glass of one of these cabinets. Seán Kilkenny says, 'Jesus Christ we're going to get fuckn landed in some trouble here now.' And next thing, BANG! The glass in the cabinet exploded in a shower of smithereens. Down we dropped to our hands and knees under the desks, laughing away like eejits. It was the right move, because next thing every glass cabinet started exploding. *Boom boom boom!* It was like someone had taken a fuckn submachine gun to the place. It was raining glass and we were on the floor, wondering how the hell we were going to get out of there. Of course, no one had thought to open a window in the room to let in a bit of air. There was an awful toxic smell now and we figured we'd better get out of there for fear that if we didn't get hit by flying glass, the fumes would poison us or something. So we started crawling like fuckn rats for the door. But before we had time to reach the door, didn't one of the big windows on the other side of the room explode. And then another, and then another. Holy shit! It was a war zone now, like a bomb had hit the place.

We made a run for it and shot out the front door like bats out of hell. But the teachers' cars were all parked under the science lab and some of them had heard the noise of the glass smashing on to the bonnets. Some of them were already out there, wondering what the jaysus was going on. Next thing, there we were all out there, standing around like muppets looking at a room that had exploded out of the blue on a clear day. And acting like innocent altar boys as if it had nothing to do with us.

Needless to say there was an inquest. And an inquiry and an inquisition too. One by one we were all marched up to the principal's office. Pat McGarry knew damn well who the ringleaders were. Anyway, I was marched into Pat's office and I sat down and I could hardly keep my face straight. Says Pat, 'Shane, you know who did this, don't you?' knowing well that it was me and a few of my confederates. I told him I hadn't a clue. He said he'd give me one more chance to own up. I told him again I hadn't a clue. He said if I came clean and told the truth, he wouldn't tell my mother and father. But if I didn't, they'd be called in to the school and given a hefty bill for the damage. I straightened up fairly lively when I heard that. So I admitted that I might have had something to do with it. I said it was a bit of innocence that went wrong. He said that an awful lot of damage had been caused, and who was going to pay for it? I said, well, it's not a great situation all right. But then again, if Mr White had turned up on time, none of this would've happened in the first place. I suppose I could've been a bit more contrite. But I did own up, and this seemed to get me some brownie points. He knew I wasn't going to snitch on all the other lads, and none of the other lads were going to do the same either. In the end we got off lightly. We were all reprimanded, one by one, but I can't remember any of us being suspended, much less expelled.

Normal life in school quickly resumed and the incident of the exploding classroom was forgiven, if not forgotten. Well, I've never forgotten it anyway, and to this day I break out into a fit of laughing every time I think of it.

The thing is, for all my complete and total indifference to books and learning, I loved school. I don't think I missed one day in my five years at the Tech. And I loved school because I was, and still am, a social animal. I love meeting people, be they friends or strangers. Even as a small boy I never had a shy phase, I was never stuck for a word. I just seemed to have a naturally sociable, outgoing sort of nature.

And I don't have a dark side. I never get depressed and I don't even get down very often. I just happen to be blessed with a sunny disposition and an optimistic outlook on life. I'm a happy sort, you could say. I love laughter and wit and conversation and a few drinks and good company. I like the bright side of the road, I've always gravitated towards positive thinking and positive people. In my experience, the more optimism and positivity you project outwards, the more it comes back to you. Maybe it's a form of naivety, in ways, but I always think there's good things round the corner, that there's a bright day up ahead. Maybe I came out of the womb that way. Or maybe it's because I had a happy childhood in the innocent world that was our town in the 1970s and 1980s.

I came into that world on 8 April 1971, the first of three boys born to my parents, Tommy and Pauline. Jason is a year younger than me, Evan five years. Dad grew up in Church Road and that's where we lived until I was twelve. Mam grew up in the townland of Arm, on the outskirts of Castlerea, and we relocated there in 1983. Both my parents worked in the old psychiatric hospital, what's now the prison: Dad in the power house, Mam in the kitchen.

The hospital was opened in 1943, a fine, cut-stone building established on a lovely swathe of wooded parkland just outside the town. It was used as a sanatorium in the late '40s and early '50s under the TB eradication campaign pioneered by the great Dr Noël Browne. It then reverted to its original purpose as a psychiatric hospital. The power house was a separate premises on the grounds. It was a massive building and inside it was this enormous, tunnelled furnace that heated the whole hospital. It was fed tons and tons of turf and all sorts of other materials that could be burned. It needed fitters to keep it in good working order, fellas who could turn their hand to plumbing and to mechanical, electrical and general maintenance work. It had to be kept going seven days a week and usually had four men or so on shift at any one time.

And it was down in the power house that I got the best education of my life. From the age of six or seven I was running down there from our house on Church Road, especially at weekends. It was always warm there, even in the depths of winter. Inside it was a small little wooden hut, and that's where the men would congregate to drink tea and smoke and talk football, politics and the news of the day, local or national. I'd sit there and soak up the conversations. At the centre of it all was a wonderful man who made a big impact on me, the general foreman, Larry Cummins. I was in awe of Larry, and not just because he'd played corner back on the Roscommon team that won the All-Ireland in 1943. I'd say the first bit of history I ever learned, about anything, was about the legendary Roscommon team of that era which won All-Irelands in '43 and '44 and which took Kerry to a replay in the final of '46.

In the eyes of a child, Larry was a king. He was a massive man, big and broad, then in his mid-fifties. And he was just a magical presence; he had this aura about him that made a profound impression on me. And on top of that, he was a lovely, gentle soul. He was the gaffer, the main man in the power house, but I never heard him raise his voice to anyone. Everyone deferred to him, not just the men in the engine room, but the medical staff and patients too – doctors, nurses, administrators, everyone. He had a wealth of knowledge. And he had an authority and a humanity about him that just radiated outwards and attracted everybody to him. It was Larry's presence and personality I think that united the whole institution and brought together all the people who worked and lived there.

I realized as I grew older that psychiatric hospitals had a sort of stigma about them; people were afraid of them, and sometimes half afraid that they might end up there. But the patients were lovely people, and everyone who worked there interacted with them naturally and freely. I made friends with a lot of the patients just through meeting them around the grounds of the hospital; you'd go walking with them and chatting with them and you got to know them as real people. Most weekends we would have a patient or two out to the house for dinner, and during the summer a few of them would come to the bog for a few days' work turning the turf and bringing it in. This was long before the time when it became normal to try to integrate the mentally ill into the wider community. But they loved the day out and we enjoyed having them. Some of them were mighty crack altogether and in fact a lot of them had been put into the hospital for reasons that weren't to do with their mental health at all. They may have come from broken or impoverished homes; they may have been abandoned in one way or another. After years in hospital they'd become institutionalized in a way that was sad to see. But they just didn't seem to have any other outlet in life or any means of supporting themselves and keeping a roof over their heads. From what I could see, they were looked after very well by the staff. Most of the nurses were from the Mayo/Roscommon/Galway area and they brought a lovely bit of country decency and warmth to their work.

In 1994 the Government took the decision to convert the hospital into a prison. By then the care-in-the-community policy had also taken over and the numbers in the hospital were dwindling. It no longer needed all the maintenance staff it once had and Dad took a job as a bus driver, transporting the patients to various day-care centres and outpatient facilities. So he retained his connection with them more or less throughout his working life. Most of them are gone now, but I remember them with great fondness to this day.

I was a fairly giddy young fella, as you can imagine, but when the power-house men gathered of an evening to smoke and talk in the wooden hut, I knew enough to sit still and listen to what they had to say. I must've felt intuitively that these were wise men, talking about important things, and I loved being in their company. To this day I seek out the company of older people; I always feel comfortable in their presence. And I really believe that listening to older people is a great natural education for children. I'd hope that Ireland as a community doesn't lose this link between the young generation and the old, because it's a vital connection and a wonderful influence.

The wooden hut in the power house had another attraction: an eighteen-inch black-and-white television. I rarely missed a Saturday night down there, because we didn't have a television at home – and because I knew that they'd be faithfully tuned into *Match of the Day* on the BBC. The men in the hut were mad for *Match of the Day*, and so was I.

Needless to say, I was mad keen to play sport as well as watch it: soccer, Gaelic football, it didn't matter to me, I was out on the street with my mates or down at Hanley's Field, playing morning, noon and night. We had street leagues and parish leagues in those days, and I'd have started playing those when I was only five or six. I was kind of reckless in the way I threw myself into tackles against the bigger, stronger lads, because I had no sense of fear at all. I'd be chasing after the ball like the proverbial dog chasing a scrap of litter on a windy day. I think they put me in goals to keep me out of harm's way. So virtually from day one I was a goalkeeper in soccer. In Gaelic, I was a natural forward from the start. That's where they put me, that's where I played.

The Church Road gang included the Hayden brothers Luigi and Paul, Gerard McLoughlin, P. J. Carroll, Gerry Kelly and several more. Then you had the Patrick Street lads, who always thought they were the most talented, the likes of Myles Hawkshaw, Enda Collins, Eugene 'Lulu' Collins and Paraic Newman; Main Street had Andy Leyland, Dara Bruen, Frankie Hestor, Michael 'Freddie' Doyle and Teddy Browne. Then you had Barrack Street, Knockroe, who were a mixture of the good, the bad and the downright useless – easy pickings for us (sorry, boys): Michael Harvey, Seánie Connell, Dermot O'Connell and Donie Duignan. Am I leaving anybody out? Apologies if I am. The street league matches were ding-dong affairs: lots of bust-ups and rows and spills and thrills. And when we weren't playing in the leagues, we were playing out on the street, more or less seven days a week.

Match of the Day only fed the obsession. I remember, when I was starting playing in goals, my father telling me that there were only two goalkeepers in the world worth talking about. One of them was the great Pole, Jan Tomaszewski, who'd become an overnight sensation after his famous exploits against England at Wembley in 1973. The other was Pat Jennings. I remember asking Dad who he played for. Jennings had just transferred from Spurs to Arsenal in the summer of 1977, so I was six years old at the time. Dad told me he played for Arsenal and that was it: I followed Pat Jennings and because he played for the Gunners I became a mental-mad Gunners fan. In the next few years a lot of Irish lads, from north and south, played for Arsenal, and this of course added to the attraction: Brady, Stapleton, O'Leary, Jennings, Pat Rice, Sammy Nelson and John Devine. Of course, since then, English football has become a globalized industry and I doubt we'll ever see such a large Irish contingent again at any one Premier League club, let alone Arsenal. But that doesn't matter: my great love affair with the club continues to this day. I've travelled all over the world to see them play and I'll go to see them at the Emirates a couple of times every season too.

Highbury and London might as well have been on another planet for a small boy in a rural Irish town back in the 1970s. Castlerea was my universe and I didn't know anything of the world beyond its boundaries. And within those boundaries it had more than enough to keep me happy and content. My first school was St Anne's, where we were minded by two lovely teachers, Bonnie Garvey and Sister Anthony. The caretaker was our next-door neighbour on Church Road, Annie Pidgeon, and Annie took care of every child who passed through the school like they were her own. At lunchtime I'd dash home to our grandfather because Mam and Dad would be out at work. He was Granddad Curran, Thomas Curran, and he'd have a good cup of thick soup ready for me and a couple of those thick arrowroot biscuits that you don't get any more. Granny Horan on our mother's side was also hugely involved in our upbringing, and I loved being around them both. When Granny Horan died I was about twelve or thirteen, and it left a deep void in our lives because we treasured her so much.

I had an Uncle Martin, who died young, when I was only four, but I've a vivid memory of him bringing me around the town on the handlebar of his bike. Martin liked his bottle of stout and on a Sunday he'd bring me into McLoughlin's shop, one of those old-fashioned grocery shops that had a bar at the back, and he'd put me up on one of the high stools and buy me a bottle of orange. You'd have farming men in there after Mass with their caps and pipes, and I'd watch them packing the tobacco into the pipe and billowing out clouds of smoke. I was fascinated by this adult world, listening and looking and taking it all in.

After our infant years in St Anne's, St Paul's was the next level up. An all-boys' national school, run by the Marist brothers, and this was where my formal education in Gaelic football began, under the tutelage of Brother Mel. He taught us in sixth class but he'd already been teaching us the arts of Gaelic football for three or four years by then. And he did recognize very early that I had a bit of talent out on the football pitch, if not in the classroom.

There was a Brother Ronald as well, a very nice man. And there was another teacher whom we knew as Brother Gregory; only later was he identified by his lay name in the courts. Martin Meaney was a

paedophile who wreaked havoc in our school and, prior to that, in a school in Sligo too. In 1991 he was sentenced to eighteen years in jail for a range of horrendous offences against boys. He taught me in second, third and fourth class. Luckily for us, our age group escaped his criminal activity. But the damage he did at St Paul's caused the most desperate grief and suffering to the victims and their families. And, needless to say, it cast a long shadow over the school too.

When I think of St Paul's I prefer to think of Brother Mel. Naturally enough, I was one of the lads in the back row of the classroom, as far away from the teacher as possible, and acting the maggot whenever possible too. If we got too rowdy, Brother Mel would occasionally let fly with the *glantóir*, the yoke with the wooden handle on it that they used for wiping blackboards in those days. I don't really know how he and all the other teachers I had over the years ever put up with me. I just could not concentrate in class. My attention span could be counted in minutes on the fingers of one hand. I don't know how to explain it fully, just that it was like a form of mental fatigue.

I remember distinctly, around fifth class, losing interest in learning altogether. I couldn't process the information that was coming at me and I didn't understand it. And the words on the page that I'd read, I couldn't retain them either. Basically I needed to be *shown* how to do things, not told how to do them. I needed it demonstrated to me in a practical way.

Eventually you find your own method for remembering things that you need to remember. You develop strategies, you find a way of seeing round the corner. For example, I became pretty good at adding and subtracting through playing darts. I played a lot of darts in Doherty's pub at the weekends and I happened to be fairly handy at the arrows. And I'd be competitive too, so the adding and subtracting was a necessary mental skill to have if you wanted to play well. I needed to know it, I learned it in a practical way, and therefore I acquired the skill.

Mind you, nobody in school seemed to notice my problem at the time, myself included. The teachers didn't pass any remarks and neither did I. I was progressing along at an average rate and my learning difficulties flew under the radar. But in fifth class I made a conscious decision just to look on school as a place to connect and socialize, not a place to be educated. I just didn't have the capacity to be educated the way the education system was educating me.

It never bothered me one iota. I was good at football, I was popular with the lads, and I enjoyed the general messing and mischief. I'd inherited the football gene from my father. He won four county medals with Castlerea, captained them to one of them in 1968, and was county footballer-of-the-year one year too. Brother Mel put me on the national school team when I was nine at corner forward, a good three years younger than some of the lads in sixth class. There was a cup competition those times called the Marist Cup, and I think I was the youngest ever to play on the St Paul's cup team. The tournament was played over a weekend against other Marist national school teams from Athlone and around Connacht. We won a couple of those tournaments and I was already playing with top-class young talents like Andy Leyland, Frankie Hestor and the late Ciaran Webb.

Along with getting that competitive experience, Brother Mel was instructing us rigorously in the core skills of the game: the kick, the catch, the blockdown. He was a brilliant coach, way ahead of his time in his emphasis on technique. And his way of imparting his knowledge made it simple and easy for us to understand. He drilled it into us that you had to be able to kick well with your weaker foot, and so we spent hours kicking left and right. Kick it direct to your teammate's chest; kick a one-bounce pass into him; watch the trajectory of the ball; hit the ball off your laces; always have a vision of the pitch in front of you; catch the ball at your first attempt; make your hands into the W shape when catching it; kill it dead in your hands every time. It was all meat and drink to me. I lapped it up and came back for more.

Pretty soon I was togging out for the Castlerea St Kevin's Under 12 team. We beat Roscommon Gaels in the county final in 1983. I was playing midfield, Fergal O'Donnell was playing midfield for the Gaels. The two of us were already developing reputations around the county. We would go on to have a long rivalry through every age grade at club level, and a good friendship as players on various county teams. We were teammates with the Roscommon seniors for many years. It's a standout memory, coming home with the Under 12 cup, getting the tour of the town with us all hanging out the windows of the cars and everyone beeping their horns and people coming out of their houses to wave at us as we passed. Conquering heroes, we were! And then ending up back at the clubhouse for sandwiches and Taytos and Cokes. I can remember the late great Billy Webb welcoming us back to the clubhouse, Liam Carlos too, Eamonn Campion, and of course the man himself, Larry Cummins. Richie Walsh was behind the bar that night, as he was on a million other nights, and you were never short of a laugh or a word of encouragement when Richie was around. His son Decky has carried on the tradition of looking after the bar and has been a great friend to myself and the club over the years.

The names keep tumbling into my mind, the more I look back on those childhood years, and it humbles me to think of all the people involved in our club who encouraged us and praised us and brought us on. J. P. 'Doc' O'Callaghan, a teammate of Larry's on the fabled Roscommon team of '43/'44, was another gentleman we looked up to and revered. Phil Gannon too, a lovely man who was a pillar of the town. I loved spending time in their company. Likewise Billy Webb, always a source of sound advice on and off the field, with his pipe in one hand and glass of Paddy in the other. The 'four kings' had four queens too in their wives, Eileen Cummins, Kitty O'Callaghan, Mae Gannon and Renee Webb. Great ladies in their own right too, and people I also remember fondly.

That Under 12 team was managed by Danny Burke, our Mick O'Dwyer, and a great stalwart of the town in several roles over many generations. And it was a team of exceptional players, many of whom went on to play for the county at underage and senior: Derek Duggan, Martin Costello, Seán Costello and Ken Duggan.

Along with the club football there were the vocational schools competitions, and our driving forces at the Tech were Mark Kennedy and the late Liam Campbell. Liam was a visionary coach and a brilliant influence on me. He taught us English in school, and he ran a pub in town as well, along with his wife Joan. The Horse and Jockey is since closed, but it was a favoured watering-hole in our young drinking years. Liam had knowledge and authority. He knew the game, he knew what he was talking about, and you knew that he knew. He seldom raised his voice and he seldom had to: one look from him was enough. If he gave you an instruction and you didn't take it in, he'd stop you in your tracks with that stare of his. We won the county vocational schools title a couple of times under Liam's guidance, and he steered us to two Connacht finals, where we were beaten by Glenamaddy from Galway. We were winning pretty much at every underage grade with St Kevin's and I was making smooth progress through the ranks.

Meanwhile, along with a lot of my friends from the street leagues, I joined Castlerea Celtic FC. The infamous GAA ban on 'foreign games' had been lifted more than a decade earlier, but it would've made no bloody difference to us one way or another. As a group of kids, all we wanted was to be kicking a ball of any kind on a field of any dimensions. We had very good sides at Under 15 and Under 16, winning various league titles and regional cups. The club has terrific facilities now, but back in the mid-'80s there was still a lot of work to be done. The pitch had a slope and usually we played with the slope in the first half if we won the toss. Most of the lads played Gaelic too, there was a big degree of crossover, and we had fellas playing with us from neighbouring parishes who we'd have played against in GAA games. My time there coincided with a great generation of young talent, fellas like Alan 'Beano' Kennedy, Seán and Martin Costello, Barry McKeon, John Regan, Gary Cunnane and Paul O'Donnell. Then there were a few senior to us, Andy Leyland, Ciaran Webb and Frankie Hestor, all good players too.

Kevin Freyne was in charge of the Castlerea Celtic first team at the time, and he gave me my debut when I was about sixteen and a half. I walked into a well-managed and well-motivated side. Myley Hawkshaw never went near the Gaelic, soccer was his game, and Myley was our predator, our fox in the box, our Ian Rush. It was unbelievable the amount of goals he got, he couldn't stop scoring. And it was always a bit of a mystery to us how he did it because he only had one foot, a left foot, even if it was a great left foot to be fair. He never headed the ball either, which should've been a bit of a drawback for a striker. I don't think Myley headed a ball in his whole feckn life. As a result, we weren't a route-one team. There was no point in me bombing the ball down on his head from sixty yards away. We tried to play it out from the back, and we had Beano in midfield, who could control the flow and the tempo: Beano was your typical midfield schemer. At centre half we had Paul O'Donnell, a player definitely gifted enough to make the League of Ireland grade, if not better. He was a tall, super-classy defender.

Castlerea Celtic were a serious club back in the '70s and '80s, consistently at or near the top of the Connacht Senior League. I often found it hard to remember the names of my teammates because most of us were saddled with nicknames and were never called anything else. My first nickname was actually 'Tiger', handed down from my dad, who was also Tiger in his footballing prime. Being a bit wild, on the field and off it, probably helped as well. Tiger lasted for most of my teenage years until my great friend, Ciaran Webb, God rest him, dreamed up 'Cake' at a training session one night. In fact, originally it was 'Cáca Milis', as in sweet cake, then abbreviated to 'Cáca', and finally translated to the English. You wouldn't need to be a genius to figure out how it came about: Curran, currant cake, cake. And it has stuck with me ever since.

Dermot Carroll was 'Kempes', after the fantastic Mario of Argentina fame at World Cup '78. You had Bill 'The Bear' Kelly, Tom 'Banjo' Byrne, Seánie 'The Badger' Connell, Paraic 'The Silver Fox' Newman, Joe 'The Dutch' Byrne, Donald 'Huda' Egan, Michael 'Pharaoh' Harvey and Seamus 'Boballoo' Egan. You couldn't make them up, but we did.

One family synonymous with the success of both St Kevin's and Celtic was the Mulvihills. The late Páid Mulvihill and his good wife Bernie ran a pub on Main Street and were the main sponsor of the soccer club for years. Their son Dermot now runs the premises, and if ever a name deserved to be on a team jersey it is 'Mull's', as it is affectionately known. Dermot's brother Billy was a valuable mentor to me in my early soccer career and a man who would do anything for you.

While the club had various managers in charge of underage and adult teams over the years, there was always one constant presence hovering over everything. Ray Kerrane was our general manager and director of football rolled into one. A larger-than-life character, a constant source of banter and crack, the scene was never dull when Ray was around.

I owe a debt of gratitude to Kevin Freyne for putting me into the first team at such a young age, but between everyone at the club I got a great grounding in the basics of the game, first at underage and then with the seniors, where I spent five years. We had a lot of brilliant times in the green and white of Castlerea Celtic, on and off the field, and a lot of those old teammates are still good friends to this day. When I took my leave of Celtic for Athlone Town, I was the first from the club to make it with the League of Ireland. I think they were proud that someone had made it to that grade, and I was certainly proud to represent them when I went to pastures new.

Meanwhile I was having a rare old time of it in school. I can honestly say that the last three years at the Tech were the best three years of my life. The crack was just relentless. It was a complete comedy circuit from morning till evening. I did the Group Cert and just about got through it. A day or two before the Inter Cert, I broke my ankle playing in a seven-a-side match on a rough old field, and I ended up in hospital in Galway for an operation. Normally I'd have been distraught with any injury that got in the way of football. But this particular cloud had a very bright silver lining. Needless to say I hadn't a thing done for the Inter: not a book opened, not a word learned, nothing only a heap of windows broken and thousands of pounds' damage done to the science room. This was 1986 and the World Cup was happening in Mexico. I got back from the operating theatre in time to see Josimar wallop home his famous goal for Brazil against Northern Ireland with my hero, Pat Jennings, in goal. It disappointed me a lot more than missing the Inter Cert, I can tell you.

If we didn't feel like sitting in class for a whole day, we often went on the mitch. We had a cunning scheme for disappearing when we wanted to. On the grounds of the school was an old public building called the Hanley Hall. The Hanley Hall had a snooker table, and snooker was all the rage at the time. People had these massive bloody aerials for their television sets to get the BBC. Come the snooker world championships we'd all be glued to the telly. Anyway, the Hanley Hall was usually locked and out of bounds. But a few of us were fairly enterprising and we managed to get a replica key cut for our own private use. As it happened, I was the fella who had the key. I had it for all my years at the Tech. And many a day the lunchtime break became a full afternoon break. We'd skip school, let ourselves in to the Hanley Hall, pull the curtains and set the balls up on the green baize.

For all of our messing, I have to say we never got into any trouble with the guards or anything like that. I didn't smoke, I never have, and there wasn't much in the line of underage drinking either because we always had games to play or training sessions to go to; our whole lives away from school were taken up with sport. One of the underage coaches at Castlerea St Kevin's was a guard based in the town at the time, Detective Garda John Morley. He and his colleague, Garda Henry Byrne, both of them from Knock, were murdered in the course of their duty on 7 July 1980. I was nine at the time and was part of the Under 12 team that John Morley coached. We were at home that afternoon in Church Road when Annie Pidgeon came in with the news that John Morley and Henry Byrne had been shot dead. I remember RTÉ breaking into their normal programming to announce it in a news flash. We were absolutely stunned. Couldn't take it in. A branch of the Bank of Ireland in Ballaghaderreen had been robbed by armed raiders. John and Henry had intercepted their getaway car near Loughglynn and were killed in the shootout. Their colleagues, Mick O'Malley and Derek O'Kelly, were also in the car that fateful day but thankfully managed to survive.

It was an outrage that shocked the nation, but it was a bit more personal for us because we knew and loved John Morley. By all accounts, he'd been a commanding footballer with Mayo during the 1960s and had won a National League medal in 1970. I was too young to remember him as a player and was just old enough to come under his influence as a coach. And he gave me this impression of a man who carried himself with real composure and class. He was a lovely man, everyone in Castlerea thought the world of him and his wife Frances. And we were also very friendly with his sons, Shane and Gordon, and daughter Gillian, which made it all the more distressing. Thousands upon thousands turned out for the state funeral. The guard of honour seemed to go on for miles. We schoolchildren formed part of the guard of honour. It was a powerful, solemn, desperately sad occasion. The whole town united in grief, and subsequently organized fundraising nights for the bereaved families. It left a wound on the town that took a long time to get over. The Morley family relocated to Galway in later years, and Gordon would go on to win an All-Ireland club medal with Salthill in 2006, beating St Brigid's in the Connacht final along the way.

The GAA's All-Star awards were inaugurated in 1971, and a year later Roscommon had their first All-Star, Mickey Freyne – Kevin's brother. Mickey was an iconic forward with the Rossies and a great inspiration to us growing up; he would later coach our senior team to a couple of northern titles, as they were known at the time. Then there was Harry Keegan, a fantastic defender who won three All-Stars between '78 and '86. Alongside Harry in the Roscommon full-back line of that era was Tom Heneghan, an All-Star winner in '79. He won three Connacht titles as a player between '77 and '79 and was manager when Roscommon completed the four-in-a-row in 1980, famously reaching that year's All-Ireland final. It's the final we refer to in Roscommon as 'the one that got away'. Tom Heneghan became a great ambassador for Ireland and Roscommon in later years through his work with Bord Fáilte in the USA.

The All-Star awards had enormous prestige at the time, and to have three players from Castlerea St Kevin's winning them was a terrific source of pride to the club and community. We certainly weren't stuck for role models growing up; we were surrounded by high achievers who made us believe that we could do big things too. We also had three players from that era who weren't as well known nationally but who were outstanding footballers. One was Padraic O'Callaghan, the second was Adrian O'Sullivan, who by general consensus is one of the best the club ever produced. I wouldn't have seen him play but everyone talked about him in reverential terms. Adrian played a couple of years with the county but a serious injury cut him off in his prime and he never made the great career his talent deserved. The third, John Kerrane, later a distinguished academic with DCU, was by all accounts another top-class player, who captained the club to their 1973 county title.

If history in the Leaving Cert consisted of the story of Roscommon and Castlerea football, I'd have got an A in honours. If the entire syllabus consisted of football, soccer, snooker, darts, badminton and pool, I'd have been a star pupil. They'd probably have put a mortar board on my head and a scroll in me hand. Unfortunately they didn't form any part of the curriculum, for some strange reason. We had a lovely Irish teacher who told us she'd never had a student who failed to pass Irish in the Leaving. There were seven or eight of us in her class. She did her best with us, but we all failed. And it wasn't hard to see why: none of us wrote a word on the paper during the written exam. Not a single fuckn word. Like, you could waffle away in the English paper but you couldn't in Irish. I passed four subjects out of the seven in the Leaving Cert, which actually wasn't bad going for someone who never opened a book. But you needed five to 'pass'. So I failed the Leaving Cert, that great rite of passage that every Irish teenager has to endure. It left me psychologically scarred for life – not. I was never going to need it anyway, where I was going.

Pat McGarry came to me one day and asked me to come back to the Tech the following year, to repeat the Leaving. If I just studied two or three subjects and passed one of them, I could add it to the four I'd got and hey presto, I'd have passed the Leaving. I wasn't too interested in that, but the school had a very good team and they were going to make a serious rally to win Connacht the following season. The prospect of winning the provincial championship for vocational schools proved irresistible. So I registered to study biology, and physics and chemistry, and Pat said grand – with the proviso that I didn't blow up the fuckn science lab again.

Sure enough, we won Roscommon and reached the Connacht final. This would've been around March or April '89. But a week before the final I broke my collar bone, playing a league game for Castlerea Celtic FC. Poor old Pat and Liam Campbell were both distraught and I was devastated too. I'd have loved to have won it for them, and alongside the teammates that I'd shared so much fun with over the previous six years. We were beaten by two points in the final. And I didn't even re-sit the Leaving Cert — once was plenty.

A few months later I faced an examination, a test of a different kind, in MacHale Park. I think I passed that one okay in the end — and it meant a lot more to me too.

3. Birth of a Salesman

I wasn't long out of short trousers when I started making my own few pennies and pounds. My first job was helping John Leonard on his milk round during weekends and summer holidays. I was ten or eleven at the time. You were out of the cot fairly early for this gig, up at half four, down to John's house on Main Street for five, and head for Frank Ward's distribution depot to pick up the consignment of milk. You'd load up to 400 crates in the back of John's Hiace – 20 pints a crate – and head for Ballinlough, Cloonfad, Dunmore, Williamstown, Ballymoe, and back to Castlerea. I loved the excitement of heading out on the road and feeling you were on a bit of a tour of the countryside. I'd be hopping out of the back of the van on every street, dropping crates at shop doors and skipping over walls to drop bottles on the doorsteps while everyone else was still fast asleep. John was a decent man who paid me the first few quid I could call my own. I spent two years calling to John and Geraldine's house, and doing that milk round was one of the most enjoyable experiences I had as a child growing up in Castlerea.

Then I swapped milk for high heels, so to speak. I was thirteen when Tom Byron gave me the start in his shoe shop on Main Street. The Byron name is synonymous with shoe shops in the midlands and further afield. I loved the job from day one because you were dealing with the public, and there was nothing I liked better than chatting to anyone and everyone and knocking a bit of crack out of the customers.

Castlerea was a big market town back in the '80s. It was a centre for shopping in the region, it had a few factories and a cattle mart that is still doing good business. On Saturdays the town would really come alive. You'd have a street fair, a vegetable market, and people piling in from all parts of the surrounding countryside. It was Roscommon's version of the famous Smithfield market in Dublin.

In Byron's I got my first lessons in selling. And I learned fairly quickly: the ladies' shoes and the gents' shoes, the brands, the styles, colours and prices. I understood intuitively that selling was all about talking: making a connection with the customer as soon as he or she came through the door. Basically I took to it like a duck to water. Anyone who came in, I'd find out their name and where they were from as soon as I got an opening for some chit-chat. Usually you'd be able to make some sort of connection; you'd know someone that they knew, you were at school with someone they knew, you played football against their local team. Whatever common ground there was between us, you'd try and find it. With the men it was often football; with the women it was often flattery: you told them how well the pair of shoes they were trying on suited them.

If they didn't like one pair, you'd bring them ten more pairs. All the time you'd be having a bit of gallery; if they had any sense of humour at all you'd be cracking a few jokes and one-liners. If the price was competitive, and it usually was, you were then well on your way to making a sale. I sold a lot of shoes in that shop and it wasn't long before Tom was trusting me to run it on my own. Many a Saturday I opened it and closed it and looked after the cash and the stock.

Next door was Tommy Gaynor's pub and grocery, and Maureen Gaynor, God rest her, would often bring me in a mug of tea and biscuits if I was there on my own. If business was quiet you'd be out on the street, shooting the breeze with whoever happened to be passing. I think that's one of the great advantages of growing up in a small town: you learn to talk to everyone, from the solicitor and priest to the latchicoes ducking in and out of the pubs and the bookies' in the middle of the day. There isn't what you might call the class segregation you find in cities, where the rich live in one part and the poor in another. In towns like Castlerea you're mixing with the whole cross-section of your small society; you take everyone as you meet them and learn to have a civil word with everyone. And you learn that a bit of comedy helps to grease the wheels of every conversation.

I was fifteen when I moved from Byron's to Scahill's on Patrick

Street. By then I was getting used to having a few pounds in my pocket. You felt you were independent, you felt a bit important in yourself. You could buy a few groceries for your mother; you could buy twenty Gold Bond for your father. You could buy a shirt for yourself or a nice pair of football boots. I liked the independence of it and I liked not being stuck for a few bob when a lot of my mates hadn't a rex between them.

Scahill's was a big home-supplies operation that sold everything from carpets and furniture to electrical goods, giftware and domestic appliances. I'd heard on the grapevine that they were opening a second store, so one evening I called to Liam Scahill's house and asked him if there were any jobs going. Apparently this impressed him; I'd shown a bit of gumption and a bit of initiative. Anyway, I started doing weekends there, then school holidays and summer holidays, and by the time the Leaving Cert came around Liam had offered me a full-time job. Liam's father had opened the business in 1954 and I joined during a period of expansion in the mid-'80s. I spent twelve years there and learned a huge amount about the business of running a business.

From day one I was put on the shop floor selling, which of course suited me down to the ground. It was the same formula as before: put people at their ease, get to know them, gain their confidence, make them feel comfortable – and seal the sale. We had brilliant crack there over the years, but I learned very early that I had to pay my way like everybody else. Cash flow was crucial and we all had to sell. Now, I had never as much as opened a washing machine in my life at that stage, but pretty soon I was selling fifteen or twenty washing machines every week. A lot of the customers knew me and, as the years passed, my exploits on the football field for Castlerea, and especially in that Connacht minor final, meant my name sort of went before me. It helped a lot to have this sort of ice-breaker. But then again, there were lots of people who didn't know or care what you did on a foot-ball pitch. They were watching their money like everyone else and you had to be able to wheel and deal and think on your feet when the selling got serious. Naturally enough, I laid on a fair amount of guff when I'd be giving them the tour of the goods. It didn't come hard to me, and it didn't come hard to smile either, and to be friendly and as helpful as you could. You can't fool all of the people all of the time and you couldn't cross the line with too much bullshit or sales patter either. Mind you, I'd say I came close to the line a fair few times over the years. But I took pride in doing my work well and I was competitive when it came to the numbers at the end of the week. If I made my pitch to a customer and they walked out without buying anything, I nearly took it as a personal insult.

You had a bit of leeway to negotiate on price. You knew what the item cost, you knew what the retail price was, and you knew you had to make a profit on it. It was up to you to figure out what sort of discount would swing the sale. There's an art to this process, and one part of it is straightforward commerce and another part subtle psychology. I found I was fairly inventive or imaginative in the way I could present the product and negotiate with the customer.

I remember one couple came in when I wasn't long in the job full time. They were newly married and had just bought a house that was empty and needed filling. I sold them the lot, from carpets to cutlery and all points in between: tables, chairs, wardrobes, beds, white goods, electrical appliances, sanitary ware, pots, pans, crockery, the works. Liam wasn't there that day. When he came in the next day I told him to take a look in the order book, which was the bible. He opened up the relevant page and started going down through the list of stuff I'd sold. You could see he was delighted, but he did his best not to show it! It was a great boost to my confidence, but he wouldn't give you too much praise; if he did, he knew he'd have to pay you more.

I was on commission and always felt I could do with a few extra per cent. Liam says I never undervalued myself and that in fact I sometimes overvalued my contribution. Well, there was no point in hiding your light when what you did was directly linked to what you earned. But we never fell out over it because I got on famously with Liam and Madeline, his wife, business partner and better half by far.

In fairness they were very flexible with me, and in fairness too, they had to be. I was hard to pin down at times, but they had the good sense to keep me on a long leash and not a short one. I just don't work that well on a short leash. I don't like too much structure or too many regulations. For example, I was inclined to be late of a Monday morning, especially if I had a match the day before. The day would turn to night, and Monday morning would come around just a fraction too soon. But I could always trust my loyal colleague, Jimmy D'Arcy, to step into the breach and man the fort while I was in recovery mode. Then I'd have to bunk off early sometimes of a Thursday, or a Friday, or a Saturday, for a match or a training session or something, and they'd let me off. But generally I'd have my work done and my quotas reached. I usually kept myself ahead of the game in that regard.

There was one time (at least) when I was a bit too smart for my own good. I had liberated the company van for a weekend in Dublin without telling the boss. I must have forgot. Anyway, Roscommon were playing in Croke Park that weekend and wasn't I spotted tearing down O'Connell Street in the van with the side door open and half a dozen Rossies hanging out of it with their flags, roaring and shouting like lunatics. Of course the word got back to Liam and Madeline fairly quick. In fact they knew about it before I was back in Castlerea. I got some land when I arrived in to work to be faced by the pair of them, looking none too impressed. There was no asking for a wage increase that week. Or indeed many another week when Jimmy and I went cap in hand to the boss man.

I'd like to think they were happy with my contribution, and I'd like to think that the customers also were happy with the deals they did with me. Even the women whom on one occasion I talked into buying frying pans that weren't quite as prestigious as I suggested. A rack of frying pans had been sitting on the floor for weeks and they weren't moving. And I was at home one night watching television when Darina Allen came on with her cookery programme. It was one of her early series and Darina was just getting well known at the time. So the following Saturday, when a rake of women came into the shop, I very helpfully steered them towards the rack of pans. And I said to them, do you know that Darina Allen one, the lady who cooks on the television? And of course they did, they were all big fans. 'Well that frying pan there, that's the one Darina uses on the telly. It's a mighty frying pan altogether. Non-stick, great for the old rashers and sausages, and it'll last a lifetime.' Or words to that effect. Well, those frying pans walked out the door. And I'm sure they produced many a good feed for the families lucky enough to have one in their kitchen.

Then there was the bed department. Needless to say, I knocked outrageous crack out of selling beds. Any couple that came in looking for a new bed, be they twenty or eighty, I'd start the saucy talk with them. The brand leader in those years was Odearest, with their famous advertising slogan: 'For the rest of your life'. Now, you could buy a bed at the time for less than a hundred quid. Odearest had a top-of-the-range model that went for around £650, £700. But we also stocked beds from a rival company in Tuam called Home Lee Bedding. And Odearest were up against it in our shop because (a) we got a better margin on the Home Lee bed, and (b) the sales rep from Home Lee would treat you better at Christmas, and (c) we had great crack with the Home Lee crew. So you were inclined to push one brand more than the other. Anyway, Home Lee brought out their own top-of-the-range job to compete with the Odearest version. It was more or less the same price, and at that money the profit margin was reasonably generous.

A young married couple came in, looking for a bed one day, and I established soon enough that they were up for a bit of fun. So I told them that this Home Lee luxury bed was the job for them. It had a quilted mattress, a chiropractically wonderful mattress that would stand up to whatever circus acts they wanted to get up to in the bedroom. It was built for gymnastics and it was built to last. And it had a double divan bottom with a base in it that you could store your blankets and bed linen in. The woman was mad for it; her husband, the fella writing the cheque, was a bit dubious; but they went for it anyway, and when they got to the till your man said he couldn't believe he was forking out £650 for a bloody bed. I told them they'd never regret it. And I bumped into them years later in a pub after a match and they were still laughing their heads off at the sales pitch I'd blinded them with that day. Mind you, they still had the bed, and they'd made three babies in it, so they were more than happy with the deal too.

For other customers, I'd try a more philosophical line. I'd ask them: 'How long do you intend to live?' And they'd look at you like you had ten heads on you. But I'd ask them again and they'd say eighty at least, they hoped to live to a good eighty or more. Grand. And I'd say to them, 'Well, you are going to spend at least a third of your life in bed, so the least you can do is treat yourself to a nice bit of comfort when you turn in for the night after another hard day at work. Yes, a third of your life will be spent in the cot. So buy a good one now and it'll be the best investment you'll ever make.' I wasn't saying anything original, mind you, but it was the way you said it that made the difference.

I sold a lot of beds in my day, and I hope that they gave my customers a lot of happy nights. In fact, you could say I played an important part in the love life of many a couple, over many years, in that particular area of the west of Ireland.

You were always dragging beds and mattresses out of the storeroom and Billy McCormack was often the lad helping me at the other end. Billy was a great friend and colleague. He was a successful graduate of the training programme run by the Brothers of Charity in Castlerea for people with learning disabilities and became a treasured member of the staff in Scahill's over many years. Billy met every customer coming in the door with a big smile and a warm welcome. And no matter how shook you were after a night on the town, Billy's first words to you would be: 'Shaneen you're looking well!' He loved Roscommon football and was a staunch Rossie himself, rarely missing a game. We were all mad about Billy and were desperately saddened when he passed away in February 2014.

Liam and Madeline Scahill were great friends to me over those years and we are still good friends to this day. It went way beyond the employer–employee relationship. I had a great time working with them, I learned a huge amount, and basically I grew up in that shop. I matured, my confidence soared, and it gave me a solid foundation for the next stage of my working life. Around the time I told them I was leaving, I remember Madeline saying that the pupil had taken over from the master. No, Liam was still the top man, but it had been a brilliant business apprenticeship for me.

4.   A Box in the Jaw

I made my senior county debut for Roscommon in Hyde Park in the winter of 1990. It was against a Down team that would go on to win their historic All-Ireland title some ten months later. They were assembling a formidable side at the time.

Roscommon were managed by Martin McDermott. Castlerea had reached the county final earlier that summer, where we were trounced by the all-conquering Clann na nGael team of that era. But I'd been in free-scoring form during that championship campaign and Marty had drafted me into the squad later that autumn for the 1990/91 season.

This was one of those horrible dank November Sundays where you'd be sat in this old-fashioned concrete dugout in the Hyde, down in a hole basically, with pools of water lapping up around your boots and you freezing your nuts off. I was wearing a pair of white shorts instead of the official blue-and-yellow combination. And if I recall, I was also wearing a number 28 or 29 jersey. So I wasn't exactly dressed for the occasion. I was well down the pecking order as far as I was concerned. So I was surprised when Marty turned to me early in the second half and told me to get warmed up. After a few minutes I was sent on for Gerry Cregg.

I was nineteen at the time, skinny as a rake and an innocent ginger head on me. I'd say I looked about fourteen. I'd say, for the Down full-back line, I looked like an antelope fawn would look to a lion on the African plains: easy prey, a handy kill, a gosson sleepwalking into a man's world. As soon as I went in to corner forward, the corner back lamped me with a box in the jaw. A scattering of Rossie supporters saw it and started shouting and roaring. But a far bigger roar went up when I turned around and lamped yer man back. A good proper skite to the head. No big deal: it was just my way of telling him I wasn't going to be bullied. It was the only way of telling him. We settled down after that, I clipped a point and had a decent debut.

I came off the bench the next day as well, against Dublin in Croke Park. We got a fair old pasting that day. I was marking Mick Kennedy, a real old-school corner back and a great Dublin stalwart. And when I landed in beside Mick he says to me, 'Don't worry, sonny, I'm not going to be giving you a slap today.'

We were well beaten at this stage so I say back to Mick, 'Well, it'd be hardly worth your while anyway.'

I was more or less a semi-detached member of the squad for the rest of that national league campaign. Roscommon qualified for the play-offs and in April '91 played Tyrone in a league quarter-final in Breffni Park. We won by a point, but I didn't play. Well, to be strictly accurate, I came on to the pitch during the half-time interval and played a bit of ball with the other subs. And the game we played, in all innocence, was soccer. We were just tipping it around. There was fuckn war afterwards. Some of the Ulster GAA contingent seemingly took great umbrage at the fact that the Roscommon subs were playing soccer, in Breffni bloody Park! It was sacrilege, apparently; you even had some bollocks giving out about us in the national newspapers.

On a Sunday in May, Castlerea St Kevin's played a league match against St Aidan's. We won with a score of 2-12 and I'd hit 0-11 from frees and play. That evening Roscommon were playing a challenge match against Monaghan, in Monaghan. I was absolutely knackered, and so I bailed out of the trip to Monaghan. My Castlerea teammates on the Roscommon panel, Derek Duggan and Andy Leyland, headed on without me. I told them I'd see them at county training the following Tuesday. But the next day I received a fairly hostile phone call from one of the senior members in that Roscommon team. He gave out shite to me for not making the Monaghan game. I bottled out of training the next night. I didn't want to have to go explaining myself to certain people over why I missed the match. I felt bullied by this senior pro who was having a go at me because I was an easy target. So I skipped the session and that was the end of it. Marty McDermott didn't make any contact and I didn't play for

Roscommon again that year. Looking back, I'd say the management had decided I wasn't ready for senior championship football anyway. I was a squad player, one for the future, not the here and now. In hindsight I should've turned up for that training session and faced the music. But the lesson for me out of this episode is that young players often have other stuff going on in their lives. If they're not turning up for games or training, it's often because they're dealing with other issues. They need to be handled with a bit more tact and understanding than this senior player showed.

Anyway, Roscommon won Connacht later that summer and took the great Meath team of that era to the wire in the All-Ireland semi-final. Duggan scored a fantastic goal that is still widely remembered, but we missed far too many chances in the first half when we had Meath on the rack. We lost by a point. I felt I could've made a difference. Thrown on with twenty minutes to go, in that atmosphere, on that stage, I know I'd have done something; I'd have made something happen. But that ship had well and truly sailed by then. This was a settled and mature Roscommon team with a lot of veterans on it and I never really felt part of the set-up that season. I'm a great believer anyway in the old saying: what's for you won't pass you by. It wasn't for me that season, it passed me by, and no regrets.

McDermott asked me back in the autumn of '91, but I had joined Athlone Town that summer and was excited about giving soccer a serious shot. I declined the offer, but in fairness to Marty he left the door open and the following April he brought me back into the panel. I played in a series of challenge matches and forced my way into a team that was debilitated with injuries going into the first round of the Connacht championship against Leitrim. The Roscommon full-forward line that day was all Castlerea: Duggan, Leyland, Curran. We won the match but it wasn't a particularly happy championship debut for myself. About five minutes before half time I was fuckn creeled by the Leitrim goalkeeper, a proper butcher's job. I'd got off to a lively start and was going fairly well. Junior McManus got on a ball and I was screaming for it inside. Junior let it in but there was a red cross on the ball – it was a bit of a hospital pass. I had to stretch for it and leave myself wide open. I knew I was wide open.

And sure enough, out came Thomas Quinn and he ploughed into me around the midriff; he nearly broke me in half. It was a blatant penalty; of course no penalty was given. I met the referee at a do in Belmullet twenty years later and I made sure to remind him of it as well, because I never forgot that hit. I was down for a few minutes. I actually walked off, vexed that I'd been taken off 'cos I thought I was able to continue. But that was only the adrenalin masking the pain. In the dugout I started to get weak and faint. I was taken to hospital in Galway that evening, where they found a broken rib that was pressing against a lung.

I was still hoping to make it back for the Connacht final against Mayo. But, a week or so before the final, that suddenly became the furthest thing from my mind. Ciaran Webb was found dead in the swimming pool in Castlerea on a Sunday morning. He was only twenty-five. I'd been out with Webby the night before, he'd actually left me home that night. Duggan picked me up for county training the next morning and broke the news. We were dumbfounded. We'd played with Webby for years, with St Kevin's and Castlerea Celtic. He was the life and soul of any party: a lovely lad, an engineer, mad about Leeds United, and a really popular character. His death hit us all hard. I'm glad to say that he is still remembered and beloved in Castlerea, where an annual soccer tournament is played in his name, the Ciaran Webb Memorial Shield.

I started on the bench against Mayo and came on late in the second half. Andy didn't start either. He was a great friend of Ciaran's and his heart just wasn't in it. Mayo beat us by seven points and this was really the end for a generation of Roscommon veterans who'd given the county team long and distinguished service. Terrific servants like Gay Sheeran, Paul Hickey, Seamus Killoran, Pat Doorey, Paul Earley, John Newton, Joey Connaughton and others were nearing the end of their careers. A few weeks later the greatest of them all, Tony McManus, announced he was retiring after sixteen seasons. Most of that generation was gone within a few years and it left a huge void in the Roscommon county team for more or less the rest of the decade.

Lean years lay ahead as one cycle ended and another began. Marty

McDermott also stepped down, replaced by the legendary Roscommon figure that was Dermot Earley. But I had made up my mind that I was committing full time to Athlone Town, which left me in a sort of self-imposed exile as regards the county team for the next season. This was my one chance to make a real go of a professional sport and I wasn't going to take any half-measures.

5. Athlone Town

In January 1992, aged twenty, I made my first-team debut for Athlone Town in the Premier Division of the League of Ireland. This was the big time, or so I thought anyway, and a great crowd of my Castlerea friends and teammates had come down to St Mel's Park to support me. A lot of Roscommon GAA supporters from around the county had come down to cheer me on too.

The manager, Pat Devlin, came in at half time and reared up on me. Ate the shite outta me altogether. And there was me thinking I'd been doing a great job between the sticks.

I felt like saying to Pat, 'Listen, no one told me, I'm just going on instinct here, I've never had a minute's goalkeeping coaching in my life!' And I hadn't either. We were playing Shelbourne. Athlone's regular keeper, Josh Moran, had a niggle and they'd decided to throw me in at the deep end. Sink or swim. And I was swimming.

'Shane Curran,' reported Frank Roche in the following week's *Westmeath Independent*, 'making his first-team debut, belied any early nerves with an acrobatic fingertip save. The young Castlerea custodian grew in confidence as the match progressed, especially when dealing with high crosses, and the occasional injudicious advance from goal can be forgiven in view of his tender years.'

It was the 'injudicious' advances off my goal line that had Devlin blowing a gasket at half time. I was attacking every ball into the box, coming for every cross. One of our centre halves that day was Colm Phillips, a good, battle-hardened operator. At one point a cross came in that was nearer to the edge of the box than to the goal line, and I came for that one too. Colm was jumping for it, and I went flying over his head to grab it. I couldn't hold on to it and we just about scrambled it clear.

It was basic inexperience and basic lack of specialist coaching in what is obviously a specialist position. I was raw, natural but raw. A few of the Castlerea Celtic lads, myself included, had been selected to represent the Roscommon & District League in the FAI's Youth Inter-League Cup, the rough equivalent in soccer of the Roscommon county minor team. And we did very well for a couple of seasons, reaching the All-Ireland semi-final as it was, having beaten a Dublin team along the way. A fella from Ballinasloe by the name of Noel Gannon, who was PRO with Athlone Town, had been keeping an eye on me, and our chairman, Pat O'Connor, had been promoting my name to anyone who would listen. Pat saw potential in me and always believed I could play at a higher level. So when Athlone came calling, Pat paved the way for my transfer. I was brought down to play a few games with the Athlone reserves and they seemingly liked what they saw. I started training with them and was then put on the bench for a couple of first-team matches.

But I was by no means a polished professional keeper. I enjoyed the job, I loved the acrobatics of it: springing across the goal and touching shots round the corner and over the crossbar. I was six foot one and I could command my area. The years playing Gaelic football made me very confident in the air, in terms of handling the ball and timing my leaps – I could get up high and hold on to the ball. I had no fear of leaping into a crowd of players in the box, all of them attacking the cross, and claiming the ball. Crosses were meat and drink to me. In fact, I was winning so many of them that day I distinctly remember a crowd of Shelbourne fans behind my goals shouting at Padraig Dully to stop putting in crosses. They were roaring at him in their Dublin accents: 'That fucker's a bleedin' gah man!' 'That ginger cunt plays gah for Roscommon so he does.' 'Will ya stop crossing the ball into him for jaysus sake!' Dutchy had started out in league football with Athlone Town. And I remember him looking back at the Shels fans as if to say, 'What can I do about it?!' Shelbourne went on to win the title that season and their team that day was peppered with top names in the domestic game at the time: Jody Byrne, Mick Neville, Dessie Gorman, Mark Rutherford and Gary Howlett, who scored the winning goal that day.

Despite Devlin's criticism, I was buzzing about it all, and leaving St Mel's Park that day I was on cloud nine. I met up with my hometown mates after the game. We stopped off in Jimmy Murray's in Knockcroghery for a few pints on the way home, and the celebrations continued when we got back to Castlerea.

A few weeks later we beat St Francis in the Leinster Senior Cup final, but that was as good as it got that season. We were in relegation trouble right throughout the spring – which meant I was a busy boy between the posts. The upside was that I had lots of chances in every game to show what I could do, and I was in flying form. The match reports in those months are littered with accounts of the saves I was making to keep us in games. They are dotted as well with references to mistakes – paying the price for my inexperience at this level. But overall I was making my mark and generating a buzz for my style of goalkeeping, which was commonly described as flamboyant, sometimes spectacular and occasionally 'enigmatic'! You were coming up against serious players at that level, the likes of John Caulfield and Pat Morley at Cork City, Pat Fenlon, Paul Osam, Derek Swan – talented, battle-hardened professionals. You could only get better playing against them, and I could feel myself getting stronger, more confident in my judgement and concentration.

Pat Byrne and the great Jim McLaughlin were joint managers of Shelbourne at the time, and Jim had a lot of connections in the English game. Rumours started flying around pretty quickly that Jim had been scouting me for Manchester City and there was a lot of talk of me getting various trials cross-channel. I heard the talk but didn't pass any remarks. It had never crossed my mind at that stage that it might be a possibility. I suppose I had low expectations, not having grown up in the soccer culture the way a young lad from Dublin might have. I mean, even getting to play for the Athlone Town first team was a quantum leap for me in terms of where I was coming from. It was an alien world to me, the professional soccer culture – I was the first fella from Castlerea ever to play League of Ireland. I was happy enough with that.

Later that season the club decided to put me on a professional contract. They'd been paying me £30 a week to cover my expenses, which barely covered my petrol up and down from Castlerea. But they put me on a pro contract, mainly, as I understood it, to make sure they cashed in if an English club came looking for me. The more they paid me, apparently, the more money was on my head when it came to the negotiations. So they offered me £150 a week. This was solid money at the time; I was getting £120 a week from Scahill's. I was chuffed. The idea of getting paid to play sport was a dream for me. I had been doing it for nothing, but now someone was paying me money to do it. Athlone Town might have had ulterior motives, but that didn't bother me. I asked no questions. I felt this was tremendous validation of my ability. I was actually a professional sportsman, even if I had a full-time job in civilian life too.

Mind you, it didn't take long for the reality of so-called professional soccer in Ireland to dawn on me. It was professional in name only, at least as far as Athlone Town were concerned. The facilities were a joke, the training a shambles. There were no training facilities whatsoever. The club had to beg, borrow and steal a place to train. Sometimes we'd train under floodlights on a spare pitch at Athlone RTC. Well it was basically a field masquerading as a pitch. We had no dressing rooms there. And if it wasn't available we'd use a GAA pitch on the grounds of the Marist College secondary school. It had two rigged-up lights so we could just about see where we were going. And if that wasn't available you'd find yourself driving round the town looking for a place; more often than not we'd end up training on a tarmac car park on Connaught Street with just the street lights for illumination. Afterwards your gear would be covered in muck, you'd be soaked to the skin, and you had to drive home before you'd get a shower. And usually you'd only have six or seven lads there anyway because most of the squad was based in Dublin and they only showed up the day of a match. They'd be training on their own in Dublin.

We were sponsored by the cake company Gateaux, and in fairness the MD, Tom Burke, a native of Athlone, was more than generous with his effort and commitment. But the set-up in general was a farce. The games were great, especially the home fixtures where we had a hardcore fanbase that came out in support. But behind the façade, you had a seriously dysfunctional operation. Everything was a struggle, everything was a fight.

In April '92 we were beaten 6–3 by St Patrick's Athletic at Harold's Cross, and it was a fitting place to be relegated: a dog track with a pitch in the middle of it, miles away from the crowd, and a wind blowing through it that would cut you in two. It was a bleak place to play football, and worse when you had hailstones falling on you and sheets of wind blowing into your face, as we had that day. Next season we'd be sampling the delights of Division One football from Finn Harps in the north to Cobh Ramblers in the south: Monaghan United, Longford Town, Galway United, Kilkenny City, Home Farm, UCD and St James's Gate.

Pat Devlin resigned in May. Mickey O'Connor took over as player-manager. That summer I got a call one day from Mickey. He wanted to meet me for a chat. I met him in the Royal Hoey Hotel in Athlone. Mickey told me straight up that the club could no longer afford to pay me my wages. Being the naive culchie from Castlerea that I was, I just accepted it. I didn't point out the obvious: that I had a three-year contract with the club and they were duty-bound to honour it. No. I just said, fair enough, all I want to do is play football, so whatever you can afford, it'll do me. He put me back on £50 or £60 a week, I can't remember which. I don't hold it against O'Connor or anyone else. Playing for money was still something new to me. I loved playing and had never expected to get paid, I just saw it as a bonus rather than a basic entitlement. Money wasn't the be-all and end-all for me then, or now. If you have it, grand, if you don't, you'll survive all right until you do.

That was my attitude, but the League of Ireland was full of mercenaries. The older guys who'd been around the league for years knew the system and cornered the budgets. You had an old boys' network operating everywhere. It was a merry-go-round where the same faces would fetch up at different clubs from season to season and every manager would have his own few favourites who he'd bring with him wherever he'd go. The manager would look after these players at their new club; it was all a bit of a closed shop. Managers took what they could get for themselves first; they looked after their mates in the dressing room next; then they dribbled out the remainder to the rest of the suckers in the squad. It was like they were all second-hand car dealers, except they were wheeling and dealing with players instead of cars.

Athlone Town operated in a cash economy. Occasionally, if they'd got a good crowd in through the turnstiles that particular week, you'd get a cheque. But most weeks if they gave you a cheque it'd bounce like a fuckn ping-pong ball. So it was usually cash in a brown envelope. I mean literally a brown envelope. You'd go up to the clubhouse after a home game for your money, which was the only time they could afford to pay you. Because the next game was an away game and they wouldn't have any cash coming in the following week, they'd try to cover you for two weeks after a home game. But often you'd only get paid for that week and wouldn't get anything the next week.

There was always war when fellas didn't get paid. The bitching and the arguments would start: we're not putting up with this, those cunts are robbing us, I'm getting to fuck out of this kip, we're supposed to be professionals, etc., etc. But they weren't professionals, there was fuck-all professionalism anywhere as far as I could see, certainly off the pitch. The players were semi-professionals, which is a loose term anyway, and the whole thing was run by amateurs posing as professionals. If someone had a bad run of games, one of the excuses for him would be that he hadn't gotten paid. This was seen as a legitimate excuse for not bothering your hole in a match: I haven't got paid, so why should I bother. That used to rile me. I could never accept that excuse and I don't know any GAA player who would: go out and play your best anyway and at least keep your pride in yourself. Having said all that, some of the senior pros who came to Athlone Town couldn't be faulted for their attitude. The likes of Frank Darby and Barry Murphy were top players who'd put their heart and soul into every match.

Another great lad was my rival for the keeper's jersey, Anthony 'Jelly' Keenan, a local hero who'd been part of the Athlone squad that won the club's first ever League of Ireland title in 1980/81. Jelly had huge experience, and Mickey decided to install him as first-choice custodian for '92/'93. But there was no edge between us. We were part of the goalkeepers' union after all, and Jelly was very good to me in terms of mentoring me and passing on a few tricks of the trade. He was really the first guy to give me specialist coaching in the position and I learned a lot from him. Sadly, Jelly passed away in 2010 after a long illness.

I saw very little game-time that season but, despite that, rumours of a transfer deal kept resurfacing. The strongest talk was of a move to Blackburn Rovers, who were then managed by Kenny Dalglish. Pat Devlin had a long association with Kenny and, although he was no longer managing Athlone, it would've been normal for him to alert Dalglish to any good prospects on this side of the Irish Sea. In March '93 the local press raised the Blackburn connection but again nothing came of it, and I never inquired further about it either. The season was a total anticlimax for me personally and for the club: I spent most of it warming the bench and the club got mired in the mediocrity of the division. We didn't make a serious run for promotion and were left treading water for most of the campaign.

I was still playing Gaelic for Castlerea St Kevin's, and in October '93 we reached another senior county final, only to be beaten again by Clann na nGael. I was feeling the call of the county jersey too and there was no longer a huge incentive to put all my eggs in one basket with Athlone. The set-up in terms of training, facilities, coaching and finances was still a shambles. And Jelly was still holding on to the number one jersey. You had more camaraderie with the Gaelic lads too, and everything was better organized and, ironically, more professional. Division One of the League of Ireland, playing on shit pitches in the depths of winter with two men and a dog looking at you, was a wasteland. I loved a crowd and found the empty venues soul-destroying.

Athlone got promoted back to the Premier Division for '93/'94 but the season was another washout for me, sitting on the bench and playing with the reserves. For all the talk of England, my much-touted big career in soccer had run into the sand. As a result, I'd migrated back to the Roscommon set-up that season and was involved in their league and championship campaigns. But that was another washout too. The team was going nowhere. Bad and all as things were at Athlone, at least they were going to be in the Premier Division for '94/'95. And now that they were, the club wanted the strongest squad it could muster. They wanted me committed as the number two goalkeeper behind Anthony for the season. They would even bump my wages up to £80 a game – or was it £70? – and sure how could I resist? Anyway, I bit the bullet and made that commitment.

The season had barely started when Jelly got injured. I got back into the first team and stayed there more or less for the rest of a season that would culminate in an almighty drama at St Mel's Park. It was the match that decided the title race, and which left me public enemy number one among Derry City supporters for years to come.

6. Roscommon: The Lost Years

My fellow Castlerea St Kevin's clubman, Mickey Freyne, was a Roscommon selector with Donie Shine, the manager, and Mickey had always maintained that one day I'd end up a goalkeeper in Gaelic too. He'd seen me playing for Castlerea Celtic over the years and reckoned it was my natural position. And now he and Donie were sizing me up for the number one jersey on the county team. I was still knocking over plenty of points for Castlerea in the full-forward line, but they were trying to build a new Roscommon team and they wanted someone who could nail down that key position once and for all.

Dermot Earley had stepped down as manager at the end of '93/'94. It hadn't worked out, but it wasn't his fault. Managerial success or failure has a lot to do with timing, and Dermot was caught between the end of the previous era and the start of the new. The old team was disintegrating, and in a county like Roscommon you're not automatically going to get a new wave of players coming through as good as those they're replacing. These things come in cycles. A lot of very good players with strong leadership ability had bowed out, and the next generation struggled to fill what had become a major void. We were on a downward spiral.

The mood in the county wasn't helped by the death in February '94 of the county board secretary, Paddy Francis Dwyer. Paddy Francis was an absolute gent, and very nice to young players, which wasn't something you could always take for granted from county board officers. The committee men often viewed players as fellas not to be trusted, smartarses who had to be kept down and only grudgingly looked after when it came to welfare and expenses. But Paddy Francis was very good to us.

I remember, I think it was around December 1990, when myself, Derek Duggan and Enon Gavin were only young bucks fresh on to the senior panel. We were all stuck for a few quid coming up to Christmas so we decided to approach Paddy Francis in the Royal Hotel after a league game. The team wasn't going well, so we went to him with a fair bit of trepidation. We needn't have worried. He said to us to write out a few expenses on a bit of paper and there and then took out his cheque book. Without further ado he gave us a cheque each for £300 if I recall. He could've made a big song-and-dance about going through the official channels and all that nonsense, but he didn't; a gesture like that is something that means a lot, especially when you're that age. Paddy Francis smoked a pipe, drove his Ford Granada like he was Jackie Stewart, and usually referred to us affectionately as 'gossons'. I've never forgotten his decency to us.

Paddy Francis was also a top-class administrator and I could've learned plenty from him when, still in my mid-twenties, I became chairman of St Kevin's. Things had gone a bit flat at the club, and they reckoned some young blood and fresh thinking was needed. I'd like to think I had a safe pair of hands as a goalie but no one would've said I was a safe pair of hands in this particular line of work. I wasn't the most political or diplomatic of people. Pretty soon I was nicknamed 'Chairman Mao'. But I was really only the front-of-house fella. The work was done by our secretary, Brian Stenson, who later went on to become secretary of the county board. I did drive things on the financial side, setting up a new club lottery draw which I think was one of the first of its kind in the country. It proved to be very successful and is still going strong.

Dermot's regime came to an end after Leitrim beat us in the first round of the Connacht championship in June. I was in the full-forward line that day alongside Don Connellan and Dermot Washington; I did not play well. Leitrim would go on to beat Galway and Mayo that summer to claim their first Connacht title since 1927, so there was no disgrace in losing to them. I opted out of '94/'95 to concentrate on Athlone Town, and when I came back in the winter of '95 it was with the proviso that I'd wear the goalkeeper's jersey. I was happy enough with that arrangement, and Donie was happy enough for me to continue in my dual role with Athlone as well. If fixtures clashed, we'd come to a compromise, otherwise it was all systems go.

I made my goalkeeping debut against Wexford in a league game that December. When I'd first come into the panel, five years earlier, we were a Division 1 team. Now we were in Division 3 – and failing to get promotion out of it too. Mayo beat us in the first round of the Connacht championship that summer, a game I missed because of a groin injury, and another season slipped away with a whimper.

Hopes were higher going into the '97 championship the following summer after a good league campaign that saw us gaining promotion. But our performance against Sligo in the Connacht semi-final was a disaster. We took out the shotgun that day and shot ourselves in both feet. We were five up at half time and more or less dominated the third quarter; but we missed chance after chance after chance. Then on the hour mark I caught a ball and came out about fifteen, twenty yards and passed it off to our full back, Martin Feely. Next thing the ball was on the ground and I was caught in no man's land as Dessie Sloyan pounced and kicked it into an empty net. Sligo drove on from there in the last ten minutes and we were gone again, another championship summer stillborn.

Donie Shine stepped down after that and I felt really sorry for him because he'd put a lot into it and I think we let him down in many respects. Gay Sheeran took over in September, and pretty soon we had a disagreement over where I should play. Gay wanted me back playing outfield, but that ship had sailed; I was a goalie now and was very settled and happy in that position. We had a conversation and he was adamant that he saw a future for me only in the full-forward line. I don't know what his thinking was. Maybe it was something to do with the fact that he'd been Roscommon keeper himself over many years and didn't agree with my style of play. He certainly had a much more conservative mindset than I had and I'm not sure he was able to see the value of a keeper who did anything more than stand between the posts and take the kickouts.

The game was changing and keepers like John O'Leary of Dublin had already shown that you could be more proactive than just spending your time standing on the goal line. O'Leary liked to operate as a sweeper behind his full-back line and so did I. He wasn't afraid to come off his line to cut out balls over the top and start attacks from there with short passes, rather than just belting the ball as far as you could downfield. I had the confidence to take that kind of initiative because I had the footwork and the speed and the ball skills to do it.

I could bring more to the table as a GAA goalkeeper because it was a much easier job than its equivalent in soccer. The soccer goalkeeper has a broader range of functions and a more complex set of challenges. You are commanding a much bigger area of the field on your own. You are guarding a goal that is higher and wider. You are much more involved in the action. Your concentration levels are tested more often and more intensely. The ball is moving at different angles and coming at you from a wider variety of trajectories, angles and heights. You have to be aware of where the ball is at all times because that dictates your positioning. And all the time you have to be in touch with your back four. The offside line keeps changing, depending on whether your defence is playing a high line or dropping deep. You might go for long periods of time without making a save, but you cannot afford to let your concentration drop at all: you very rarely get away with a slip-up in soccer, very rarely. Your decision-making is tested all the time: when to come off your line and when not; when to come for crosses and when to hang back. Then there are the set pieces, organizing your defence for corner kicks, setting up the wall for free kicks. And that's before you consider the bread-and-butter stuff, the common denominators it has with Gaelic: your shot-stopping, your handling and your kickouts.

After developing some mastery of the technical and tactical challenges in soccer, goalkeeping in Gaelic football came easy. I was very comfortable in that position. But I didn't want to stay in my comfort zone. I wanted to bring a bit of added value, as it were, to the position. It didn't have the same prestige as its counterpart in soccer. It didn't have the same specialist coaching either. Traditionally, it was often the most useless footballer on the team who got the goalkeeping gloves in Gaelic. But I knew that you could do more with the position, and I wanted to do more. I didn't just want to catch a ball in my square and lamp it seventy yards down the field to no one in particular. Most goalkeepers too would let a ball dribble harmlessly over the endline if it was going wide and that used to annoy me. Why not pick up the ball and set up an attack from there? But there weren't too many people thinking in those terms at the time, and certainly not in Roscommon.

Of course the game has changed a lot in the last ten years or so, and the position has changed with it. The traditional six backs/six forwards formation is gone. The keeper will often end up with the ball in space, and so he has to have the skills to carry the ball out and make the right pass. He has to be able to solo the ball well, pass it well off both hands and both feet, and look to set up attacks from there. I saw the sense in this at the time. I saw how it could help a team. I was willing and able to do it. But Gay Sheeran didn't see it that way. I could've brought all of this to the position, but the simple fact was that he didn't want me there at all. It was his way or the highway. The net result was that the Sligo game under Donie Shine was my last senior championship match with Roscommon until 2001. I was out in the cold for the next three years.

Castlerea were dumped out of the '97 county championship not long after the Sligo shambles and I decided to head to America that summer to play a bit of ball and have some fun on the famous GAA circuit Stateside. A businessman originally from Roscommon invited a load of Rossie players out to play with the Galway club in Boston: myself; Derek Duggan; our Castlerea teammate, Niall Finnegan; Nigel Dineen; Luke Dolan; Niall O'Donoghue; the Garvey brothers from the St Croan's club. This fella who invited us out promised us the sun, moon and stars. He was a bit of a chancer as it turned out. We were put up in this house in Dorchester among the big Irish community there. The house was a rough enough shack. It was rougher by the time we were finished with it. There were about fifteen of us kipping down in it. There was no air conditioning, and this was at the height of an American summer. The place stank like a sewer. It couldn't be any other way with fifteen clatty Paddies sweating and living like livestock in it. You were tripping over beer bottles and pizza boxes and Chinese takeaway cartons and dirty jocks and socks and smelly football gear everywhere. The mattresses were disgusting, the floors were a health hazard, the bathroom was a silage pit.

One night we were coming back from the pub and didn't someone notice a skunk lurking in the front garden. And of course nothing would do a few of our boys but to go over and annoy him. Now I had enough sense to keep out of the firing line. But sure enough, a buck from Dublin and a buck from Galway got sprayed by the skunk. And Jesus the stink was utterly horrendous; it was absolutely shocking; it was unnatural. It stayed in your nostrils for days. In fact I can still smell the bastard. The two lads who got hit, any slim hopes they had of a holiday romance that summer were dead. They took several baths and bought new clothes and everything, but the smell still hung around them. Eventually they had to get into a bath with yogurt and milk because someone told them that was the best remedy.

I had got engaged just before I came over and my fiancée thought it'd be a lovely idea if she joined me for a week or two later on. I thought it was a lovely idea too until I saw the state of the kip she'd be arriving to. During phone calls home I kept trying to tell her in the nicest possible way not to come out: this was no place for a woman. I was very conscious of trying to impress my new fiancée in every way, and landing her in a slum not fit for man or beast was no way to impress anyone.

I first met Sharon on 18 June 1994, a Saturday. I remember the date precisely, not just because I met my future wife that night, but because it was the famous day that Ray Houghton put the ball in the net for Ireland against Italy at World Cup USA '94. Myself and the usual crew of Saturday-night layabouts and pissheads watched that famous match in the Horse and Jockey in Castlerea. With the soccer celebrations in full flow, we decided we'd hit for Rockfords emporium in Roscommon town. Anyway we piled into the nightclub and partied on with the usual buffoonery. A great night was had by all, and it got even better when I bumped into this lassie at the door. It was Sharon Curley from Brideswell. She was looking a million dollars that night. And there was no way I was going till I got her number, which she kindly gave me on the back of a cigarette box I picked up off the floor. Romance, how are ya! Sharon had just begun her nurse's training in the Beaumont Hospital in Dublin. She'd given me her home number, and every time I rang she wasn't there. I ended up getting to know her mother Rosie better than Sharon herself, until I met her a second time on the night of the All-Ireland football final that year, in the great Jimmy Murray's pub in Knockcroghery. We had a lot of things in common, we got on very well from the start, and our relationship developed strongly over the next few years. We dated in Dublin, Athlone, Castlerea and Roscommon — none of them Paris or Rome, in fairness, but we had plenty of laughs and good times along the way.

Anyway, she had great hopes for our few weeks together in Boston. I did my best to tidy up the joint but she got some land when she walked in the front door of our palace in Dorchester. Poor Sharon spent the week trying to clean the place up.

Meanwhile, we'd come out to Boston on the pretence that we were going to work as painters and decorators and carpenters and bricklayers and the like. But basically we were getting paid about $700 a week to play football. Which is more than I ever got in a week, or even a month, playing for Athlone Town. We were supposed to do a bit of training midweek but it wasn't too onerous: a bit of a kick-around, followed by ten or fifteen bottles of Budweiser was the order of the day. It was all financed by the GAA mafia out there. Most of them were in construction and they were happy enough to pick up the tab. Despite all the boozing and late nights we played well at the weekends because I suppose we had the reserves of fitness, and the overall standard wasn't great anyway. So the Galway club in New York thought it'd be a good idea if we could come down and beef up their team for a couple of championship matches in Gaelic Park.

The only problem was that the GAA back in Ireland was trying to regulate the flow of player traffic to America every summer and, while we'd got an exemption to play in Boston, we didn't have clearance from Croke Park to play anywhere else. And we knew there could be serious repercussions back home if we breached the regulations. Croke Park could suspend you, once you got home. But the fee per head for playing in New York was $1,500. And our man in Boston said there'd be no problem. He was looking after all the arrangements. We could all play under pseudonyms and no one would find out because no one was too bothered one way or another. The $1,500 was an all-in package: it was supposed to include the cost of your flight down from Boston. But this bucko figured it'd be smarter for him to drive down and pocket the cost of the flights. We'd still get our cut and he'd charge New York for flights that were never taken.

Anyway myself, himself, Dineen, Dolan, O'Donoghue and Finnegan all bundled into his car early one Sunday morning for the drive down to New York. We'd all been out on the tear the night before, and a few more cans were consumed en route too. We were all given names that were connected to various Irish rebels and republicans, with their Christian names and surnames mixed around. I don't know who came up with that bright idea, and I can't remember whether I was some fella from 1916 or 1798.

Myself and O'Donoghue played together in the full-forward line in the first game, then adjourned to the bar in Gaelic Park while the second match got underway. Dineen, Dolan and Finnegan were playing in the second game, and it was fairly obvious before too long that Dineen was a bit off-colour; in fact he didn't look too steady on his feet at all.

Some genius had come up with the pseudonym of 'Johnny Sands' for our Nigel. And there was a fella on the tannoy doing a running commentary, a lad who had delusions of being Michael O'Hehir, Micheál Ó Muircheartaigh and Willie Hegarty rolled into one. And every time 'Johnny Sands' got on the ball, O'Donoghue and me broke into a fresh fit of laughing. Anyway, his team at one stage was awarded a free on the 14-yard line, dead straight in front of the goals, and Dineen decided to take it. So he puts the ball down and starts pacing back from it. And I'm saying to Niall, 'Jaysus, he doesn't look too steady in himself at all.'

So he begins his run-up to the ball and just as he's about to pull on it, doesn't he trip over himself and land in a heap on the ground. And yer man on commentary was going, 'Johnny Sands now, Johnny Sands with the free, this should be a simple point – and Johnny Sands has missed the fuckn free! Johnny Sands has fallen over!' Well, we were nearly on the floor ourselves with the laughing. It was one of the funniest sights in all my days playing football.

A while later, one of the New York fellas who had financed our trip came over to me in a fairly agitated state. He said that our fella, the fixer from Boston, was looking for $1,500 a head for us, but he wasn't going to pay it because we hadn't taken any flight down from Boston. He'd seen the bucko's car in the car park with its Massachusetts plate and he wasn't one bit happy that yer man was trying to pull a fast one. And he asked me, where were our airline tickets? I played innocent; I said I didn't know what was going on. And he said that this fella was going to get killed once he appeared. And I said, as long as *we* don't get killed I don't mind. We just wanted our money and to get back to Boston in one piece. He said he'd meet us in a pub in the Bronx later that night with the money. Grand, said I.

Next thing, there was a commotion and I looked around and there was our Boston friend on the receiving end of several wild swinging punches. A few more members of the New York branch of the GAA mafia weren't happy with him either, and they'd decided to take the law into their own hands. They were shouting and roaring and swinging at him and as he was trying to get away he sent several tables and bottles flying in all directions. It was like a scene out of a John Wayne cowboy film. It was cat altogether; they were batin' him black and blue. Several punters then jumped in before it could get too serious, and pulled them apart and calmed things down. We rounded up the troops fairly lively after that and got out of there and headed for downtown Manhattan.

We still wanted the money, so we showed up in the pub in the Bronx that night. And the New York fella turned up with a wad of cash and divvied out the money. He said he'd pay us a grand each for turning up, but he was keeping the rest. We were more than happy with that. But didn't our Boston friend stick his oar in too, demanding his cut for his troubles. Well, that was a red rag to a bull and suddenly the New York lads started fucking him out of it and getting very belligerent with him all over again. Now this fella was about six foot two and twenty-two stone and he had drink taken too and started getting belligerent back with them. Next thing, the row was up again. He was jumped on by three or four fellas and they grabbed him and hoisted him over the counter of the bar! They threw him over the counter and he landed down the other side. And when his head appeared above the counter they started firing bottles at him, pelting him with bottles, and roaring and shouting that they were going to fuckn kill him.

It was getting serious now and I said to the lads, let's get to fuck out of here. So we grabbed yer man from behind the counter and said to the other cowboys that we'd take him straight back to Boston and get him out of their hair. It turned out that there'd been bad blood between him and the New York lads in previous years; apparently he'd tried to pull this scam before. In fairness, they'd no beef with the rest of us, so they gave us the go-ahead. We bundled yer man out of the pub and into the car and got back on the road. It was time to get out of Dodge.

Yer man was all scratched and bloodied and bruised about the face. And there wasn't much chat out of him after that; he was fairly shook. To be honest, between the drink, the travelling, the football match and the brawling, we were fairly shook ourselves too. Everyone apart from Johnny Sands, of course, who at this stage was comatose in the back of the car.

Boston is a beautiful city and we had six weeks of fantastic crack there. But later that year our American jolly came back to bite us in the backside. For some reason those exotic pseudonyms we'd chosen hadn't worked. We were ringers – and they had the photos to prove it. The long arm of the GAA law had reached as far as New York and collared us. We were handed twelve-month suspensions for our illegal jaunt in Gaelic Park. We appealed it. We had to face a kangaroo court in Croke Park and state our case. But of course we didn't have a leg to stand on.

I didn't know whether to take this charade seriously or not. These GAA committees can have the effect of bringing out the joker in you. You're supposed to be serious, but it's hard not to have a smile on your face when you're looking across the table at these fellas with their sombre faces in their Sunday suits and pioneer pins. But we did our best, stumbling and shuffling through a few explanations before heading outside while the committee adjourned to consider the gravity of our offence. We were then informed that the sentence had been reduced to six months. And then one of our county board officers told us afterwards that an arrangement had been squared away and the six months would later be reduced again, on the QT, to three. This was around November/December. And seeing that it was now the off-season, it wouldn't really affect us at all.

This was GAA justice at its nod-and-wink best – and its nod-and-wink worst too, it must be said. Because when really serious stuff happened, like when fellas were getting assaulted left, right and centre on the field of play, GAA justice was often nowhere to be found.

7.   Crime and Punishment

While researching this book I came across a report on a club championship match in the *Roscommon Herald*. It was August '93 and Castlerea were playing Shannon Gaels, a club from the north of the county on the Leitrim border. The final scoreline was 2-21 to 2-2. I'd scored 2-5 from play and, according to the report, I'd put on a bit of a show. It seems I was up to my usual tricks, pulling off a few flashy moves, celebrating the goals with somersaults, a general bit of showboating.

For my sins I nearly got my jaw broken. And in the GAA culture it *was* a sin to try to entertain the crowd. I can't imagine there were more than a couple of hundred, but probably in my head I was performing to adoring thousands in Highbury or Croke Park. I liked putting on a show, when the chance arose. I enjoyed laying on the shimmies and dummies and sidesteps, sending defenders the wrong way, doing things with a bit of style and class. Sometimes people told me to tone it down. I used to argue that sometimes the flamboyant way of scoring was also the most efficient way of scoring.

Anyway, in a one-sided game like that you could play around and enjoy yourself, not just play to win. For our second goal their keeper hit his kickout straight to me. And seemingly I got it into my head to lob the ball back over him, run around the other side of him, and stroke it into an empty net.

Later on I ended up on the ground, going for a ball. According to the *Roscommon Herald*, one of their defenders 'quite deliberately ploughed into a grounded Curran with his knees. The dazed full forward was helped from the field holding his jaw.' I can't recall the incident but I can recognize the kind of tackle: running into a fella's face with the knees, accidentally-on-purpose, is a mean, dangerous act.

It was the same in most counties at the time, I suppose, but skilful forwards were routinely targeted in club matches in Roscommon. You'd be punched, kicked, pulled and dragged, on the ball and off the ball. You were seen by some clubs – not all clubs – as a punch bag, as fair game for all sorts of thuggery and intimidation.

In 1994 I got sent off twice in the space of two months for retaliation. We were playing Elphin in a championship match. I'd scored two points, but one of their defenders was absolutely dogging me. Midway through the first half I turned round and flaked him with a box. Of course, the umpires, who'd seen nothing up until then, saw that, and I got the line. Then against Strokestown in August I was sent off again for a second bookable offence, having been on the receiving end of more rough treatment.

Basically you learned young in club football that you were never going to get adequate protection from umpires and referees, so you ended up taking the law into your own hands. Match officials were often incompetent or cowardly, or both. They wouldn't see blatant skulduggery, or they'd see it and ignore it, or they were too afraid to send players off because of the abuse they might get in return. But some of them seemed to take pleasure in seeing you getting half killed. Someone like myself was seen as too cocky for his own good. I was a county man, I was a flair player, I probably wasn't humble enough for their tastes. So you'd get hammered by ruthless defenders and they'd get away with it in front of referees who'd just look the other way.

In a 1997 championship match, again against Shannon Gaels, they assigned not one but two players to man-mark me. If one didn't get me, the other did. Any time I got near a ball I was hit from all angles with boxes to the body; when I wasn't on the ball I was pulled and dragged every time I ran a couple of yards. Basically it was a pre-planned tactic to intimidate me out of the game. It was the worst doing I ever got on a football field. But they got away with it, and it was one of those games that would leave you totally disillusioned about the sport.

The atmosphere in those games was often toxic. There was little or no control of the sideline. You'd have subs, mentors and supporters all congregating there, shouting vicious abuse at the referee and his linesmen. You'd have incursions on to the field of play. You'd have fellas squaring up to each other, you'd have the supporters roaring from the stand, you'd have women screaming like demons. You were often just a hair's breadth away from a fracas or a melee of some sort.

In 1998, not long after I transferred from Castlerea to St Brigid's – a story I'll tell later on – Brigid's played Kilmore in a county semi-final. The match went to extra time and was abandoned by the referee with a minute to go, officially because of fading light. But in actual fact he called it off because there was serious danger of a full-scale brawl breaking out. Richard Canny reported in the *Herald* that the game

> descended into near-anarchy at the finish against a backdrop of a side-line that was overflowing with players, mentors and a sprinkling of supporters. A number of players, finally reacting to a niggly undercurrent that coursed through the exchanges, took leave of their senses and vented their aggression in the form of a number of harmless and not-so-harmless squabbles. Even one of the linesmen became the brunt of one player's pique in an incident that had a strong resemblance to the infamous Paolo Di Canio push in the English Premiership. The fading light and [the referee's] decision to call a halt to proceedings with a minute left of extra time was a blessing in disguise. Such was the tinderbox atmosphere that the creeping darkness was a convenient expedient to bring a sorry mess to a close.

Two players were sent off, and there could have been five or six more sent off along with them. Another player needed prolonged medical attention after an off-the-ball incident.

Off the ball was where the real damage was done. If you were on the ball you'd always be expecting a skite. But if you were just standing there, looking down the field, you could be done if some fella was bad enough to do you like that, when you had no warning and no means of protecting yourself. I remember once playing a championship match for Castlerea against Tulsk in Frenchpark. The play was down the other end of the field. Next thing, I heard this horrible sound and I looked over and there was one of our players, Dermot O'Connell, lying on the ground. I jogged over to him. His face was a mess. His mouth was full of blood. His eyes were all watery and glassy.

It turned out his jaw and several of his teeth were broken. It was probably the most hateful act that ever happened on a field while I was playing. It was a despicable act. I remember distinctly meeting my father after that match and he telling me there was a bunch of Castlerea supporters waiting outside to get at the player who'd done it. They were going to kill him stone dead if they got their hands on him. Thankfully, it never came to that. And in fairness to the referee that day, he showed some real courage when it was needed. Seán Mullaney didn't see the incident, he couldn't have seen it, and of course the umpires behind the goals hadn't seen it either, surprise surprise. Mullaney came down the field and we weren't long pointing out the culprit. It was obvious who had done it because the only player in Dermot's vicinity at the time was the player marking him. I said to Mullaney, 'Seán, you can't leave that bastard on the pitch.' And I think Seán was shocked at the sight of Dermot's face. He called over the player and sent him off, despite not having seen the incident. Dermot O'Connell, as far as I'm aware, never played football again. He was in his early twenties at the time.

Andy Leyland had his jaw broken on another occasion. A county footballer who played with Strokestown suffered a horrific facial injury in a club match. Lots of players got bad doings. Fellas who wanted to assault players had more or less *carte blanche* to do it. Personally I think it took the edge off my outfield play in the end, especially as I got older. It just drained you, as much mentally as physically, knowing you were going to be in for another afternoon of abuse from whatever vigilante was handed the job of marking you. I just got fed up with it.

But in my early years as a senior player I made a decision that I wasn't going to be the victim. I wasn't going to take any of it lying down. I think the incident in Frenchpark that day left a deep imprint on me. I think I was only nineteen at the time and hadn't become hardened to this sort of lawless environment. But I figured out fairly quickly that the best way of dealing with it was to hit back. Let them know you were going to give it back if you got it. So I did. Over the years I raised my hands, I retaliated. But I never hit first and never did it in a sly, cowardly way. It was upfront and face to face.

Another way of dealing with it was to ridicule them. Usually the worst thuggery came from the worst teams. The top teams didn't have to resort to it. So it was normally bad players who'd be trying to take you out. For starters they'd be far too slow for you. I was blessed with raw speed and sharp feet. I'd often torment these fellas with dummies and shimmies, letting them think they were about to get to me, before swerving away. I'd get great satisfaction out of it. And I'd taunt them; I'd be laughing out loud and smiling into their faces. And after twisting them into knots and finishing with a score, I'd come back out to them and tell them how useless they were. The more ignorant they were, the more they got it. If I was after getting a few boxes and kicks, I loved nothing more than sticking the ball in the net and then telling them how fuckn useless they were. 'D'you know what, sonny? You are one red raw useless fucker.' 'You are fuckn full class useless.' 'You're not able to fuckn walk, never mind run, you stupid wanker.' Naturally enough, this would drive them mad altogether. And of course you knew well you were really in the firing line when you'd come out with stuff like that. But then again you'd be on fire yourself, too. You'd be flying around the place. And I wonder sometimes if they were half afraid for a finish to try and do me, because I gave them the impression I was half mad myself. That I was liable to do anything. And if they were to do something to me, they wouldn't know what I'd do back. They weren't sure what to make of me.

Referees and umpires didn't know what to make of me a lot of the time either. I mean, at club level especially, a lot of the officiating was so bad it was downright comical. You learned eventually that you were better off laughing at it than taking it too seriously because otherwise you'd blow a complete gasket.

Many's the time I stood between the posts of a Sunday afternoon, and pretty soon I'd be getting the whiff of alcohol drifting towards me across the goalmouth. The umpires would've been on the piss the night before. Believe it or not, I even got the telltale aroma in big county championship matches, and on National League days too.

But it was more commonplace in the club game. They'd be standing there beside the uprights in their white coats with big red faces on them, goggle-eyed from porter and their heads bursting with a hangover. And they'd no more want to be there of a miserable ould Sunday when they could be back in the hotel with the carvery dinner and the spuds and the gravy and the jelly and ice cream and the few pints to settle them. I'd say they'd be dreaming of the big feed while they were standing there beside the posts, yawning and scratching themselves. Well, there had to be some reason why so many of their decisions were high-class unbelievable.

Any GAA keeper will tell you that part of his job is to get chatting to the umpires. Because a lot of them were so half-hearted about the job, and so weak-minded in doing it, you knew you could get to them if you could engage them in a bit of old chit-chat and small talk. You had to plamás them in case any fifty–fifty decisions had to be made. Some of them wouldn't bother engaging with you. You can smell a prick a mile away, and you just knew by the cut of these fellas that they had no interest in being there in the first place, let alone in talking to you. But most of them were ready enough ould skins and you could get the banter going with them no bother. If I smelled the drink off them, that'd be the opening gambit. 'Jaysus, there's a right smell of porter off you! You were out last night, bucky?' 'I'd say you had a right few pints?' 'Where were ye anyway?' 'Did ye have a late one?' They'd usually laugh along with you. And you wouldn't mind a fella like that because at least you had him on your side.

If a shot for a point looked any bit off target you'd be waving your arms and shouting that it was wide, hoping you'd introduce a bit of indecision into his thought processes. To be fair, I'd say most umpires have a pain in their hole listening to goalkeepers telling them a shot is wide when it has sailed over the black spot. But you did it mainly because you couldn't trust them to do their job properly. The amount of times over the years I've seen them raising the white flag when a ball was wide and waving a wide when it went between the posts is hard to credit. You'd just shake your head in disbelief at the calls they'd make. That's why you had to keep on top of them, one way or another, either by being all pally with them, or arguing your case with them over every dubious decision. Personally, I know I've changed an umpire's mind numerous times over the years. I don't think I was abusive to them – you were better off just trying to remain friendly with them and hope that a crucial call would go your way. One decision from an umpire could have serious consequences in a game. It might just be giving a 45 to the opposing team when the ball has in fact gone wide. But when the margins are fine, every call is vital. And if the call went against you, I often told an umpire that he should've stayed in the fuckn pub the night before.

One thing I could never understand was the umpire who wore glasses turning up on a rainy day and not as much as a handkerchief in his pocket. He'd never think to bring a cloth with him to give them the odd wipe. No, he'd just stand there, trying to follow the game with the water dripping off the front of his lenses and the steam clouding them up on the other side. That was criminal altogether; there was no excuse for it at all. And you'd see him taking them off when the play was at the other end and trying to wipe them on the sleeve of his white coat. Then he'd put them back on again and two seconds later they'd be as bad as ever. Then a high ball would drop and he'd be looking up at it and twisting himself this way and that to try and get a proper gander at it. And he was as well looking up at the moon. And he's fuckn soaking wet and pissed off and you're wrecking his head and all he wants is to be back in the hotel, sitting down to the couple of pints and the big feed. I actually often did think of putting a few pairs of glasses in my glove bag and bringing them with me on rainy match days. But then I realized that if you offered them to him he'd think you were being a smartarse and give you no decisions at all.

You had to walk a sort of diplomatic line with umpires to stay on their good side. Same with referees. In my experience, the worse the referee was, the more important he was in himself. There was one little fella in Roscommon, five foot two or three, and he'd strut his way on to the field like he was ten foot tall. And he'd walk off it an hour later, having made a litter of woeful decisions. The more abuse he got the more he'd puff his chest out. He solid loved his authority. He loved tooting on his fuckn whistle.

There's another referee who had this unbelievable ability to rile half of Roscommon. Every game, he'd have supporters and players – on both sides – ready to tear their hair out. And when the full-time whistle would go, you'd be ready to hang him up by his heels. You'd be thinking he's the greatest prick that ever wore shoe leather, and you'd love to take the fuckn head off him if you got half a chance. You'd walk off the field, fuming with the temper, you'd take a hot shower and you'd head to the clubhouse bar, promising to rip him apart as soon as you'd see him. Then he'd stroll into the bar like Sergeant fuckn Bilko and the first thing you'd say to him is, 'Do you want a pint?' And then you know you're going to get an explanation for every decision, and you know the explanation is going to be as long as a novel. And he is going to be right, every single time he's going to be right! You wouldn't know whether to laugh or cry, listening to him.

In fairness to club referees, it has to be said there's not much in it for them, apart from the ego trip with some of them. There's no great glory or status in being a referee down at the grassroots. Usually there's nothing in it but hassle and abuse. So you're better off just having a bit of crack and a few pints with them afterwards. They are ordinary Joes doing a fairly unpleasant job. I generally make a point of buying them a pint. Mind you, I usually tell them too that they were good for fuckn nothing an hour earlier. They take it well; they're used to it, I suppose.

Seán Mullaney was the best of the Roscommon referees in my day. He was a great ould character, you could have a row with him on the field as long as you did it in a joking sort of way, and he wouldn't take it personally. He was old-school; he had a sense of humour and you could talk to him.

The best county referee by far that I came across was Pat McEnaney. Most players of my vintage will say that (apart maybe from the Mayo lads). His judgement of situations on the field was generally very sound. You could trust his decision-making. He just had the ability to read a tackle and call it the right way. He made lots of mistakes too – but we all do – and by and large his instincts were reliable. And he treated you with respect. This is more important, in terms of discipline, than people might think. Because the thought processes of a player are completely different if he's treated with respect. Players don't trust referees with big egos. They're more inclined to challenge them and undermine them. With McEnaney, the respect went both ways, which made players easier to handle. If there was a rumpus he'd come in and sort it out with some straight talking. He'd talk your language, he had a good way with players, and he'd lay down the law fair and square.

You contrast that with an incident from the 2013 Connacht club final. St Brigid's were playing Castlebar Mitchels in MacHale Park. After about ten minutes Castlebar were awarded a point that was a full yard and a half wide. It wasn't even close. And I turned to the umpire and told him it was a mile wide. I asked him how could he make a decision like that. And his words verbatim were, 'Whether it was a point or a wide, I'm giving the point, full stop.' I was shocked to hear that. Basically he was saying it didn't matter whether it was wide or not. Anyway, the match referee, the great Marty Duffy, then arrived on the scene. And he says to me, what are you mouthing about? And I told him the ball had gone a good yard and a half wide. He snapped at me, said it wasn't my job to decide that. And I said it was the umpire's job and he's doing it wrong and he knows it's wrong. And Duffy is all business putting me in my place until the linesman comes in and has a word with him. And he tells Duffy that it was actually a wide. It was only then he relented. The decision was reversed, the point was ruled out.

You get this kind of confusion all the time. You get referees and umpires who think it's more important to take you down a peg or two rather than admit they might be wrong. Bad officiating is a plague in Gaelic football. And as for umpires, Jesus they'd bate Banagher. When you see them looking at one other like lost sheep and wondering whether to put up the white flag or wave a wide, it's like a scene out of *Father Ted*. Most referees, instead of admitting to uncertainty, will tell you to shut up; they'll talk down to you and treat you like a schoolboy. But I don't like the sight of players hounding referees like a pack of dogs; that's horrible to see. There has to be more respect on both sides.

It's a fact of life that the tackle in Gaelic football is always going to be a big source of aggravation. If you make a tackle that you believe is fair and the next thing you get is a referee blowing the free, I think a player should be entitled to ask why the free was given. He should ask it politely, the way they do in rugby, but he should be allowed to ask because players need to know what they're doing wrong. They need to establish where the boundaries are with this particular referee because every referee has his own interpretation of when a tackle is legit and when it's not. But more often than not they'll try to put you down when you ask. They'll just dismiss you or tell you to shut up, or they'll move the ball forward thirteen metres to punish you.

I admire the way referees and players communicate in rugby union. The captain has permission to go up to the referee and ask him for an explanation. And the referee will explain his decision. Unfortunately, this wouldn't work in Gaelic football because it's a completely different game. The pitch is bigger, the ball is moving up and down the field at speed, and the captain isn't going to be able to arrive at every scene where a free is given. For that matter, the referee is often not at the place where the alleged foul occurs either. He could be forty, fifty yards away. So appointing the captain as a sort of official spokesman probably wouldn't work. But they could come up with some new protocols, some way for players to query decisions without being dismissed by the referee with a wave of his hand. The players in turn would be obliged to talk to the referee in a non-confrontational way: no raised voices or abusive language or invading his personal space. It would take a bit of thinking and planning to come up with some such protocol, but it would be worth a try because the current climate on the field is a mess.

But I'm glad to say that the GAA has got its act together big-time over the last twenty years on the burning issue of match violence. There is far less tolerance for it now. Gradually they've gotten a grip on it, starting at the top, at national level. Television helped accelerate this culture change. The county game was in the shop window every Sunday on TV, and the old-fashioned melees were just becoming embarrassing for Croke Park. They didn't want parents with young children watching this stuff and deciding that they'd take their kids to soccer or rugby instead. What's more, the cameras were able to pick up on the off-the-ball stuff too and expose the culprits. So the clampdown had to get serious. It's taken the GAA a long time but they've got their disciplinary system in much better working order. There are consequences now for a player if he steps out of line, there are deterrents that make the hitmen think twice.

The standard of football has improved as a result. There's far less pulling and dragging. Instead of gouging corner forwards, corner backs have to be able to do things. You know, football things, like soloing the ball, passing it to a teammate, kicking it straight, and even coming upfield to score the odd point. The standard of ball play in general has gone way up since the 1980s. That's why I can't understand the pundits who go on about how terrible it is nowadays. Maybe they're harking back to their own days and letting sentiment cloud their judgement, like the umpires with the mist on their glasses. But back in the '70s and '80s, and even the '90s, some of the football played by county teams was piss poor. It was full of rooters and mullockers and fellas drop-kicking the ball and other fellas afraid to get their hands on the ball for fear they wouldn't know what to do with it. You won't get away with that nowadays. You can't build a career on just stopping your opponent by fair means or foul. You actually have to be able to play the ball. You have to have some measure of skill and speed.

All of this has percolated down to the club game as well. It's a much safer environment. The standard of officiating is still cat, mind you, but referees and even umpires feel empowered nowadays to police games a lot more strictly. And maybe society has changed here for the better too. There's just less savagery on GAA fields. Fellas aren't quite as thick and ignorant – or cowardly – these days.

No one can afford to be complacent on this, not for a second, because you'll still see some dirty stuff going on here and there. But by and large the culture has improved and it's good to be able to say that. If a corner forward gets a box in the jaw these days, there's a fair chance that the bollocks who did it is going to get the line.

8.   Champagne Showdown

I was only doing my job, but if I hadn't seen the champagne I mightn't have done it with quite as much gusto in the end.

It wouldn't have been so bad if they were only bringing in a few crates of humble bottled stout, or Marcardles Ale itself, or a few dozen cans of Tennent's Extra in plastic supermarket bags. But no, it had to be the champagne. I suppose, in fairness to Phil Coulter, he was from the showbiz world and he probably liked to do things with a bit of style.

It was the end of April 1995; it was the last game of the regular season. Derry City had arrived into Athlone with thousands of fans in tow, fully expecting to leave as league champions. We were deep in relegation trouble at the other end of the table. Second-place Dundalk meanwhile were hosting Galway United at Oriel Park and needed us to do them a favour. But the title was in Derry's hands: all they had to do was get a result at least equal to what Dundalk would get at Oriel, and a win would guarantee them the title.

I landed in the car park at St Mel's Park just as the Derry City team coach also pulled in. Phil Coulter was following in a fine swanky car behind. I think Phil was honorary president of the club at the time. Barry Murphy, our centre half, pulled up in his car beside me. We looked on as the Derry players and their manager, Felix Healy, spilled out of their coach and started gathering their gear from the underneath storage compartments. Then we noticed Coulter pulling a crate of champagne from the boot of his car, and another, and another.

And as soon as I saw it I could feel the hackles rising in me. They were hot favourites to roll us over, but it stuck in my craw to see the champagne. I thought it was a bit presumptuous and a bit premature. And Barry said to me in his Dublin accent, 'Jaysus, Cakeo, they must be expecting a big bleedin' party here today.'

And I said back, 'There'll be no fuckn party here today only our fuckn party.'

We were damned with inconsistency that season, but we'd managed to find a fairly decent run of form in the weeks leading up to this showdown. We'd beaten Shamrock Rovers 1–0 in March, then Sligo Rovers 1–0, Galway 1–0 away from home, and drawn 1–1 with Cobh Ramblers. And on our day we had enough good players to trouble any team in the league. Our Dublin contingent were a bit untypical in that they were really committed to the club and the team. They didn't just turn up for the money every week. They put their hearts into it. Barry Murphy and Frank Darby were formidable defenders, among the best players I ever lined out with. The two of them gave me rock-solid protection. I wasn't much more than eleven and a half stone at the time and I was agile, I could spring across the goal. But you'd have centre forwards piling into you for crosses and corner kicks, trying to rough you up, and Murphy and Darby would be in there, giving it back to them with good measure. And Rod de Khors in midfield didn't hang back either. Rod knew how to put his foot in; the only problem was that sometimes he put his two feet in, and an elbow, if it was needed.

At the same time you could see why Derry and their supporters came down fully expecting to take the three points and the title. They had a power-packed team at the time, strong from back to front, with the great Dermot O'Neill in goals, Paul Curran, Stuart Gauld, Paul Doolin, Peter Hutton and the star man himself, Liam Coyle – the Lionel Messi of the League of Ireland before Lionel Messi was ever heard of. We'd already played them three times that season and, in a quirk of the scheduling, all three games happened in not much more than the space of a week back in November. They beat us 3–1 in a League Cup game, 1–0 in the league – both those matches at St Mel's – and 3–0 up at the Brandywell. They were a better team; by far a better team.

And for most of the first half that April day they threatened to overrun us completely. There was a massive crowd in the Park that day and a tremendous atmosphere. But we had something to hold on to: Donal Golden had scored for us inside the first minute with a deflected shot. After that, Derry came storming into the game. Liam Coyle equalized with a brilliant goal on fifteen minutes. From then on they were coming at us in waves. I was busy. I was making save after save. It wasn't just that I was extra motivated, having witnessed the champagne in the car park. The like of that will only get you so far. As it happened, I was in great form that season anyway. It was probably the best season of my career in soccer. And I always loved big crowds and a heaving atmosphere. It was on the quiet days when you were playing in front of empty terraces that my mind was in danger of wandering.

I was totally immersed in this match. I was completely in the zone. The Derry supporters brought fantastic noise and colour to the occasion. But the Athlone fans were making an unbelievable racket too. They gave us a standing ovation, going in at half time. The home crowd cheered me in as I walked from the goals towards the dressing rooms. Six minutes before the break I'd tipped a Pascal Vaudequin free kick round the post; it was a pile-driver heading for the top corner. I remember that save. I don't remember the two I made from Kyle Maloney in first-half added time when, according to the *Westmeath Independent*, he looked certain to score. I caught up with Peter Hutton going into the dressing rooms, and he looks at me and says, 'Fuck's sake, are you playing like that all season?'

'I am,' says I, 'see you in the second half ould shtock.'

About seven minutes into the second half, Derry were awarded a penalty. Stuart Gauld stepped up. There were about 2,000 Derry fans in the shed behind the goals, baying, and I mean baying, for the ball to hit the back of the net. I decided that he was going to hit it to my right. I didn't know whether he was going to hit it high or low, but I was going to my right anyway. He hit it low, it was skidding along the ground; I got my right hand to it, it hit the post and went out for a corner. Apparently it was Gauld's thirty-ninth penalty in three seasons and only the second he hadn't scored. Having battered us for so long, and then having missed the penalty, it seemed to knock a bit of the stuffing out of Derry. Maybe they felt it was just going to be one of those days. Meanwhile the word came through that Dundalk were ahead in their game. Dozens of Derry fans had transistors with them and were listening to updates from Oriel Park. The whole ground was seething with tension and anxiety.

I'll let the *Westmeath Independent* take it from here.

> As the game wore on, Athlone grew stronger and Derry looked a beaten team. Rod de Khors, who rivalled Curran for man-of-the-match, dictated events in midfield. Tommy Keane ran his heart out. The anguish of the Derry players was palpable as the game ticked into its final minutes. Deep into stoppage time, Gauld's cross from the far left was met by Curran but somehow the keeper succeeded only in [turning] the ball towards his own goal, to prove that perhaps he was human after all. The crowd held its breath for the inevitable goal. Agonisingly for City it was not to be as De Khors stepped into the breach to clear it off the line, and that was that.

The match ended 1–1. Dundalk had won 2–0 at Oriel Park. The only problem from their point of view was that the league trophy was down in Mel's Park! The FAI had reckoned that this was where the trophy was going to be needed. And they weren't alone in thinking that.

'There were red faces all around among football's hierarchy,' wrote the *Independent*, 'when Athlone forgot the script and promptly set about writing their own version of events that could have been a classic remake of David and Goliath. After a hectic and pulsating game, Derry were condemned to the runners-up spot in the league for the third time in six seasons. The Bord Gáis league trophy was subsequently taken out of St Mel's, covered up red and white ribbons attached. Tempting fate can be a dangerous thing.'

The Derry lads were shattered afterwards. In fairness to Liam Coyle, he came down to me in the goals and congratulated me. It was very magnanimous of him after losing the title in those circumstances. And in hindsight I'd have preferred it if Derry had actually won the championship that season. They'd brought a lot to the League of Ireland since they were admitted to it ten years earlier. They'd given the whole scene a shot in the arm with their big support base, their resources and the colour and noise they brought to games. They'd brightened it up and I'd always found them a friendly old crowd, all in all. And on the other hand I didn't really have a lot of time for Dundalk. But at the time, on the day, I was fired up; the team was fired up, we played out of our skins.

Back in the dressing rooms you could hear the silence in the Derry room next door. We were happy but we weren't celebrating; nobody was rubbing it in their faces. At the same time, I couldn't resist it when I saw Phil Coulter in the corridor, about an hour or so after the match. We were showered and togged in at this stage and heading for our cars. And Phil was mooching around outside when I passed him. And as I say, I just couldn't resist it: 'Phil, any chance of a bottle of that ould champagne?!' I didn't stop to hear the reply; I kept going.

There was big money sloshing around the league in those days, silly money, and the top players were rumoured to be on a couple of grand a week. Dermot O'Neill, my opposite number in the Derry goals, was a senior pro, highly rated, and was probably picking up ten times what I was getting every week. They had spent a lot of money trying to win that title. Felix Healy was asked by the media afterwards what he'd thought of my performance. He said I'd done 'quite well'. The poor man was haunted too by the 'certain goal' that was cleared off the line by Rod in the dying seconds. I think they were all haunted by the events of that day for a long time afterwards.

The following November Athlone travelled up to the Brandywell for a league game. Every time the ball came near me I was roundly booed. The abuse in the stands was vitriolic. I couldn't hear exactly what they were saying, but my poor mother and girlfriend Sharon could. Coming off the field at half time, you had to go through a gate and walk up a sort of pathway to the dressing rooms. There was wire fencing on either side of the walkway. But a couple of dozen Derry fans had congregated down there to vent their feelings as I came through. Jesus it was vicious stuff. What they didn't call me: the c word, the f word, the b word, all being fired at me by the men behind the wire. They'd have practically ate their way through the wire to get at me. And next thing I was splattered with a gobbet of flying spit; it landed right on the side of my face. I was rattled.

But then I felt an arm around me and a fella shepherding me up to the dressing rooms. It was that gentleman, Anthony Tohill. The one and only time I'd come across Anthony before that was in the 1989 minor All-Ireland semi-final when he and his team demolished us. Anthony was also a fine soccer player and was doing a stint with Derry City at the time. He ushered me away from the mob that day, and I've always appreciated that gesture. I got sent off in the second half for taking down Liam Coyle and the fans were so delighted, it took the poison out of the atmosphere. They waved to me and sang 'Cheerio' all the way on my lonely walk back to the dugout.

The '94/'95 season didn't end for us that day in St Mel's Park. We were facing a promotion/relegation play-off with Finn Harps from the First Division. It would be played over two legs, home and away, two cup finals basically to decide our fate for the following season. Finn Harps in fairness had most of the chances and played most of the football over the two legs, but both games had ended in 0–0 draws. The second leg was at St Mel's. We had a chance to win it in extra time with a penalty, but Frank Darby's shot came back off the cross-bar. It went all the way to a penalty shootout. I took our second penalty and blasted it to the top corner. One of their players blazed his over and Mickey O'Connor, our player-manager, had the fifth penalty for us to seal the deal. Mickey slotted it, cool as a breeze. One of our drinking hangouts at the time was the Shack bar on the Dublin road and Mickey had famously written in his programme notes that he was either going to end up 'in the Shack or the Shannon', depending on the outcome. It was the Shack; we'd survived in the Premier Division for another season. I received the player-of-the-year award at our annual club dinner in May.

Off the field, things still hadn't improved much. The club was always flying by the seat of its pants. Sometimes, when you saw some of the cock-ups and witnessed the general cheapness of the culture all round, you got the impression that the whole league was flying by the seat of its pants. But at least we'd established a stable training base at the Marist school that season. The club had come to some arrangement with them and we no longer had to go driving round the streets of Athlone, looking for a place to do our work.

The much-travelled Tommy Gaynor joined us in October '95 and scored two goals on his debut. Tommy was a class player, but he was thirty-two at the time and any bit of pace he had had was more or less gone. You'd see him the day of the game and you wouldn't see him again until the next game. Tommy was slow around the pitch; but the irony was, there was no man faster at getting off the pitch! He'd always be first in line to get his match money. And if there was a poor crowd at St Mel's there was a serious danger that there wouldn't be enough cash to go round. Which was why Tommy would show an unbelievable turn of foot at the final whistle. He'd been around the block; he knew the score.

I hated this ritual they had where you'd have to go back to the pub after a game to wait for your money. Whatever pub had sponsored us that week, that was the pub to which you returned to collect your brown envelope. I found the whole thing a bit undignified. You'd be hanging around for a couple of hours, feeling a bit like a prostitute, waiting for the club officials to sort out the takings and lock up the ground before they'd arrive. And if the gate receipts were poor you wouldn't get what you were entitled to. They'd be coming to you with all sorts of excuses and promises. 'Listen we can only pay you fifty this week but we'll have the other fifty for you next week.' Blah blah blah. 'We're expecting a good crowd next week and we'll sort you out then.' Right. Eventually I stopped hanging around the pubs waiting for my fee. I wasn't in it for the money anyway and the whole thing was a pain in the arse, knowing that a lot of the time there was no point because they wouldn't be able to pay you.

In fairness, the fellas running the club were doing their best and it was a constant struggle for them. They were probably out of pocket as well, and they were giving an awful lot of their time trying to keep the show on the road. One of those club stalwarts was Michael 'Mickey' Francis, and another was Paddy McCaul, now the FAI president. The likes of Mickey and Paddy put in endless hours running the club. In addition, Mickey and his wife Geraldine also doubled up as my hosts any time I had to stay overnight in Athlone. They showed me nothing but the best of hospitality; staying with the Francises was often the only highlight of the week if things on the pitch were going bad.

But for all their efforts a huge swathe of the town never bothered to turn up for matches. There was just this deadening apathy every-where. One article in the *Westmeath Independent* in September summed up the reality at the time. We'd played Galway the week before at St Mel's. The attendance, wrote the reporter, 'was a disgrace'. He continued:

> One is entitled to ask whether the people of Athlone really give a damn for football or for Athlone Town Football Club. The club has never done more to promote itself within the town. The best young playing talent is being nurtured and catered for like never before with two teams in the Dublin schoolboy league. Local players have been afforded every opportunity to play in the first team. A soccer acad-emy is being established to further raise standards. But this all seems to be met with total and blind indifference.

That just about summed it up.

Mind you, that same Galway game got the blood going of the few supporters who'd bothered to turn up because it featured an almighty melee. I was on the bench that day, Anthony Keenan was in goals. Rod de Khors and Mark Herrick had been kicking lumps out of each other nearly from the kick-off. It was just one of those games where there was needle and aggro flaring up all the time. Mickey O'Connor and the Galway manager, Tony Mannion, were having a go at each other on the sideline too. Then, down in one corner of the field Rod went flying, studs up, into Herrick and threw him up into the air with the impact. It was an awful act of vandalism altogether. The Galway bench went fuckn ballistic and suddenly some of them were racing in to swing a few punches and throw a few shapes. The referee pulled Rod out of the ruck and flashed him a red card. Rod had to take the walk of shame – except he wasn't exactly ashamed by the time he landed beside me in the dugout. He winked at me with a big grin on his face as he came in: 'What'd ya think of that one, Cakeo?! He won't be fuckn playing for a while after that!'

The season was going pear-shaped. In October we had three play-ers sent off against UCD and in the next game I was sent off in that match at the Brandywell. Funnily enough, we played Derry a week later in a turnaround fixture and they got another penalty. Stuart

Gauld took it, and I saved it again. Not that it was much use in the overall scheme of things. In December we clocked up our tenth defeat of the season and, by Christmas, Rod, one of our mainstays, had left for Shamrock Rovers.

In February '96 Mickey O'Connor was let go as player-manager. It was inevitable in the end. The chairman, Paddy McCaul, who in 2010 rose to the position of FAI president, really had no choice if we were to have any chance of saving our season. I'd had my ups and downs with Mickey. Anthony Keenan and he were great buddies, so it was always a dilemma for him when it came to choosing me or Jelly for the goalkeeper's position. But he'd given me my break in the first place. He'd taken a chance on a small-town lad from a GAA background and put his faith in me. I'd like to think I repaid that faith along the way.

Tony Mannion took over. There wasn't much diplomacy needed to build bridges after the bust-up in September. It was water off a duck's back for everyone involved. The team was changing and a lot of younger players, like Warren Parkes, Donal Golden, Ray McLoughlin and Adrian Carberry, were starting to come through. Mannion had a really nice way about him and an enthusiasm for the game that was contagious. He was always talking, always full of beans, and the team got a bounce from having a new voice in the dressing room.

In March we played Manchester City in a friendly at St Mel's Park. A crowd of about 4,000 turned up, obviously lured by the star quality of an English Premier League team. We beat them 2–1, with goals from Michael Collins and Warren Parkes. City lined out with well-known names like Nigel Clough, Alan Kernaghan, Steve Lomas and Garry Flitcroft. The great Georgi Kinkladze also graced us with his presence that day. Needless to say, he wasn't too bothered about the result, but he did show a few mesmerizing flashes of his class. None of the City players were too bothered about the result, they had bigger fish to fry, back in England. But we did have one thing in common: we were both involved in relegation dogfights, and both of us would end up going down that season.

We fought for our lives in the final run of games and a steely 1–1 draw with Derry at the Brandywell in late April left us with a precious lifeline. Again we'd avoided automatic relegation, and again we would have to face a promotion/relegation play-off – but at least we were still alive. Derry had taken a 1–0 lead through a Paul Curran penalty, but Parkes equalized for us eleven minutes from time. Paul Curran came up to my face after he put the ball in the net and was shouting and grinning and taunting me. This was pay-back time after the drama of twelve months earlier – the bitterness was still there.

The play-off match was against Home Farm Everton. They won the first leg 2–0 at Whitehall, we won the second leg 2–0 at home; the tie finished 2–2 on aggregate after extra time. To penalties again, then, for the second year in a row. And this time we ran out of luck. Home Farm held their nerve just that little bit better, and suddenly we were gone through the trap door. We were back in the coal mines of the First Division. And there was feck-all champagne to be found down there.

9.   Travelling Roadshow

In the late 1990s the construction industry in Ireland was a jumbo jet on the runway waiting to take off. She was revving her engines; she was about to go ballistic.

I didn't know it at the time, but I was about to be sucked into the downdraft and get taken along on a magic carpet ride. It was great while it lasted. Then, like a lot of fellas, I was eventually swallowed whole and spat out the other end.

In 1998 Sharon and I got married and moved from Castlerea to her home place in Brideswell, outside Athlone. I also transferred clubs and changed jobs. Within a few months my circumstances had changed completely.

My new job was with Ganly's Hardware in Athlone. Ganly's were builders' providers. The economy was expanding and Mike Ganly was expanding his business along with it. They were building a new facility in Athlone, on the Roscommon roundabout, a massive operation that would supply just about everything the building trade needed in the whole midlands region. Plumbing, electrical, heating, insulation, cement, timber, floors, tiles, bathroom ware – the works. My brief was to build up sales in my designated area, which was all of Roscommon, more or less, plus east Galway and parts of Longford. I would be dealing with developers, contractors, roofers, plumbers, electricians, second fixers, all kinds of builders and contractors. I had a suit and tie, a mobile phone the size of a brick and a Volkswagen Caddy van.

I wasn't long in the job when I left the same Caddy van in the middle of a field one night coming home from the pub. I hit a country stone wall coming round a bend, bounced across the road and vaulted a wall on the other side of the road and down into the field. Cleared the wall like Eddie Macken on Boomerang back in the day. I was a lucky boy to walk away without a scratch. But I got away with it and learned my lesson.

The hardest part of sales is cold-calling potential customers, but my sporting profile was a big help. It was often the ice-breaker. The first man I cold-called was a builder-developer by the name of Peter Owens. He'd faxed in an order for a quotation and my brief was to call down to the site in Ballinaheglish, just off the main Tulsk–Roscommon road, where Peter was working. I introduced myself and gave him the spiel.

'Are you Curran the footballer?' says he.

'I am,' says I. It turned out he was a big Roscommon supporter. Sure I was halfway there already. We had the chat about the football and I showed him our price.

He said the rep from Chadwicks had called already and given him a better quotation. Could I do any better? I said I didn't know, I'd have to ring Ganly. He said to me in fairly colourful language not to bother my backside ringing Ganly. 'Just knock fifty quid off it and you can have it. I'd like to give it to you.'

So I did, and I went away, chuffed with an order that was worth over £3,000.

Peter Owens was very good to me thereafter: he connected me with loads more people who were happy to place orders based on his recommendation. And it was in this line of work generally that I felt the power of the GAA business network. It was everywhere, especially in the construction industry. The business connections in the GAA are huge, not just in Ireland but all over the world. Rugby was always famous for its old boys network, particularly in areas like banking, finance and insurance. In my experience the GAA presence is to be found more in industry and enterprise, fellas who set up their own companies and build them from scratch. Anyway, it was an absolutely invaluable asset to me at Ganly's. People would at least take your call on the basis of your name, which meant you were in the door anyway. If you could back it up with price and service, you had a great chance of sealing the deal.

I spent my days on the road, calling on to building sites, meeting developers in hotels, visiting the offices of quantity surveyors, architects, contractors. A major breakthrough happened for me later in 1998 when I called one day on to the site of a brand-new housing development in Athlone. The developer was a young local business-man who became a great friend and loyal backer of mine, Pearse Gately. He was just starting ground works on the site. It was a big development and the dogs in the street were fighting for the business: Chadwicks in Athlone, Garveys of Roscommon, Barretts in Balli-nasloe, other builders' providers in Galway and Sligo. They were coming from everywhere. I didn't put any pressure on Pearse, we did everything by the book, and our quotation was a bit higher than some of our rivals. But we got on well, we could have a few pints and a bit of crack, and he knew I'd look after him on the after-sales ser-vice end of the deal. So he gave us the deal, worth over £13,000 at the time, and it was the beginning of a long relationship between us in the building game.

I learned the ropes fairly quickly as I went along, and part of the learning was knowing if you'd get paid or not. It was hard to get money out of people, especially the cowboys who'd jumped on the construction bandwagon without the knowledge or expertise to back it up. Some of these fellas would price a job without knowing what they were pricing or what were the true costs involved. They might have an engineering degree or some such, but they wouldn't have the actual on-site experience. They'd price a job too low and they'd find themselves in way over their heads. As a result, suppliers and sub-contractors would be left dangling for money they were owed. At Ganly's you always kept an ear out on the grapevine to see if someone had come in too low; you'd try and avoid them. It was due diligence of a sort. The general tendency in Irish business is to take fellas on trust, but you could get burned easily.

Mike used to call me 'the Scarlet Pimpernel' because I was some-times hard to get hold of. But generally I was let do my own thing, once I was bringing in the business. And I grew my customer base from an initial fifteen names to about 300 over the two years I worked there. In the second year I started building relationships with other sales reps on the road who wanted to sell their own product into Ganly's. One of these was connected with a company called Capco who were trying to get a foothold in Ireland. Capco were in the roof tile and slate business. They were based in Castlebar and they wanted to get their product into Ganly's. But they had zero traction in the Irish market. Tegral were the dominant slate company in the country, they were the industry leaders by a mile. And Ganly's stocked Tegral only.

Meanwhile I was aware of a new housing development going up in Roscommon town. I knew the developers, Cormac and the late John Hoare. The Tegral slate was going on the roof. But I made a pitch to Cormac for a lovely Capco slate called Berona, manufactured in Czechoslovakia with a classy finish. The acid test was getting it up on a roof. Cormac liked its colour and texture and price, and he went with it. So I ordered several pallets of the slates for Ganly's yard. The Tegral rep wasn't long finding out and he wasn't long ringing Mike. Then I got the call from Mike. I knew it was coming. What the fuck was going on here? And I just said that Cormac Hoare had seen the Berona and liked it and wanted it for his development. And I told him we were getting a better margin with Capco than with Tegral. And that calmed Mike down.

It was huge for Capco, because now they had a breakthrough. Someone had broken with precedent and plumped for them over Tegral. Their product had been used by a reputable builder. The next sell would be easier; they were in the ball game now. Two weeks later, Capco came to me with a job offer that would double my wages. I didn't need long to think about it and when I went to give my notice to Ganly he said he knew I'd been hatching a plan. 'When I saw those bloody slates in the yard I knew well there was something going on.' He didn't stand in my way, I told him it was an offer I couldn't refuse, and we parted on good terms.

I started with Capco in early 2000 and spent six years with them. My territory was similar: Roscommon, Longford, parts of Galway and Mayo. They also threw in a nice new Land Rover with the transfer fee.

My sales target for my first year with Capco was £1 million. It was a phenomenal target, to try and sell a million pounds' worth of product in that first year from a standing start. It wasn't practical to supply direct to the trade: you needed builders' providers to stock the stuff. It needed to be a centralized operation in order to collect the money.

It wouldn't be feasible to go around collecting money from thirty or forty customers. The builders' providers had an invoicing and collection system, and that was the only way to go. But it was a huge challenge getting them to stock it. They had long-established relationships with Tegral and they didn't really want to know about this new competitor in the market. The trick therefore was to persuade the developers, contractors and sub-contractors of the merits of Capco, so that they would go looking for Capco from the providers. I spent a fair bit of time wining and dining them and building up personal relationships with them. The old mantra in business is that people do business with people, and it's true. You have to get to know your customer, get them to like you, get them to trust you. I knew a fair few of them anyway from my days with Ganly's, and pretty soon I was starting to make headway.

At the end of my first year I'd sold £960,000 worth of product. I thought it was a great achievement. But the head honchos came back and asked me why I was £40,000 short! They always seemed to be a bit wary of me anyway. My immediate manager was one of those control freaks who wanted every i dotted and every t crossed. He wanted to know everything you were doing, everyone you were meeting, your every day written up and accounted for. This didn't suit me at all, having to write up reports and fill out forms. It was complicated by my dyslexia, too. I just didn't like doing it. The only thing that should've mattered was your bottom line every month, and I was doing well in that regard. But it was bugging them that they didn't know how I was doing it. They wanted to know my modus operandi.

About six months in, one of their managers came down to meet me one day. He wasn't happy that I wasn't conforming to their methodology. And he said that they were happy with my sales but that they'd a certain way of doing things and why couldn't I do it that way? And I told him that their way wasn't my way. And I told them too that I had an offer on the table from another company and if they felt that strongly about it, I'd fuck off out of the place so. I wasn't bluffing either. A competitor had heard that this new Capco product was starting to make inroads and they decided that they wanted a slice of the slate action too. I'd met their top man and he'd offered me a good package to move. When they heard this, Capco backed off and gave me my head.

My target for year two was £1.1 million. By now I was getting the builders' providers to take a container of slate at a time. Previously they might take four or five pallets, but a container had eighteen pallets. Sales of natural slate were climbing too. This was a more expensive slate than your normal cement fibre job, but the housing developments were getting more ambitious and house buyers liked the idea of having a natural slate finish on their roof. It fitted in with the sort of luxury, aspirational lifestyle that every Tom, Dick and Harry was aiming for. And I had a few great roofing contractors who were sizeable operators in their own right and who preferred the Capco range. The man who would become my business partner some ten years later, Ger Brennan, was doing some roofing at the time and that's how I first got to know him. The Roscommon football team was starting to do well again too and my own profile got another shot in the arm.

By the end of the second year my sales quota started to come easy to me. I had my own system down pat, and it was working smoothly. The first week of each month I'd make my phone calls and arrange to call in on all my suppliers in Roscommon, Longford, Galway and Mayo. It wouldn't be a business meeting as such. I liked to keep it fairly informal. So, depending on the time of day, I'd have coffee, lunch or dinner with them, followed by a few pints. I had about fifteen to twenty core suppliers, and they were all taking an order in on a monthly basis. Then I had my foot soldiers on the ground, the developers, builders and sub-contractors, calling in to these suppliers and asking for their load of Capco slates. Essentially, they were putting pressure on the suppliers to stock the product. The suppliers had to meet the demand; and there was a nice margin in it for them too.

It was a simple enough formula. Pretty soon the system was driving itself. Pretty soon I was enjoying a lot of leisure time. I'd be off playing golf in the middle of the week, going to the gym, heading to Galway for a night out, heading off to training sessions or matches, without work getting in the way of any of it. I was also networking with various business people, exploring some business options myself and getting involved in some property speculation too. And it used to drive the management in Capco mad. They knew I was doing damn-all work a lot of the time. And I'd stopped writing up any reports whatsoever. But they couldn't say anything because my figures at the end of every month couldn't be challenged. In fact I was hitting phenomenal targets. The other reps, I was blowing them out of the water. And some of these lads would literally be on the go from seven in the morning till ten at night, chasing their tails up and down the roads of Ireland, trying to make their target. The second year I did £1.6 million in sales – half a million beyond the quota. In 2002 I did €2 million. And I was doing it without breaking a sweat. In my mind it was far better to work smart than to work hard.

So when they told me that I could trade in the Land Rover for a new commercial vehicle, I decided to treat myself. Anything up to the level of the Volkswagen Passat, in or around £30,000, was the directive from HQ. My first car ever had been a 90D red Toyota Corolla. I'd consistently traded up since, and this time was going to be no different. So I went into Moore's showroom in Athlone and the salesman showed me the standard Passat. Have you anything bigger, says I? I have, says he. So he showed me the de-luxe model, and I ordered it there and then: a 1.8 turbo diesel 170 bhp Passat worth about £35,000; an 03 MO reg, a magnificent black machine. And I told no one in the company. So when I landed down at the first meeting of the year in January 2003, they were all staring at it with their mouths open. The managers were fuckn fuming because they were only driving middling buses in comparison. One of them told me I hadn't got clearance to buy a car in that range. I said they'd told me to buy a Passat, so I bought a Passat. And I told them I'd brought in €2 million the previous year, so what the hell about it?

You were supposed to carry sample slates in the boot of your company car, but this machine was far too good for that; it carried my golf clubs and my football gear, and that was it!

Sorry, correction: it carried something else very important too – a baby seat for our beautiful daughter Lauren, who'd come into the world on 13 December in the year 2000. On 24 March 2003 she was joined by her lovely sister Abby. Sharon was brilliant with them from day one; she seemed to know automatically what to do and how to hold them and how to care for them. I did my best to catch up. It knocked me for six when they arrived into our world and the two girls have been the light of our lives ever since. I had a family now to provide for and, if anything, it made me even more competitive in terms of driving sales and seeking fresh opportunities.

My six years with Capco coincided with their share of the natural slate market jumping from five per cent to something like forty-five per cent. We had zero per cent of the fibre cement slate market at the start and ended up with almost forty per cent. My sales in that time came to almost €16 million in total. All of it was fuelled by the building boom which, by 2005, had gone into the stratosphere. It was absolute madness out there. Money meant nothing, there was so much of it flying around. Everyone was on a credit craze. Everyone was spending, everyone was buying, everyone was building. We were all up on the back of the Celtic Tiger, and she was a rampant animal. And I was looking around me, seeing an awful lot of ordinary Joes – and in some cases downright fuckn eejits – making fortunes. Or at least you thought they were making fortunes. I was doing well too, very well. But I figured I might as well join the party good and proper by opening up my own business and cashing in while the going was good. There was serious money to be made. Everyone else was doing it, so why shouldn't I?

10. Slip Sliding Away

When Athlone Town fell through the trap door and into Division One at the end of the 1995–6 season, we had no way of knowing the club would remain there for the next eighteen seasons. But there was a definite sense that the club was drifting. Morale was low and there wasn't much positive energy about the place.

Tony Mannion stepped down as manager after we were relegated, and Dermot Keely took over later that summer. Keely had already been around a fair few houses by then, and he'd go around a fair few more of them before his long career in management came to a halt. Immediately he set about doing what a lot of managers like to do when they take over a new club: he brought in a few of his own cronies. The much-travelled Mick Byrne arrived. He was thirty-six at the time. Mick didn't hang around long. The much-travelled Peter Eccles arrived. He was only thirty-four at the time. Peter didn't hang around long either. Both had played for Keely at Shamrock Rovers. Byrne had also played for him at Dundalk and Sligo Rovers.

Keely then signed John Connolly. Athlone Town already had two proven goalkeepers in myself and Anthony Keenan. And I remember Jelly, God rest him, saying at the time: 'What the fuck's he doing, bringing in another keeper, when he has two already here?' John Connolly was no better than me and Jelly. But the manager obviously felt that a relegated and cash-strapped club could do with a third keeper. Connolly had been with Keely at Dundalk the previous season.

I didn't like the vibe around this set-up at all. To me it smacked of the League of Ireland's Dublin cartel looking after each other. And then, lo and behold, in late September Keely walked out on Athlone and straight into the manager's job at Home Farm Everton. Good luck and good riddance. Byrne and Eccles disappeared too. I don't know if they'd even signed contracts by then, but it didn't matter one way or another because contracts weren't worth the paper they were written on. I had signed a new two-year contract that summer, but I'd have been as well signing my name on the back of a beer mat. It was a charade; it meant nothing; they still didn't pay you when money was short.

Keely was replaced by Terry Eviston, another veteran of the domestic game. Terry was a nice man who did his best, but it rapidly turned into a soul-destroying season for everyone involved. You were playing in front of miserable crowds in shit facilities and against a backdrop of complete public apathy. The people didn't care, the press didn't care and very often the players themselves didn't care.

That season was the start of my long goodbye from Athlone Town, and from the world of so-called professional soccer. I played a few games in the autumn, but then John Connolly took over in November and I ended up playing with the reserves, the stiffs. I got back in the first team in January after Connolly picked up an injury. We made a bit of a late charge for promotion in the spring, but two defeats in quick succession to Kilkenny City, followed by a loss at home to Waterford Utd, knocked that on the head fairly lively. Galway Utd also beat us at St Mel's and Longford Town turned us over too, at home, in the last match of the campaign. 'Dismal conclusion to season for Athlone Town' was the headline in the *Westmeath Independent* the following week. But the season had had a fairly dismal beginning as well, and it was fairly dismal in the middle part, too. It was all fuckn dismal as far as I could see.

Terry Eviston resigned and Liam Buckley took over as player-manager for '97/'98. I got very little game-time until November, and then I stayed in the first team until Christmas. In January '98 I picked up a groin injury. It was just collateral damage from my ongoing back problems, but that was more or less the end for me in an Athlone Town jersey. The team reached the FAI Cup semi-final that season under Buckley but I was detached from the set-up by then. Gary Connaughton, who went on to have a great career with the Westmeath senior Gaelic football team, replaced me in goal as my days at St Mel's came to a halt. At the end of that season I packed up my soccer career. I played a few games for them in 2002 at a time when they were stuck for a keeper, but effectively I was finished by Christmas of '97.

Six years earlier I'd broken into the first team, full of excitement and wonder about the road that lay ahead. I was playing in the top league in Irish soccer. Every week you were coming up against well-known faces and seriously good players. A lot of these lads had been to England and back. You were in the mix, you were part of the culture, you were rubbing shoulders with the professional game in Ireland – and it was only one step removed from the big-time glamour across the Irish Sea.

I really enjoyed those early years in particular. We had some great times, a lot of big-game drama and plenty of crack along the way. Some of the lads I shared a dressing room with at Athlone Town were unbelievable characters and top footballers. It was a pleasure playing with them and hanging round with them and I remember those years very fondly.

But realistically, where we were was pretty much the underbelly, the other side of the glory game. So much of it was shoddy and cheap. Facilities, by and large, were pathetic. Imagine not having a place to train of an evening? I mean literally no regular place to tog out and do your training. And no manager most of the time because he was in Dublin. And only a handful of teammates to train with, because most of them were in Dublin as well. And no proper coaching either.

And all around you was the smell of fairly low-level corruption when it came to money. The League of Ireland had a sort of hustling culture, with fellas jumping from one club to another, and getting money under the counter, and signing-on fees that were off the books, and cash into the hand, and all that sort of second-rate carry-on. It was a kind of hand-to-mouth environment; nothing was ever straightforward and above board; there was always a problem, a complication, an excuse for not paying what you were owed. And at the end of the day it was all pennies anyway. It was a sort of back-alley culture, or like the old pool halls with fellas ducking and diving and hustling for a few quid here and a few quid there.

Eventually I found it demeaning, and the whole culture more than a bit demoralizing. I have come across few businesses as badly run and dysfunctional as League of Ireland soccer. And everyone involved in it seems to be in some degree of denial about how shabby it all actually is. Maybe they have to be, to maintain their delusions about it. And in fairness I think they're all in it because they just love the whole scene. And there's a lot to like about it, especially the camaraderie and the crack and the different people you come across. But Jesus, when you turned up on a winter's day at Gortakeegan or Buckley Park or the Strokestown Road in Longford or St Francis in Dublin, and no one there but a few hardy souls trying to keep warm, you knew you were on the wrong side of the tracks. If the cold didn't kill you, the drabness eventually would.

I was pleased for Athlone Town and its long-suffering supporters when they finally made it back to the Premier Division in 2014. I still keep an eye out for their results. And I still feel grateful to them because it was the club that brought me into the League of Ireland and gave me a new dimension to my sporting life. I got to play soccer at the highest level that this country has to offer. I learned a huge amount about the goalkeeper's trade and I'm glad I was able to test myself in an environment which, for all its faults, demanded the best out of you. Playing for Athlone took me well out of my comfort zone, and I'm happy that I went through it.

The much-touted move to England never materialized, but I never took the speculation too seriously anyway. If I started at St Mel's with a bit of a bang, it all ended in a bit of a whimper, to be honest. But it didn't bother me then and it doesn't bother me now. I had plenty of good times and I learned a huge amount. It was a life experience that left me a better keeper, and a good deal wiser in the ways of the world.

11. In from the Cold

It was a damn strange way to get a championship call-up; it was a damn strange way to solve a problem that had been festering for a long time.

The day before Roscommon played Leitrim in the Connacht semi-final of 2000, I got a phone call. I was in Carrickmacross on a weekend with Sharon. I didn't recognize the number, and the voice on the other end had me stumped for a moment. It was Gay Sheeran. We hadn't spoken in almost three years. But here he was, out of the blue asking me if I'd sit on the bench in Hyde Park the next day. They needed cover for the goalkeeper.

Now I'd been aware of rumours concerning the goalkeeping position for several weeks. Derek Thompson was a good keeper, but apparently his form had dipped. And the sub keeper had picked up an injury. At this point I was a full-time keeper: a year earlier I'd moved back into goals for St Brigid's.

About three or four weeks before the Leitrim game I'd got a call from one of the senior Roscommon players. He was worried about the goalkeeping situation. With the sub keeper injured there was no one to fall back on if anything happened to Thompson. The senior player asked me if I was interested in coming in and shoring it up. I said of course I was. I'd missed being involved. I loved playing with the Rossies. I said I'd do it in a heartbeat but that it wasn't up to me, or him. It was up to the management – where did they stand on this? He said he'd talk to them.

Weeks passed and I heard nothing. Management knew full well what would happen if they asked me back. They knew I'd make a strong claim for the number one jersey. I'd make an instant impact. A lot of players would be looking at me as the obvious choice. And it would make things very awkward for the management. They'd come under pressure to play me, and it might expose them to criticism: for three years they'd ignored me, and now they were calling me up a few weeks before a Connacht semi-final? It would've been seen as a panic move. They just didn't want to go there.

But now, some twenty-four hours before the game, Gay Sheeran was coming to me, cap in hand. So I say to him, 'Why the fuck didn't you ring me a month ago?'

And he says, 'Well, we didn't want to cause a furore.'

It was a farcical situation. I should have turned him down. I shouldn't have been party to this kind of amateurish carry-on. But the lure of a big championship match swayed me; it was too tempting to turn down. And I didn't want it said that I'd walked away when I was needed. So I said yes.

Leitrim beat us 1-13 to 3-6. We'd been leading 3-3 to 0-5 at one stage. But that was the day the chickens came home to roost. The team had been mismanaged. Players, not just me, who should've been on the panel had been marginalized. Roscommon weren't putting out their best team.

The irony now was that, once I was back in his good books again, Gay became my number one fan! He had to muster a team in double-quick time for the junior championship; we were due to play Sligo a few days after the Leitrim debacle. So he asked me if I'd captain the team. And in fairness I was honoured to be asked. And I was determined to make a go of it. I suppose I wanted to show that I still had something to offer, and that Roscommon football still had something to offer too. We had a fairly young bunch of lads who were pretty quiet and maybe lacking in a bit of confidence. So I took over in that dressing room. I galvanized them as best I could. We drew with Sligo, won the replay and got on a roll. On a Saturday evening in Nenagh we beat Kerry in the All-Ireland final; it was a brilliant game of football too. A huge crowd came down from Roscommon to support us. That's the thing about our support: they're so starved for success and so mad about football that they'll turn up if there's even a whisper of a chance.

I've been critical of Sheeran, but he deserves great credit for sticking with it when he must've been devastated by the Leitrim result. It might only have been the junior championship, but it gave everyone associated with Gaelic football in the county a great boost. There were four or five players on that team who should've been on the senior squad, and their performances in this campaign were proof of that. One of them was Andy McPadden and there was a funny incident in the final involving me and Andy. The match was nip-and-tuck. Kerry had just gotten an equalizer and I saw Andy free for a quick kickout. I had the ball in my hands and I noticed that the referee had his back turned, running out the field. So I took the kickout to Andy from my hands – totally illegally, of course – and the Kerry forwards started shouting and roaring. But the umpires, once again, saw nothing. Andy carried on with the ball and it ended up with Roscommon getting the point that put us in front again.

It was Roscommon's first national title in twenty-two years, the first since the All-Ireland Under 21 title of 1978. I lifted the cup and declared in my speech that this was the beginning of a new era for Roscommon football. We came home that night to a rapturous reception. We stopped off in Jimmy Murray's in Knockcroghery to share the moment with the man who'd famously lifted the Sam Maguire in '43 and '44. From there it was on to a reception in the Hyde Centre in Roscommon town, where a big crowd came out to greet us. And, naturally enough, the celebrations were rounded off in Rockfords nite club, where all of Roscommon's beautiful people hang out – thousands of them.

Sheeran and his management team stood down, and in September John Tobin took over. I was reinstated in goals, against a lot of internal opposition, it must be said. I had antagonized a lot of people over the previous few years. I'd given interviews in which I'd been publicly critical of the Roscommon management set-up, and this was not appreciated by certain people in the county board and beyond. In general the GAA committee class likes players to be seen and not heard. And there were a number of influential former players with big reputations who felt I was too big for my boots. I know for a fact that Tobin came under pressure not to bring me back in. But in fairness, he made his own mind up. And I had an ally too in Frank Grehan, who had gone for the manager's job himself but who ended up as one of John's selectors. Frank stood by me and argued my case. When I got the call to return, I was absolutely delighted. The years spent in the wilderness had left me hungrier than ever to do something in a Roscommon jersey. I was still only twenty-nine which, in goalkeeping years, was young. So I was up for it: I was mad for road and mad to get going.

In November we played Louth in a national league game in Drogheda. John had a few concerns about my style as a goalkeeper. He'd asked me to tone it down a bit; I was shouting and roaring too much, apparently. I took that on board. But then we let in a goal against Louth that I felt could've been averted if I'd given our defenders a bollocking and ordered them to drop back as the move developed. I didn't; I kept quiet; fellas left forwards loose and suddenly the ball was in the net. I made it clear afterwards that I wouldn't be keeping quiet from then on.

Tobin was a great coach and he soon enough revitalized the whole atmosphere around the county squad. He brought in seven or eight players, there was far more competition for places, and the change gave everyone a lift. In February 2001 we beat Dublin in Parnell Park, which was a huge result. In April we faced Donegal in Ballybofey; a national league semi-final was waiting for us if we won. Donegal were ahead going into injury time. They were attacking again and one of their players took a kick for a point, which fell short. I took possession and came soloing way out the field. I picked out Gerry Lohan and a couple of passes later the ball was in the net. It was a flowing move that had begun in our own full-back line. The win was a fantastic confidence boost. A lot of good young players were starting to find their feet and make their mark: Seamus O'Neill, Clifford McDonald, John Whyte, John Hanly, Ian Daly, and the three Lohan brothers – Gerry, Stephen and Eddie. I think the goal was also a vindication for my own philosophy as a ball-playing goalkeeper. And in fairness to Tobin, he never discouraged it. He was a progressive, forward-thinking coach and he saw the value in it. Being an outfield player for so long had given me the skill set to do it, and Tobin knew I *could* do it. He didn't see any problem at all with it.

Mayo beat us in the semi-final, but our league campaign sent us into the Connacht championship with real belief. We were supposed to have a handy run-out against New York in the first round in Hyde Park. But New York had other plans, not many of them to do with actually playing football. They came with one agenda, and that was basically to hit everything that moved. They resorted to all kinds of skulduggery. New York were a disgrace that day. And, unfortunately for me, I got caught up with it in a way that had awful bloody consequences.

I had been fouled coming out with a ball in the first half and was given the free. One of their players held on to the ball and wouldn't give it back. I lunged in to get if off him and he went down on the ground like he'd been hit by Muhammad Ali. I can absolutely say, hand on heart, that there was no contact with his head or face at all. He had the ball in his hands. I was trying to pull it out of his hands. I was miles away from his head. But he was rolling around and holding his face like I'd poleaxed him. Next thing, the umpire behind my goals was calling in Jimmy McKee, the referee. And wouldn't you know it, the one time they actually do decide to intervene, they get it totally wrong. Next thing McKee walked towards me and produced a red card. I could not believe it. I was stunned. It was a farcical decision.

We beat New York, but I was fearing the consequences of that red card. Derek Thompson would come back in for the semi-final game against Galway and, if we won that, he would retain his place for the final. That was the rule with our position: the keeper in possession of the jersey holds on to the jersey unless he makes a big mistake. In the dressing room afterwards everyone else was happy but I was devastated.

But I also made up my mind there and then that I wasn't going to mope around. The team had a great chance of winning Connacht and I did not want to detract at all from the positive energy that was around the camp. In fact I made up my mind to do the opposite: I would redouble my efforts, I'd bring all my energy to the group, I'd be absolutely positive in everything I did and said, starting the very next morning: the New York game was played on a Saturday, the panel had a scheduled get-together Sunday morning.

Another of our players had a very unhappy experience in the New

York game. Kevin Keane had come on as a sub early in the second half. Some twelve minutes later he was taken off again: the sub was substituted. It's an embarrassing thing to happen to any player and I felt sorry for him. So I made a point after the match of talking to him and emphasizing how important it was to put a brave face on it and turn up for training the next morning. And I'm proud of the fact that we were the first two there in Ballyforan on Sunday morning. It would've been very easy for both of us to drop our heads and become detached from the group. But we trained like dogs that day and I did everything I could to make sure that we did nothing to take from the positive energy in the camp. I tried to lead by example.

But unfortunately it wasn't reciprocated. Tobin's coaching skills were top notch; as a man-manager, however, he lacked some of the personal skills required. I asked him at the time if they were going to appeal my red card. There was a culture of appealing every suspension in the GAA and I assumed they'd do it as a matter of course. But Tobin told me they'd decided not to; he reckoned it wasn't worth the hassle. I was disappointed with him: most managers would go out and bat for their players in that situation. I felt it was disrespectful and insensitive of him.

That having been said, his coaching pedigree came to the fore against Galway in the semi-final. He'd identified definite weaknesses in the Galway defence and set up our team to exploit them. Our full-forward line that day was brimming with talent: Gerry Lohan, Nigel Dineen and Frankie Dolan. The team in general delivered a fantastic performance on the day. Derek Thompson came in and did a sound job, and I knew he was going to hold on to the jersey for the Connacht final. But we trained well together, Derek and I did a lot of goalkeeping drills, we worked exceptionally hard during those weeks before the semi-final and final, and he was right on top of his job for those matches. I wasn't going to be playing, but I very much felt part of the squad and part of the process; I had a sense of ownership, as did we all.

We beat Mayo 2-10 to 1-12 in a rip-roaring final. It was a match of incredible drama. Mayo struck for a goal in injury time that left them two points up. The match should've been over; we should've been beaten. Hundreds of Roscommon supporters started heading for the exits. But then, deeper into injury time and in total desperation, we mounted one last attack which culminated with Gerry Lohan burying the ball in the corner of the net. The roar that went up in Hyde Park that day was one of the loudest I ever heard at any football match. A few seconds later it was all over. The place went berserk; the Rossies went ape-shit. I wasn't exactly a model of calm and composure myself. I raced on to the pitch and did a cartwheel and was lying on the turf, looking up at the sky, laughing and roaring like a lunatic. And Tom Mullaney, our county board secretary, starts shouting at me: 'Get up, you fuckn eejit! Get up, get fuckn up, you're going to cost us fifteen hundred quid!' The GAA had a schedule of fines for pitch invasions.

But I said to him, 'Never mind your fifteen hundred quid, there's fuckn thirty thousand people going mad here!'

It was Roscommon's first Connacht title in ten years. The celebrations went on for the most of the week. My father was driving a bus for the Western Health Board in those days, ferrying the patients here and there, but that night it was commandeered for a rake of the players to take us up with the Nestor Cup to the Abbey Hotel, where the party was already in full flow. Unfortunately, the party probably went on a little bit too long that week. We never fully got back the intensity in training and preparation that we'd brought to the Connacht semi-final and final. This was the first season of the new qualifiers system, the so-called 'back door' that gave beaten teams in the championship a second chance. And as bad luck would have it, we were drawn to play Galway again in the All-Ireland quarter-final. We had ambushed them the first day in Tuam and they weren't going to get caught again. That was a great Galway team that had won an All-Ireland in '98 and would finish the 2001 season as All-Ireland champions again.

In December of that year I underwent surgery for a longstanding back injury. A couple of discs in my back had been plaguing me for years, and it had to be sorted. I got back in training towards the end of the 2002 national league, but I think John had mentally written me off by then. He told me one night that I probably wasn't going to be part of his championship plans; it had come too soon for me. He more or less said to me that if I wanted to train, then train, and if I didn't, then don't bother. He wasn't pushed one way or the other; which is just another way of telling you that he doesn't want you about the place. Again, terrible man-management skills in my view. But the team was going well anyway in my absence, and he probably felt I was surplus to requirements. Roscommon reached the National League semi-finals, playing some top-class football along the way, so everything was more or less on track for a good championship campaign. Then Cavan ran riot against us in that semi-final on 15 April, racking up a massive 5-13 in Mullingar.

Later that month the panel went off on a bonding weekend. They played Donegal in a challenge match and repaired to a hotel in Derry for the night. A few weeks later, all hell broke loose when a tabloid newspaper published a big spread on a few so-called shenanigans in the snooker/pool room of the hotel that night. Photos from the hotel's security cameras had been leaked, showing a couple of the lads in a state of undress as they played a game of pool.

The controversy culminated in Nigel Dineen and Frankie Dolan having to make public apologies, a few days before Roscommon played Galway in the Connacht championship. Now, I wasn't there that weekend. I was out of the squad. In fact I was in London that weekend if memory serves. But I think the panel in general, and the two lads in particular, were horrendously treated in the whole sorry escapade. They were hung out to dry. The lads had done nothing to anyone. It had just been daft, innocent stuff. We hear from time to time of sportsmen in America or Britain or even closer to home going off the rails on a weekend away. There are awful stories of women being sexually assaulted or people being verbally insulted or physically beaten up. There was nothing remotely like that in this case. Nobody got hurt, nothing sinister happened at all. But the media went to town on our lads. Absolutely humiliated them and embarrassed their families. They were held up to ridicule. Various rugby players and soccer players have got up to all sorts of shenanigans and piss-ups and high jinks over the years, and nothing was ever said, no one was ever named and shamed. The Roscommon lads were named and shamed when there was feck all to be named or shamed about.

And it went on for years afterwards. The damage was done. It was dragged up time and time again. Mud was thrown, and it stuck. The name of Roscommon football was tarnished over nothing. I think the county board and the team management could've done a lot more at the time. They could've come out in support of the players and nailed their colours to the mast. They could've pointed out the obvious: that it was much ado about nothing and that the players had nothing to apologize for. But they were left on their own. Luckily enough, Frankie and Nigel are resilient, jovial characters and they were able to put it behind them pretty quickly. But the wider families get dragged into it, too; they've to watch their loved ones being hounded and ridiculed; they've to put up with a lot of innuendo and slagging and general ignorance. It was a very unpleasant time for everyone involved.

The upshot of it was that Roscommon's preparations were totally distracted and undermined, going into the biggest game of their season. Galway duly won by ten points and Roscommon had lost their Connacht crown by the middle of May. They ended up drawing Waterford in the qualifiers and beating them in Dungarvan. The next team out of the back-door hat was Mayo. It's amazing how often this open draw format ends up pairing teams from the same province who are fed up with the sight of each other.

There'd been another change in the goalkeeping situation: Derek Thompson had been dropped in favour of the number two, Enda Daly, and just a week before the Mayo match I was recalled at the insistence of Frank Grehan. I was picked between the sticks for that second-round qualifier in MacHale Park and, for my sins, could only stand and watch as Mayo rained twenty points over the bar. We were a fairly pitiful outfit that day. In the space of six weeks, a team that was going places had fallen apart; the bottom had fallen out of the barrel.

Tobin and his management team stepped down after the match.

To put the tin hat on it, another story emerged ten days later of more so-called bad behaviour, this time the night of the Mayo match. Rumours had been swirling around for days about some 'incident' or other on the team bus. The Derry controversy had given the dog a bad name, and now the slightest whisper had tongues wagging everywhere. And this latest was an outrageous scandal altogether: one or two lads had seemingly urinated into a bottle on the way home. The *Roscommon Herald* carried the story of the rumour, and by now the county board seemed to be spooked. Early in July the board announced that the squad was being formally 'disbanded'. Now, what this meant in practice I wasn't so sure, because our season was over anyway. But the board obviously felt that they had to draw a line under all the negative publicity; they had to lance the boil, and this was their way of doing it. Stephen Banahan was county board chairman at the time, and a very good one, too. The players never wanted for anything when Stephen was in charge. He released a strongly worded statement in which he rightly condemned the media for the public lambasting we'd got. But he also announced that the squad had been disbanded. Any players who were still interested could rejoin later that year if they were selected by the new management.

And the new manager turned out to be the best I played under during my time with Roscommon. Tom Carr was a breath of fresh air from the start. He was appointed in September 2002 and a few weeks later I got a phone call from him; he wanted us to meet for a chat. So we met over coffee one day in Mullingar, and from the get-go it was obvious that we were getting a manager who was a serious operator. That first meeting immediately filled me with confidence. Carr was eloquent, intelligent and fired up with belief in what he could do for us, and what we could achieve together. And he made it clear to me that I was very much part of his plans.

It was a great vote of confidence in me, and it came at the right time. Having felt unwanted and discounted a number of times over the years, I badly needed to hear it. Carr had a reputation for being a dour, intense sort of individual, but I warmed to him straight away. I felt we were on the same wavelength. Here was someone who wasn't afraid of my reputation; this was a manager who wanted strong personalities and was strong enough himself to know how to deal with them. After a horrible year of injury, rejection, low morale, bad defeats and stupid controversies, it was finally ending on a hopeful note. I was thirty-one by now, but I still had a future, and not just a past.

12. The Zoo

There was a player in the Athlone Town dressing room and his party piece was . . . I've thought about this, and the only fairly polite way of saying it was that his party piece was urinating on fellas in the showers.

You'd be in the showers and everyone would be buzzed up from the adrenalin of the match we'd just played, yakking away about some incident or other. You'd have clouds of steam from the hot water and yer man would come in and if he was standing beside you he'd give you a wink and a nudge. Then he'd turn round to the fella standing under the nozzle on the other side of him and piss down his leg. The fella would be covered in shampoo suds and his eyes would be closed and he wouldn't see anything. And with the hot water running he wouldn't notice the difference. And the bucko who'd be using him as a lamp post would be laughing away. He'd be delighted with himself. He'd think it was great crack altogether. Other times he'd just wave his mickey around, spraying indiscriminately at anyone in the vicinity.

Needless to say, one day he got his comeuppance. Another player copped on that the liquid running down his leg wasn't all water from the shower above. And as soon as he copped it he turned and flaked yer man with a haymaker to the jaw, sending him flying out through the double doors of the showers. They were like the double doors you'd see in a saloon in an old Western, halfway up the wall, and it was as if John Wayne himself had sent him flying with one good right cross. Yer man landed on his back, and there was a bit of a commotion and someone said, 'What the fuck is wrong with you?'

And he said, 'I'm after getting a box, boss.'

And everyone knew why he got it and everyone chimed in with the same reaction: ''Twas about fuckn time you got it.' And that put an end to his particular brand of toilet humour. Or at least it did until he left for another club.

There was another fella who used to love waving his mickey about because of the sheer ludicrous size of it. It was a ridiculous-looking yoke altogether. He was skinny as a rake but this thing had the dimensions of a fairly stout curtain pole and it was an endless source of fascination, especially to himself. He loved parading around after a shower, proud as punch, swinging it around; it was literally a big swinging mickey. And he wore a special pair of jocks under his togs to keep it wrapped up during games for his own protection. They were a sort of rubberized jocks with industrial-strength padding. I never saw the like of them before – and I never saw the like of it before or since either.

With some of the soccer lads, the old John Thomas was a constant source of commentary and a constant subject for jokes and general banter. They were nearly obsessed with it. And they were always up to some sort of mischief to try and get a laugh. Real childish stuff like putting itching powder in your socks or hiding your boxer shorts or taking your towel. If you came in with a nice fluffy white towel, you'd come out of the showers only to find some fella drying himself with it and making a big show of wiping his arse with it too. Anything to get a reaction from you that'd have the other lads in stitches.

In terms of pure crack and comedy, the soccer dressing room was generally livelier than its GAA equivalent. Of course you'd have loads of hilarious stuff going on in GAA dressing rooms too, but it was just at another level with the soccer lads. And the main reason, the main difference, was the Dubs. The dressing rooms in soccer were filled with jackeens, and there's not too many people in the world with the wit of the jackeen. I mean, every weekend in Athlone was a pure barrel of laughs. You just wouldn't stop laughing, and you'd be looking forward to the Dubs arriving in the door. The likes of Barry Murphy, Frank Darby, Rod de Khors and Val Keenan were brilliant jokers and messers. And it was all off-the-cuff wit. It wasn't sort of contrived, trying-to-be-funny stuff; it was just natural, spontaneous comedy. I think the Dublin accent is unique in that it makes any joke sound funnier, the way they deliver it; and the Dublin soccer fraternity has a culture all of its own too. It's the real Dublin working-class culture and I loved being in the thick of it. They'd be slagging me goodo about my culchie accent and my culchie ways and my mad gah mentality, and I'd be laughing my head off. Not just in the dressing room but in the car on the way to and from away games, or in the pub afterwards when the gargle was flowing.

I think in general they were just that bit more streetwise than your typical GAA fella. A lot of them would have left the education system that bit earlier and learned how to survive in the soccer environment from a young age. And it's a school of hard knocks, the soccer industry, it's dog-eat-dog and every man out for himself, and it toughens up fellas at a younger age. I think it makes them a bit more cynical, it gives them a harder edge and a blacker sense of humour. They love their football, obviously, but they're in it to make a living too. Most of these fellas would've had aspirations at one time or another to go to England and turn properly professional. So they'd have been brought up in an environment where there would've been a lot of jealousy and rivalry and cut-throat competition. GAA lads in general would've been a bit more sheltered in their upbringing. We would be learning at nineteen or twenty what the Dublin soccer lads were learning at nine or ten.

It made for a harsher dressing room in Athlone Town than I ever experienced with Roscommon. It was a lot more volatile, the abuse would be a lot more raw. In my time in GAA I never saw a player named or shamed in the dressing room, at half time or full time. It'd be done in a roundabout way. If a corner back was getting a roasting, the manager might say that we need to tighten things up in the full-back line. Something like that. In soccer, it was fuckn straight at you, in your face, a finger pointed at you and a manager going ballistic with you in front of the other lads. Soccer managers had a licence to go ballistic. It was part of the culture. So you'd have the manager occasionally smashing the tea cups at half time to show how angry he was. The tea would be poured out, maybe fifteen cups sitting on the table, and he'd sweep them off the table and the crockery would smash off the floor and off the walls and we'd all be ducking down. The tea would fly everywhere and ruin your clothes and the more cups broken the better. It was all nonsense really. It was like a ritual almost, something that the manager did every now and again to show who was boss. It was this fear-driver mentality and it was more prevalent in the soccer dressing room. Trying to instil fear of him into you. At its worst it was really a form of bullying and humiliation.

I never saw a manager in the GAA going completely ballistic like that. I know the GAA has a long and fairly stupid history of managers psyching up players by inciting them to violence on the field, but I personally never came across it. Managers in Gaelic football, in my experience, manage the dressing room a lot differently to their soccer counterparts. There's more silence, more analysis, less abuse and less confrontation. I've seen managers in the Athlone Town dressing room going eyeball-to-eyeball with various players. The player who'd been singled out for a rollicking would snap and give it back to the manager. And next thing, they'd be standing practically nose to nose in a stand-up row, jabbing their fingers and shouting and screaming at each other.

Now, not everybody can take that kind of pressure, the confrontational culture and verbal abuse. I think it weeds fellas out of the system, maybe very talented footballers who are quiet by nature or more sensitive or lacking in core confidence. It's a survival-of-the-fittest kind of environment, with everyone struggling to move up the ladder while ten other fellas are fighting for their rung on the ladder too.

The GAA dressing room wasn't exactly a genteel environment. You had your fair share of animals in there too. In my early days I came across a fair few unreconstructed bog men, rough as fuck and dog-ignorant. These fellas had been brought up in the old school and had no idea how to show a bit of manners or respect to friend or foe. There was still a fair amount of the old tribal savagery around when it came to parish against parish – football matches were not so much games of sport as running feuds.

When I first came into the Roscommon senior squad in 1990, a few veterans like Tony McManus were very good at making you welcome and showing you the ropes. But by and large the older generation didn't make it easy for you, and they were probably right too. Things weren't going to fall into your lap just because you were the supposed new young hotshot on the block. It was a case of the old dog for the hard road and the pup for the path. They were the alpha males and you knew your place, which was fair enough.

That's almost twenty-five years ago now, a generation in time. Society has changed, so inevitably dressing rooms have changed. I don't think they're as rough now. They're not as raw or as ignorant or as coarse. There are fellas who are not even half my age in the St Brigid's dressing room now. And, funnily enough, I don't see a whole lot of difference between how we were at that age and how they are at that age. They're mad for partying and drinking and girls and travelling and experimenting and all that malarkey. The main difference in lifestyles is probably technology-related: the internet, social media, mobile phones.

Where I think the generational difference is more obvious is between the fellas in their thirties now and the fellas in their thirties back then. I think they're just a bit more refined now; there's a bit more emotional intelligence about the place. A lot of it is probably to do with education. More fellas have gone on to third level and are working as professionals in white-collar jobs. Back then you had more fellas in farming and construction and blue-collar work. Society is more urbanized now, the GAA has therefore become more urbanized, less blue collar, less rural.

Fellas are more conscious of their looks and fashions too. You can see the male grooming fads coming into GAA dressing rooms. You always had it with the soccer lads when I was there. They were very appearance-driven. It was part of the soccer mentality, a lot of them were very vain about how they looked *before* a game, never mind afterwards. You'd have fellas getting their gel out and arranging their hair in the mirror before they took to the field. I mean, you could understand it afterwards if they were going out for the night, but some of them would be paying far more attention to their hair than to the manager's pre-game talk. If that happened in a GAA dressing room, the player wouldn't make it outside, he'd have the head taken off him for being such a stupid bloody poser. But in soccer they saw the likes of Beckham and all these other Premier League players who were big media stars, and the lads obviously felt they should be doing the same thing too, in case that lucrative aftershave contract came knocking on the door at St Mel's Park.

Mind you, I wasn't mad about the other extreme either, where fellas paid no attention at all to their presentation. Jesus, you had GAA players and they wouldn't wash their gear from one end of the year to the next. They'd come in with their ould mangy gear bags and the stink out of it would be something else. And they'd put on the same sweaty jersey night after night and the same manky disgusting socks and the dried mud falling off their boots, and they wouldn't even notice. That used to annoy me. I think it shows a certain lack of self-respect. I think it should be part of your preparation for games that all your gear is washed and clean and that you look fairly smart going on to the field.

The meat-and-drink of any sportsman's life is preparation. It's the weekly training sessions, your Tuesdays, Thursdays, Saturdays, and for a lot of fellas it is pure drudgery. That's why you find so many of them in a bad mood, coming into the dressing room on training nights. They know they're facing into the hardship and monotony of stamina running and sprints and exercises and there's no fun in it at all. It's just something that has to be got through.

There was a stage in my career when I just got fed up running. I wouldn't do it any more. I only did the running I felt a goalkeeper should be doing: short, sharp, quick stuff. But I've trained very, very hard throughout my career as a goalkeeper. I tried to keep on top of every aspect of the trade. I had all sorts of drills for shot-stopping, on the ground and in the air, for practising my angles and my fielding, for free kicks and penalties and corners – the works. And I generally enjoyed training, for much the same reason as I enjoyed going to school: because of the characters you were going to be meeting up with and having the crack with for the next two hours. The only time I didn't enjoy training was when I didn't want to be with the people who were there. I hated negative energy and I hated having to listen to fellas who were always moaning and bitching about something. These fellas are toxic; they're vampires; they drain the good energy out of a dressing room. And when there's no energy in there, it just becomes total drudgery. It was a particular danger in soccer dressing rooms if you had fellas who were there who just didn't give a shit any more. They were just there to pick up their few quid and they'd lost their passion for the game.

Or you could have a manager who just didn't know how to relate to players. He didn't have that kind of empathy, he didn't have that spark in his personality. And you had managers who had no concept of tailoring their coaching and training methods for individual players. They thought that everyone should be doing the same thing, no matter how irrelevant it would be to certain positions on the field. A lot of the work I needed to do as a keeper was different from the work being done by the outfield players, but some managers wouldn't trust you to let you work on your own with the other keepers in the squad. They were too insecure; they'd think you were trying to shirk the work, so they'd try and grind you twice as hard in their training sessions.

Or you'd have players who'd look at you doing your own thing and start complaining that you weren't putting in the same effort. Insecurity is a rampant commodity in dressing rooms and training grounds.

And a part of it is the different habits and routines and superstitions that players have. I like to be the last one out of the dressing room and I like to stand on the extreme right of any team photograph. But the one habit I very consciously developed was to walk into every dressing room with a smile on my face. It came naturally enough to me anyway, but I was always conscious of putting out the bright side, breezing in with a word for everyone and a bit of crack on my mind. It's all about bringing positive energy to the group, trying to defuse the tension if there's a big game coming up, or trying to lighten the mood if there's been a row or a bad performance that's left everyone a bit down. I'm an optimist, I rarely go round with a long face on me and the weight of the world on my shoulders. I'm just not made that way, and I've always believed it helps a team if there's someone trying to spread a bit of sunshine about the place.

It doesn't mean you don't feel the fear on the eve of a major match. You do, of course you do. What's more, you have to embrace it. You have to acknowledge that fear: the fear of defeat, of letting your teammates down and letting your people down. It can be harnessed; it can be a core asset; the fear of losing can become so strong that it drives you on to winning. But there's an awful danger that it will paralyse a team too; that it will stifle them and prevent them from expressing themselves. That's why there has to be a balance. It's why you have to put out the bright side and radiate your positivity, even if you're feeling the fear inside.

In the hour before a crunch game there's no denying that fear. Fellas are in the toilets puking and pissing and trying to take one last dump and it's all just nervous energy. Most lads are able to deal with it and get through it. But I've seen lads who have cracked under the strain and pressure of playing football and who have given it up. They stepped away from it because they couldn't cope with the demands of modern-day GAA and the pressure to play well and to win. It just gets too much; they don't enjoy it any more; and they want to get their lives back. They can do without all the time spent training and travelling and stressing about everything. And I don't blame them one bit. The strain has become excessive, the demands are unreasonable, the pressure is sometimes overwhelming. I think it has become a major issue for the GAA. Fellas are cracking up under the pressure and it's a problem that could become a runaway train that will cause a lot of damage if it's not addressed in a meaningful way.

The whole question of mental health has never been as urgent or as serious as it is nowadays. Mental illness is affecting large numbers of our young people in particular. And for those who are engaged in competitive sport, especially those in the crucial years between, say, eighteen and twenty-two, there are extra burdens attached. This is the age at which young people are trying to make their way in the world. They may be at college, they may be looking for a job, they are dealing with all the insecurity that comes with trying to establish themselves in life. Talented GAA players of this age will be playing for multiple teams in most cases. And often they have to deal with a load of different managers who are trying to pull them this way and that. And sometimes they're too timid to stand up for themselves.

Then there's the whole social media factor. Many parents are deal-ing with the very modern phenomenon of online bullying. But for lads playing intercounty GAA there is the additional stress of online abuse from faceless assassins who call themselves supporters but who are just the worst kind of bullies and cowards. Some of the criticism being levelled at players these days is scandalous. It is utterly shame-less, vicious stuff. And it's not realistic to say that players should just avoid it. For most young people, social media is an integral part of their lives. If they themselves don't see the abuse, friends or family will. It can only be desperately upsetting for the player and his loved ones when he's subjected to this kind of onslaught. It's hard to know what to do about it, but ideally you'd like to see some of these anonymous shitheads outed, exposed, and made to account for themselves.

Online bullying is one very important reason why pundits need to be very careful with the language they use and the opinions they articulate. It's a growing industry, media punditry, and thankfully a lot of the commentators are fair and conscientious about what they say. But there are exceptions – guys who are far too cavalier in their comments and criticisms. They seem to have no idea of the hurt they cause to players and their families. Which is all the more surprising, given that they were all players themselves at one time or another. They must have short memories. But they seem to have one eye on the ratings and another on the match they're supposed to be analys-ing. They are using players and managers as fodder for entertainment, while belittling and undermining them. And in doing so they are giving free licence to the online trolls to do their worst. Because if the trolls see someone on RTÉ dishing it out without much restraint, it can only encourage them to sink even lower.

Joe Brolly, for example, is someone who really needs to examine his conscience. Joe seems to think it's all just harmless fun. But there are consequences when he goes over the top with his facetious remarks. People get hurt. There is collateral damage and it can run deep. He has a massive platform on *The Sunday Game* and he needs to use it with a lot more sensitivity. Overall it's a much harsher public climate now-adays, in the stands and in the pubs and everywhere else. But those outlets for criticism were always there. The internet has taken it to a whole new level, and I worry about the damage that online abuse is doing to our young players. It's why we all need to be more careful in what we say, especially those with a public platform.

Personally, I found as I got older that I tended to let criticism wash off me without much bother. It's just a matter of becoming more mature and more battle-hardened. But at the same time you don't want to turn into the sort of cynical old pro who forgets what it was like to be young and vulnerable and insecure. Sometimes you'll see the old veterans using their status to put a young lad in his place. This is where the natural hierarchy in a dressing room can become abusive. The senior figures, the alpha males, can get away with saying things to young lads that are tantamount to bullying or intimidation. And because they're the so-called leaders in the dressing room they have licence to say a lot. They can call it tough love, or they can pose as the straight talker who isn't afraid to call a spade a spade. But if they cross a certain boundary it can be hurtful and damaging to a young lad's confidence.

You'll sometimes come across it when a big player is in the autumn of his career and he's slowing down. His own powers are fading. And he'll try to compensate by becoming more domineering. A fella who enjoyed his years as the main man or one of the main men has to be able to know when his day is done and it's time to let the next generation come through and take over the reins. That's why it's hugely important that the younger group of players is fully integrated into the set-up. When you've been through the mill yourself you're inclined to forget how it is to be starting out. But you have to be mindful of it; you have to put your arm around the young lads' shoulders and encourage them and give them the best advice you possibly can. It's in everyone's interest to do it because it makes for a happier camp and a better team. I do it my way by having a bit of crack with them, finding out what shenanigans they got up to at the weekend – the usual shite talk, really, about shifting and drinking and general messing. If you don't blend them fully into the group, there's a danger of cliques developing. And cliques are deadly to any team's ambitions. Maybe it's a bunch of fellas from the same club who stick together; or a bunch of fellas who don't like the manager and take shelter in numbers. Sometimes it is just a generational thing: the young lads in one corner, the middle-aged group in another, and then the ould fellas who've all been there together for years. It takes a lot of social awareness on the part of the manager and the senior players to make sure that everyone is blended and bonded together.

I've been through all the stages of dressing-room life, from the skinny naive rookie all the way to the senior alpha status. I would have been a very dominant personality, in the Roscommon and Brigid's dressing rooms in particular, once I became a senior figure. I was loud and talkative and demanding. I always had this feeling of frustration that we were underachieving, that there was more in us, that we could win things if we took ourselves seriously enough. I hope I led from the front, I hope it was the right kind of leadership. Sometimes it's hard to tell because your teammates are all individuals, and what you say might work with one lad and not with another. I know some fellas who were brilliant footballers but who were quiet and introspective and couldn't handle criticism. You'd have to talk to these fellas differently than to some lad who was just a messer and who you knew needed to get a good kick up the hole every now and then. That type of fella nearly enjoyed getting a good kick up the hole; he'd need it to get his batteries going.

I don't think it's that much different from any other walk of life. Every workplace has its hierarchy. The guys who've been there for a long time will have senior status because of their experience and know-how. The young recruits, if they've any sense at all, will listen and learn and gradually make their way up through the system. There's a certain amount of respect and deference for the veterans among young lads in a dressing room, especially if the veterans have the achievements to back up their talk. They've proven their ability, earned their reputation, and the young lads will appreciate this. But at the same time, they'll cop on fairly quickly if some veteran is dominating discussions but is no longer doing it on the field. If the guy is all the time talking but not delivering where it matters, he'll be told in fairly short order to shut his fuckn mouth and start performing. And rightly so, too.

13. Starting Over

I was barely a wet week with my new club, St Brigid's, when I had to face my old club, my home town, in a crunch championship match that was bound to stoke up all sorts of emotions.

This was the summer of 1998. I'd been mulling over a move for a year or so before that. Eventually I started talking about it to my Castlerea friends and teammates, and finally the time came to bite the bullet.

There were a number of factors in the move. I'd got married in May that year and moved to Sharon's home place in Brideswell, just west of Athlone, in the south of the county. Normally in these situations you'll find the new bride moving to her husband's part of the world if he has a few acres and a good stretch of road frontage to keep her in the style to which she's become accustomed. But it was roles reversed in this case. Being a townie I hadn't as much as a rood of land to my name, much less a farm, and I wouldn't be able to tell a bullock from a donkey. Sharon grew up on the home farm, and after a few years we built our own house on the family land. Learning the ins and outs of sheep farming was a tall order, and for a time I was about as useful as a newborn lamb to Sharon's parents, John and Rosie. Mind you, I've learned a bit in the years since and I even know my way around the rear end of a ewe when she's about to drop a new arrival in spring.

Meanwhile I'd started my new job with Ganly's in Athlone. I was on the road five days a week for Ganly's. I was also on the road every second weekend with Athlone Town, from Derry in the north to Cobh and Cork in the south. If I'd stayed with St Kevin's, I'd have been on the road from Brideswell to Castlerea and back again two or three times a week, for training and games. It was an eighty-mile round trip. The roads were rough, my back was giving me gyp, and it wasn't sustainable. I was already spending far too much time in the car. And things had gone stale with Castlerea anyway; I had gone stale with Castlerea. We'd lost two county finals, in '90 and '93, and that team was starting to break up. Other players had moved on or retired. I'd gotten to know a few of the Brigid's players over the years, especially the Lennon brothers, Brian and Tom. Brian worked in the bank in Castlerea, and we'd become good friends. They were neighbours of Sharon's, and long before we were married Brian was dropping hints about me transferring. I suppose it was all pointing towards one direction in the end; switching clubs made sense on every level and the time had come to bite the bullet.

But there was a taboo about moving to another club within your own county. Castlerea had nurtured me since I was a boy. My family had roots within the club that went back generations. My father had won four county titles with them. And I was a county man, one of their prized assets. No matter how much you tried to explain your situation to people, they didn't really accept your bona fides. In their eyes you were basically abandoning them for no good reason. They'd known you, man and boy, they'd coached you and taught you and invested their time in you; naturally they felt a sense of ownership and kinship towards you. All clubs do.

It's one of the sacred principles of the GAA: loyalty to your home place, your home team. There's a bit of a guilt trip foisted on someone who breaks that code, like you're committing some terrible act of treason. I reckon that a lot of fellas feel trapped by this pressure to stay when, deep down, they want to go. You're tied to this umbilical cord, it's a chain around your neck, and some fellas don't have the strength of character to make the break.

The 'one club one life' ethos in the GAA is a fine ideal, and the vast majority of people are happy to live by it and stick with it. But if a club is badly run, and the senior team is badly managed, or they just don't have the playing numbers to be competitive, good players can easily end up with wasted careers. The years slip by and they get dragged down by the mediocrity around them. They lose hope, their morale slides, their standards slip and it becomes a vicious circle. Clubs need to do more than just play the loyalty card. If they take their best players for granted and don't do enough to give them a fighting chance of winning something, then they don't deserve much sympathy if those players decide to move on. It hasn't happened a lot up to now, but it's starting to happen more and more. There's a migration of players now from the country, especially to the big Dublin clubs, and it's a trend that's going to continue. Players are getting inducements to move. Players within Dublin are moving from club to club pretty regularly too.

I have to emphasize that none of these issues were a factor in my decision to leave Castlerea. The club had a great heritage and a strong winning tradition. Winning a senior championship was always a realistic goal during my time there. If my circumstances had been different I'd never have left. But my life had changed, personally and professionally; I was no longer footloose and free. I was overstretched, trying to keep everything going. Transferring to St Brigid's, the club most local to Brideswell, would make life a bit easier and reduce the number of hours I was spending on the road. That's all there was to it. In the end it was a no-brainer for me.

I remember my first cousin, Noel, who was also a teammate with St Kevin's, coming to me one day and pleading with me to reconsider. But my mind was made up. And once I make up my mind I generally follow through. I've always been comfortable making decisions that aren't popular or that might offend some people. If I have my reasons, and I've reached my decision, I won't go back on it. I won't not do it because of fear of the consequences. You can't live your life that way. You have to take control of your own destiny. Some people in Castlerea were hurt by my decision, there's no doubt about it. And by moving to another club within the county, it was rubbing salt into their wounds.

In August '98 I made my Brigid's debut during a senior championship match against Kilbride in Athleague. I came off the bench, we were beaten by a point that day. We beat Elphin the next day out and the sequence of results meant that we'd face Castlerea in the semi-final of the losers' group. Castlerea beat us in a game that had an edge running through it because of my transfer. Naturally there was needle between my former colleagues and me. It was just inevitable. And it continued on and off for the next few years whenever we met in

With my mother and father on the day of my First Holy Communion

When I started as a young keeper for Athlone Town, I hadn't had a minute's goalkeeping coaching in my life. I was going on instinct, but despite one or two early errors I did OK *(Westmeath Examiner)*

Getting sent off by Jimmy McKee in our Connacht championship match against New York in May 2001, after a minor tussle with a New York player who wouldn't give me the ball to take a free. The decision caused me to miss our victory against Galway through suspension, and then Derek Thompson kept his place in goal for our victory over Mayo – for Roscommon's first Connacht title in ten years. I was sorry to miss out, but I celebrated like a lunatic anyway (*Aoife Rice / Sportsfile*)

In the 2003 All-Ireland quarter-final we came up against a Kerry team of all the talents – including the great Colm Cooper *(Ray McManus / Sportsfile)*

We needed all the help we could get in that match – so I humorously encouraged the umpire to signal a wide. Kerry took a big lead, but we hung in there and lost by just five in the end *(Brendan Moran / Sportsfile)*

I wasn't able to save this penalty by Sligo's Paul Taylor – a class forward and a sound fella – in a 2004 Connacht championship replay, but look at how I'm flying above Markievicz Park! Later in the same match, with our normal penalty-taker having been substituted, I scored from the spot myself – and I think I was and remain the only keeper to have scored a penalty in intercounty championship football *(Damien Eagers / Sportsfile)*

It was thanks to that Sligo match – in which I also scored a late long-range free – that I was awarded the GPA's player of the month award for May 2004 *(Pat Murphy / Sportsfile)*

As we had with Sligo, we drew at the first time of asking against Leitrim in the Connacht championship that summer. In the replay I saved a penalty and we won comfortably *(Damien Eagers / Sportsfile)*

I did what I could to rally the troops in the Connacht final against Mayo, but we missed a couple of early goal chances and succumbed to the effects of a small county's inferiority complex *(Pat Murphy / Sportsfile)*

In the autumn of 2005 St Brigid's made a breakthrough, winning the county title after some near misses – but we couldn't get past Salthill/Knocknacarra in the Connacht semi-final *(Damien Eagers / Sportsfile)*

Celebrating with my father after St Brigid's victory over Ballaghaderreen in the Connacht club final, November 2012 *(David Maher / Sportsfile)*

A crucial moment in our victory over Crossmaglen Rangers in that 2012–13 campaign: they had a gold-plated goal-scoring chance, but I caused them to rush it by first deceiving Jamie Clarke with a roar and then making myself big to cause Kyle Brennan to snatch at the shot *(Barry Cregg / Sportsfile)*

Club football is a community game, and here, after the final whistle against Crossmaglen, some members of the St Brigid's community invaded the pitch to celebrate with me *(Barry Cregg / Sportsfile)*

In the All-Ireland club final of 2013, we came up against a Dublin superclub, Ballymun Kickhams. We fell behind 2–3 to 0–1 – but as we came roaring back I celebrated every score with gusto *(Brian Lawless / Sportsfile)*

Our manager Kevin McStay delivered one of the great speeches on the Friday night before the final. He also made a few tough selection decisions – but the players trusted him, and we all shared in the joy after our victory *(Ray McManus / Sportsfile)*

Lifting the trophy with Frankie Dolan, Niall Grehan and Senan Kilbride

At home with my wife, Sharon, and our daughters, Abby and Lauren

league or championship. There's probably still a lingering seam of resentment towards me among a few diehards in the town. But the transfer was sixteen years ago now, there's been a lot of water under the bridge since, and I think the vast majority of people long ago accepted that I had genuine reasons for moving on.

In one way I've never moved on because I still have family in Castlerea, I still have so many friends there, and it still feels like home to me. The town made me, the people made me, and in my heart I still feel Castlerea is a part of my identity that will never fade.

In 1997 Brigid's won their first senior county title in twenty-eight years. Obviously I wasn't part of that squad, but the next time they reached the county final, in 2000, I was looking forward to winning my first senior championship medal. By then I'd moved back into goals. We'd beaten Michael Glaveys in the semi-final with a performance that got rave reviews.

We were hot favourites to beat Kilbride in the final. They hadn't won a senior championship in eighty-six years. We were supposed to be a powerhouse by comparison. But they won it that day. They turned up, we didn't. We were complacent, the overwhelming favourites' tag had seeped into our psyches and they ambushed us fair and square. It was my third county final and my third one to lose.

In 2002 we got back to the final again, only to lose another, this time to Strokestown: number four on the board for me. In 2003 we reached the final again, and this time there was no way we were going to lose it. We had learned our lessons, we had paid our dues, we were ready to take the last step. I was the Brigid's captain. And I had an extra, personal motivation: our opponents were Castlerea. It was unthinkable that I'd lose a fifth final to anyone, let alone to my old team. But lose we did: 1-9 to 0-11. I was a mess of emotions at the time: devastated that I'd lost, again, and to the team I'd left behind five years earlier. On the other hand I saw the joy it brought to the players and supporters and mentors I'd grown up with. Niall Finnegan, a great footballer, was Castlerea captain that day. Danny Burke was there in his band uniform, tears in his eyes. Supporters like Dermot Lyons, my uncle Eddie and uncle Johnny. My cousins Noel and Ronan were Johnny's sons, they won their medals that day too. It meant an awful lot to a huge number of people that I'd grown up with.

But it was a difficult day for my own parents, lifelong Castlerea supporters whose son was playing on the opposite team. And I must say it cut me deep at the time. Looking back now, however, I'm glad that the lads got their just rewards that day and took their permanent place in the roll of honour. Castlerea went on to win two more titles, in 2008 and '09, and they remain very much a force in Roscommon football – the tradition continues.

The hurt continued for me the following year when Castlerea beat us again, this time in the quarter-final. We hadn't played well the previous year, they were deserving winners, but this one was harder to take because the champions were vulnerable, they were there for the taking. But Ger Heneghan scored 0–6 from corner forward for Castlerea and we missed the chances that could've forced a draw or even an outright victory. Anyway, I was gone with my tail between my legs again. I had lost five county finals over a span of fourteen years and was beginning to seriously wonder if I wasn't jinxed entirely.

But, as the old saying goes, long threatening comes at last: in October 2005 we finally turned the corner. Our opponents in the final were Padraig Pearses and once again we were strong favourites. But Pearses played very well on the day and the match was still in the balance with just seven minutes left. Then Basil Mannion kicked a massive point for us and John Tiernan followed up with his second goal in a terrific performance to break the match our way. We saw it out to take the title on a 2-9 to 0-11 scoreline. At the age of thirty-four I had my first senior championship medal and I still remember the wave of sheer relief that flooded over me at the final whistle. The monkey was off my back at last. Salthill, the Galway champions, beat us in the Connacht semi-final in November, and they would go on to win the All-Ireland the following St Patrick's Day. Salthill were at a different level to us. That was the lesson from that game: once you got out of your county you were going to be running into teams operating at a different standard. This was the beginning of our apprenticeship at provincial and national level. It was the end of one journey and the start of another.

A year later we had our first Connacht title. The final at Dr Hyde Park was a mad match, with Corofin leading by two, 3-3 to 0-10, in injury time. Then Karol Mannion scored a goal that has gone down in folklore at our club. He got on to a ball down the left channel, shook off his marker and fired a spectacular shot from distance that dipped over their keeper and into the top corner. It was the first Connacht title for a Roscommon club since Clann na nGael in 1989. Anthony Cunningham, now the manager of the Galway senior hurlers, was our manager that year. He had taken over from Ger Dowd, who'd done a great job in leading us to our title the previous season.

Unfortunately I didn't play any part in that triumphant 2006 campaign. My ongoing back problem had flared up again earlier that year and it left me sidelined for months. I'd also started up my own builders' providers business in Athlone, and it was a major operation trying to get that off the ground. The new business needed all my time; my back needed a long lay-off. Between the two, I was out of the running: St Brigid's sailed on without me. I was happy to tag along as a supporter. Crossmaglen Rangers beat us in the All-Ireland semi-final and, like Salthill the previous year, they went on to win the title.

Anthony asked me to rejoin the panel in '07, and we completed a hat-trick of Roscommon championships that season. In Connacht we cruised into the final with a big win over Killererin of Galway. But in the final few minutes I ruptured a quad muscle that turned into a serious long-term injury. It kept me out of football for the best part of a year. We lost to Ballina Stephenites in the provincial final and the following summer our bid for a Roscommon four-in-a-row ended with a one-point defeat to Western Gaels in the quarter-final. Castlerea took over as champions in '08 and retained the crown in '09.

In the meantime I had taken a coaching job with a team in Westmeath. Padraig 'Oxy' Moran, the former Galway player, was the manager of Caulry and we combined to help them win the Westmeath junior championship in 2009. It was a very enjoyable experience; it gave me a taste for coaching and managing which I hope to pursue in the future.

In April 2010 I was booked on a flight to Manchester for a business meeting. Then the ash cloud erupted out of the volcano in Iceland

and all flights were cancelled. So I changed my travel plans and ended up taking the ferry from Dun Laoghaire to Holyhead. While on the ferry I collapsed: a horrendous shooting pain had taken over and I lost the power in my legs. It all happened suddenly and I was scared shitless; I didn't know what to think. Ger Brennan was with me and he was fairly alarmed too. I was wheel-chaired off the ferry. Back in Dublin I was seen by a neurosurgeon in the Mater Hospital. He diagnosed two bulging discs in the lower back. I'd been dealing with back pain for the previous seven or eight years, but now it had finally come to a head. In June I had an operation to remove one of the discs and pare down the other. At this stage all I was concerned with was quality-of-life issues: being able to walk around freely without crippling pain, being able to live with full mobility. Thankfully, the operation was a complete success in this regard. Within a few months I was walking around, more or less pain-free, but it would be over a year before I could contemplate going back to football again. I was now thirty-nine, well past the time that most sportsmen have wound up their careers. And physically I was more or less a crock, breaking down with injuries and undergoing an operation for that chronic, longstanding, back complaint. But I couldn't pack it in; I couldn't walk away from my playing career. Common sense said I should have, but I was too obsessed with it for common sense ever to win that argument.

Once again St Brigid's sailed on without me. In 2010 they won back Roscommon and beat Killererin in the Connacht final. Then they took the mighty scalp of Cork's Nemo Rangers in the All-Ireland semi-final and reached the club's first All-Ireland final. We had our chances on the day, but Crossmaglen's greater experience and craft got them home – we lost by a goal in what was a very honourable performance. The team was evolving and learning and getting stronger. But Crossmaglen were one of the best club teams of all time and they exposed a few weaknesses in our side. We knew we had to reach another level in our play if we were to take the ultimate step.

By the summer of 2011 I was back training with St Brigid's. I'd managed to stay reasonably fit, playing five-a-side soccer during the winter and spring. And thankfully I'd lost none of my agility between the sticks. My reflexes were still sharp and my eyesight was sound. The crucial assets for any goalkeeper were still there. I knew that I still had the ability to play the position at the highest level. And I'd kept in touch by coaching the back-up goalkeepers at the club. James Martin had taken over from me, and his cousin, Philly Martin, took over from him for the 2010–11 campaign. I sat on the bench for the 2011 county final, and by this stage there was no one to touch us in Roscommon. We beat Elphin without much fuss, and there wasn't much fuss afterwards either because by now we had set our sights on larger targets. But winning can sometimes paper over cracks in a team.

Tourlestrane, the Sligo champions, weren't good enough to exploit that problem in the Connacht semi-final. A week or so before that game I was asked if I'd sit on the bench for it. I point-blank refused: I was still officially the goalkeeping coach and you don't want to undermine the players you yourself are actually coaching. I felt the management should first have gone to the two keepers *in situ* and informed them that I was now officially part of the extended panel again and would be in contention for future selection. I didn't want to be involved in a three-way fight for the goalkeeper's jersey without the two lads being properly notified well in advance. So I ruled myself out of the semi-final, knowing that, if I did, I'd be out of contention for the final as well. We survived by the skin of our teeth in that final, against Corofin of Galway, with the help of a few generous refereeing decisions. This was St Brigid's third Connacht title but I had yet to win one on the field of play: injuries, non-availability and non-selection had combined to rule me out of all of them.

After beating Corofin we had to face the London champions, Fulham Irish, in an All-Ireland quarter-final in December. It was at this point that I felt management should have gone to the other goalkeepers and notified them that I was back in the panel. There was a clean break here between the county and provincial campaign, and the All-Ireland series. But they fudged the issue; it was never tackled. Noel O'Brien was our manager and I felt he was being overloaded with advice and opinions from far too many sources. Everyone seemed to be putting their oar in when it came to issues of selection. You had a lot of the sort of politicking, personality clashes and localized squabbling that are often the bane of GAA club culture. And when there's pressure coming from all quarters, it can often lead to compromises in team selection, just for the sake of keeping peace in the valley.

We won easily in London, but again the problem of our kickouts was apparent. In January 2012 we played a challenge match against Portlaoise in preparation for our upcoming All-Ireland semi-final against the Leinster champions, our neighbours Garrycastle, from over the border in Westmeath. I was put in goals for the first half. The stats, as I recall, showed that we had twelve kickouts in that half; they showed also that we had won all twelve of those kickouts.

I think the consensus among most of the panel and most of the supporters was that I was in pole position to reclaim the jersey for Garrycastle. A few weeks before that match we had another challenge, against a Donegal selection in Sligo. I was left on the bench. One of the problems, apparently, was that I hadn't been doing the 400-metre runs in training. We had a physical trainer at the time who placed great importance on 400m runs for everyone – including the goalkeepers. He was another one of these trainers, and there's a lot of them knocking around the GAA, who know everything and know nothing. I refused to do them: they weren't necessary in my position, and I had a damaged back that needed to be minded. At this stage of my career I knew my body and I knew how far it could be pushed before breaking down again. But one of the selectors told me that not doing the runs was jeopardizing my chances of being picked. I told him that I wouldn't be doing any 400m runs against Garrycastle, and neither would any other goalkeeper. I told him I hadn't done 400m runs since I'd quit playing outfield, about ten years earlier. I told him they were a fuckn ridiculous demand by a trainer who was completely ignorant of what a goalkeeper's preparation actually required.

I'd felt my best form coming back to me in the run-up to that All-Ireland semi-final. After such a long lay-off, I had the enthusiasm again of a young buck. I was revitalized, buzzing with optimism, mad for road. So I was really looking forward to that match against the Donegal selection; it would be another good sharpener before the big one that lay ahead. But after fifty minutes I was still sitting on the bench, and at that point I decided it was time to go. I left the dugout, went back to the dressing room, togged in and headed home. I was angry because I well knew that politics had played a part in the decision not to start me. And I wasn't the only player affected by club politics. It often happens: people who swear their loyalty to a club or a team are often quite happy to see that same club or team damaged in the pursuit of their own personal agendas.

We were hot favourites to beat Garrycastle, but those of us on the inside knew that there were too many issues and too much bullshit going on behind the scenes. Stuff that wouldn't be tolerated in a winning team or a successful organization. Apart from the named substitutes, our bench that day was packed with hangers-on who wanted to be seen on the pitch and in the photographs after we'd beaten Garrycastle. The dressing room was a real bandwagon job too, everyone piling in to have their say and get their slice of the action. I'd said to Sharon a few days before the match that we wouldn't beat Garrycastle, and we didn't. Anthony Cunningham was now their manager and he had his homework done on us good and thorough. They beat us by two points in Longford and our grand dreams of All-Ireland glory had bitten the dust.

We were back at the bottom of the hill. The long climb towards the summit of the club game in Ireland would have to start all over again. I was damaged goods by now: an old man with a body racked by the wear and tear of twenty years in senior soccer and Gaelic football. I still didn't want to let go. I just didn't know if anyone still wanted to hold on to me.

14. Blood and Vaseline

On a Monday morning in January 2003 my phone at work rang. It was Tom Carr, and he was ringing to tell me that the Roscommon senior team management had decided to appoint me captain for the coming season. I nearly fell out of my standing. My whole world changed in ten seconds. To captain my county team was about the biggest honour anyone could bestow on me. I was thrilled to be asked and flattered by the compliment it paid me.

My reputation as a maverick and a free spirit had always stereotyped me to some degree, but Carr was able to see beyond that. He'd sussed me out, he'd done his research and I think my off-field contribution to the 2001 provincial title win hadn't been ignored when it came to evaluating my credentials.

I was nearing my thirty-second birthday when Carr appointed me. Sportsmen tend to be fairly self-centred when they're younger, but you reach a stage later in your career when you can see the bigger picture. You realize that it's not all about you, either in life or in sport. It's about the collective, it's about what's best for the whole squad. You're there to contribute to the greater good, not just your own needs.

Carr and I had hit it off from day one. There was mutual respect. I found him an admirable man as well as an inspiring coach, so for him to give me the job only added to the pride I felt that day. He'd made his presence felt in the few months he'd been in charge. His selectors were Gary Wynne and Jimmy Deane, two fellas steeped in Roscommon football. Between the three of them they quickly started to restore morale and inject belief into a squad that had been battered by all the rubbish that had gone on the previous season. We were ready for change and they were able to deliver it.

In the first round of the national league we beat a Tyrone team that would go on to win the All-Ireland the following September. In the third round we beat Cork by a point in Hyde Park, having trailed by seven at one stage. We beat Galway by eight points, which was a massive result. I remember they got a penalty and Derek Savage stepped up to take it. Derek had two All-Irelands under his belt by this stage. As he was placing the ball I walked out to him and informed him that he hadn't a hope of scoring it; not a chance in hell. And what's more, I'd bet him €20 that he wouldn't score it. Fr Liam Devine used to do a sports column for the *Roscommon Herald*. The following week he had an account of that little contretemps:

> [Shane Curran] was at his theatrical best when facing up to Derek Savage's penalty. It was the first time I had seen a goalie coming out to shake hands with a penalty-taker as he lined up to take the kick. Even the Galway followers saw the humour in the situation. After Curran's theatrics there was only one way Derek could hit the ball – feebly along the ground.

Against Dublin in March, Frankie Dolan scored eleven points, five from play. It was the start of a brilliant season for Frankie, probably the best of his career. But a lot of Roscommon players were catching fire that season. The final shake-up in the league might contradict this assertion: we were relegated to Division Two. But we'd been keeping top-class company in Division One: the likes of Kerry, Armagh – who were All Ireland champions – Dublin and Donegal too. These teams were the cream of the crop and we'd been very competitive against almost every one of them.

No one was despondent about the relegation. We felt we were a team on the up and we could sense it in the dressing room. So we headed to Salthill for the first round of the Connacht championship with high hopes of dethroning Galway. As captain, I hit on a brain-wave the week before the match – two brainwaves, in fact. Well, I thought they were brainwaves at the time.

I paid a visit to my GP, Dr Martin Daly, a great friend to Roscommon football. Martin has been the county team doctor for many years and was a great friend to me over all the time, too. I asked him to take a pint of my blood. Naturally enough, he wanted to know why I wanted a pint of my own blood. I told him he'd find out on

Sunday. I took the blood home in a sealed plastic bag and put it in the freezer.

My second bright idea was to bring a second pair of gloves in my kit bag. And I told our physio, Adrian Tully, to bring a big tub of Vaseline with him. This was my cunning plan: I'd slather a load of the Vaseline on to my old Uhlsports, front and back, and when I'd meet Alan Keane for the traditional pre-match handshake, I'd make sure I'd clasp his hands with great sincerity altogether. Then I'd take off my gloves and put on the second pair. Keano was the Galway goalkeeper and I was looking for an edge, anything that might get under his skin. And he wouldn't be happy when he found his own gloves covered with Vaseline. It'd cause a bit of panic. Ideally he wouldn't notice at all until a high ball dropped into his square and he went to catch it . . .

'Jaysus,' said Adrian, 'you can't do that!'

'I fuckn well can,' said I, 'and I will!'

The mind is a very peculiar place. Those six inches between your ears − a lot goes on in there. And when you're thinking of all the people whose hopes you are responsible for, who are dreaming of their team winning games and winning titles, you're going to do everything you possibly can to try and gain an edge. And sometimes when there's an ability deficit between your team and your opponents, the onus is on you, the underdog, to try and think of something that might create a swing of one or two per cent.

Before the pre-match parade I donned the gloves that were doused in the Vaseline. And after it I sought out Keano, gave him the big slapstick handshake, and changed out of the gloves. When I took my place in our goals I could see a bit of a commotion down in the other goals. Fellas were running in and out from the sideline to Keano, and John O'Mahony, the Galway manager, was looking very agitated too. As far as I could see, someone brought Keano a spare pair of gloves and he changed them. O'Mahony was a great manager but he didn't do humour. He found it hard to see the funny side of anything. And sure enough, he was still bulling with me when our paths crossed after the match. He said to me that I'd never, ever shake the hand of a goalkeeper again. I told him it was only a bit of crack and not to take it so serious. The irony was that Alan Keane's father had bought a load of Capco slates from me only a couple of months before that match. I got on great with Mike Keane and Mrs Keane, and they gave me an awful slagging about it the next time I met them. It was just a bit of a stunt, really, and after the initial fuss died down I think most people could see the funny side of it. Anyway, the story about the Vaseline has done the rounds over the years since, and I still get reminded of it from time to time in Connacht football circles. And right enough, I've noticed that a lot of goalies in the years since prefer before a game to give me a fist bump rather than shake my hand.

At half time we were trailing 0-9 to 0-3. By this stage the bag of blood had defrosted in my kit bag in the dressing room. And I reckoned now was the time for the captain's speech to end all captain's speeches. It was time to literally spill blood for the cause. So I take out the bag of blood and I hold it up and I say, 'Lads, this is Roscommon blood. And we're gonna have to fuckn spill blood today to win this match.' And I ranted and raved about beating these Galway bastards and every man dying for the jersey and doing it for the pride of Roscommon. All that shite talk and mad rhetoric. And as the speech reached its crescendo, I fired the bag off the floor in the dressing room. This would be the *coup de grâce*: I'd burst the bag and the blood would spill everywhere in a powerful symbolic gesture, and we'd go out for the second half like men possessed. There was only one prob lem: the bag didn't burst, it just sat there on the ground. The lads just looked at it and looked at me and looked at it again, not knowing what to make of it all. I have to admit it didn't quite come off as I'd envisaged it. In my imagination this was going to be a seminal moment, a turning point in the fortunes of this team. But the moment had passed. I could hardly pick it up and hop it off the floor again. There'd be no blood spilled for Roscommon that day.

We lost the match 0-12 to 0-8, which meant at least that we'd won the second half. So my appeal for blood sacrifice at half time obviously worked! I'd say if the bag had burst we'd have won it altogether. Or maybe it was just that in Pearse Stadium you always get the game of two halves: one with the wind and one against the wind. It's a kip of a ground with a lousy atmosphere and a wind blowing straight in off the Atlantic that ruins just about every match. How they ever decided to build a venue there, at a cost of multiple millions, I'll never know, but it's one of the biggest white elephants in the GAA.

Dr Martin told me afterwards that he nearly got a panic attack when he saw me producing the bag of blood at half time. And he nearly got a heart attack when he saw me walloping it off the floor. He said it wasn't a pint of porter I was messing around with. He pointed out that it would leave an awful mess everywhere and, what's more, it would probably have been an environmental health hazard that'd need a specialist clean-up operation. I think to this day some of the lads reckon I got the blood out of a butcher's shop or a meat factory or somewhere like that. But the simple truth is that I got it out of my own arm at a moment when my dyslexic imagination had taken over from more practical considerations.

I think the Galway game probably came just a bit too soon for us in that season. It was a Connacht quarter-final in the middle of May. Training was going very well, but we were still at a very early stage of our evolution under Carr. That Galway team had a lot of experience and a lot of class, but even another month would've made a good difference to us.

And we proved that in the first round of qualifiers in June, when we beat Cork by a point in Hyde Park. That was a landmark result for us. The team played superbly well on the day. The likes of David Casey and Morgan Beirne were outstanding in defence, we had a strong midfield in Seamus O'Neill and Stephen Lohan, while Gary Cox, Gerry Lohan and young Derek Connellan put real pressure on Cork in the half-forward line. We were the better team for most of that match, but our inexperience in big-game situations caught up with us in the last few minutes and we very nearly buckled as Cork threw the kitchen sink at us. It helped our cause that they had two players sent off late in the game, but I think we were deserving winners anyway. That match was Larry Tompkins's last as Cork manager. Larry was a fantastic footballer and is someone I've always admired for his toughness and class on the field of play. In later years I got to know him well and would always call into his pub in Cork any time I was visiting. During the second half some idiot came on to the pitch, trying to attack him. It was an ugly situation and Larry deserved better.

Cork are one of the big guns and glamour names in Gaelic football, so beating them was a huge leap forward in our development. We were hot favourites to beat Leitrim in the next round, and we very nearly came unstuck. It took a late, late goal from David 'Jimmy Nail' O'Connor to save us that day in Carrick-on-Shannon. We were two points down with time almost up, and it was panic stations. We got the ball into the full-forward line and Frankie Dolan took a shot that was parried by the Leitrim goalkeeper, Gareth Phelan. The rebound fell to Nigel Dineen. He scuffed his shot across the face of the goal and Jimmy Nail pulled on it into the net. There was pandemonium now. Frankie tried to stop Phelan from taking a quick kickout and Phelan levelled him with a box! Frankie was stretched out on the deck and poor old Gareth got sent off. We scraped through by the skin of our teeth, 2-9 to 1-11. Jimmy Nail's goal has gone down in folklore. He'd just come off the bench in the sixty-seventh minute. He's a fellow St Brigid's man, a great character, and I often joke with him that his goal was the first and last touch he ever got in a Roscommon jersey. That was his debut, and I don't think he ever played for Roscommon again. But what a cameo!

We were on a roll now, and the summer continued with a classic match in the next round against Offaly in Mullingar. They got a late goal to bring it to extra time. But we were very fit: Carr had trained us hard and trained us well, with a lot of method to his physical regime and football coaching. He'd taken the squad off to La Manga in Spain for a week after the league campaign and worked us intensively. We did a lot of video analysis too and it was the first time that a Roscommon team had been treated so professionally. La Manga had all the sports facilities you could need and of course it had the warm weather too. Everything was well organized, the week ran like clockwork, and we all came back feeling better about ourselves and more united as a group.

All that preparation stood to us against Offaly on this occasion. We had the stamina to go the distance and the team spirit to back it up. The likes of O'Neill and Lohan in midfield, and Francie Grehan at centre half back were really commanding that day; they gave us a dominant presence down the spine of the team. Our subs came on and made important contributions too. And then Francie shot the lights out with twelve points, three from play. It was a wondrous exhibition of shooting from all angles and distances. The highlight was a sideline ball that he converted from an acute angle. It was an amazing score. But Francie was on fire that summer. Players sometimes need to be made to feel special by their managers; Carr had shown him the love and was getting the best out of him. He'd given Francie the confidence to play and the licence to express himself.

Francie has an artistic streak in him. Which means he can be moody, ratty, opinionated and argumentative. Not unlike myself at times, which is maybe why we get on so well. But if Mick O'Dwyer, Seán Boylan and Mickey Harte took over the Roscommon team together, Francie would be liable to say they hadn't a fuckn clue what they were talking about! He's just a contrary, cantankerous hoor. And he can be hilarious without knowing it when he's in one of his humours. But he's brilliant crack and a born performer. He has the skills of a footballing artist and the competitive bottle to complement them. If you need someone to nail a crucial point for you, it's Francie you'll want on the ball and looking at the posts. He will ice it for you.

We pulled away from Offaly in extra time. Afterwards we had a few drinks with them in the Greville Arms and I had a bit of a chat with one of the Offaly players, Paudie Mulhare. I'd come out of the dressing room for the second half wired to the moon. Running on to the field I rooted the ball up in the air and barrelled into Paudie on my way down to the goals. Now it wasn't the most sensible of things to do, if only because Paudie was a fairly stocky sort of a fella, maybe even carrying an extra few pounds – he was well able to fill his jersey and togs, put it that way. Naturally enough, he took umbrage at my behaviour and threw a kick at me and I ended up on the ground. I passed no remarks and neither did he. But the umpire spotted it and notified the referee, who gave us both a yellow card. In the hotel afterwards Paudie asked me what the fuck was I doing, running into him like that. And I said, 'To tell the truth Paudie, you're so fuckn wide 'twas easier to go through you rather than round you!' We had a great laugh about that.

Next up were Kildare in Round 4 at the end of July in O'Moore Park. It was another pulsating match, the best game of Gaelic football I was ever involved in, and my all-time favourite memory from my Roscommon career. John Tiernan, on as a sub in the second half, got our goal after terrific build-up play by Karol Mannion. The sides were level at the end of normal time, when Stephen Lohan had a great chance to bury a goal and win it for us. But their keeper, Enda Murphy, made a blinding save, Kildare came down the field and Padraig Brennan clipped what looked like the winning point. We were into the third minute of injury time when I came soloing out the field with the ball. I came about forty to fifty yards and shovelled it on to Morgan Beirne. The move culminated with the ball in Francie's hands. He was way out on the wing, out near the new stand, and from there he curled over a majestic point. It would've been a brilliant point at any time of a match, given the angle and distance; but in the circumstances it was an unbelievable score. It was the last kick of the game in regulation and it took us into extra time.

We were on top in the first half of extra time – Francie kicked three points in six minutes. But it was still nip and tuck going into the second half as Kildare closed the gap again to a single point. Then I came out with a ball, offloaded it and was tripped by the Kildare corner forward, Tadhg Fennin. I went sprawling to the turf and probably rolled over once or twice too often for some people's tastes. Tadhg was shown a yellow card – his second of the match – and was sent off. It was probably a harsh call, but it had definitely been a late tackle. We pulled away down the final stretch. Francie hit three more points to bring his tally to an incredible 0-13, five from play. His very first score, in the first minute, was from a sideline ball on the right, about five metres from the corner flag; he hit it with the outside of his right boot. That's the form he was in that summer: untouchable.

The Rossies came storming on to the field at the final whistle. The atmosphere all match had been white-hot, and now they were letting off steam in a big way. It was like we'd won the All-Ireland. We hadn't, but we were on our way to the All-Ireland quarter-final – we were on our way to Croke Park.

That was a really special evening in Portlaoise. We walked from O'Moore Park back to the Heritage Hotel in the town centre, and our supporters lined the streets and applauded us in the front door.

It wasn't quite all sweetness and light for me because I was waylaid en route by three women wearing Kildare jerseys, two of them I'd say in their twenties, the third a more mature lady. When they spotted me, they lit on me; they were blaming me for getting Fennin sent off; they were in a rage. They swore like sailors, called me every name under the sun. I kept walking, they kept on talking. Sure it was water off a duck's back. Nothing could ruin the buzz of that night. My father was at the game, he went to nearly every game, and we've a lovely photo at home of himself in the stand that day, alongside the great Gerry O'Malley – probably the most revered figure in the history of Roscommon football.

On the August Bank Holiday Monday we faced Kerry in Croke Park. That was a Kerry team of all the talents, an awesome outfit with some of the greatest players ever to play the game. I mean, just look at their full-forward line that day: Mike Frank Russell, Declan O'Sullivan and Colm Cooper. Their forwards in particular gave us a lesson, especially during the first half. We were chasing shadows, we couldn't cope with their movement and pace and skill. At one stage we were eleven points behind. But I took great pride from the fact that we didn't give up, we didn't collapse. We had a lot of young, inexperienced players who could have been completely overwhelmed by the occasion, the venue, the reputation of our opponents. But in fairness we hung in and managed to turn it around in the second half. Kerry won by five in the end, 1-21 to 3-10, so it was a more than respectable performance on our part. We'd salvaged our honour, and our supporters could go home happy that we'd acquitted ourselves well and given them a great summer of excitement along the way.

Two weeks later St Brigid's played St Aidan's in an early club championship round. The match was held in the rural tranquillity of the Johnstown GAA pitch, Clann na nGael's home ground. Francie

Grehan was playing with Aidan's and I remember remarking to him afterwards that there was some contrast between this and the previous few games we'd played – crowds of 30,000, give or take, then almost 57,000 in Croke Park for the Kerry game. Now we were back to a pitch that had a forest in the background and a couple of hundred supporters for atmosphere. Same game, different world.

Later in the season I was nominated for an All-Star and also received the player-of-the-year award from the Roscommon GAA Supporters Club. Fergal Byron got the goalkeeper's All-Star that year and was a deserving winner. Laois had won the Leinster championship and Fergal had a great season between the sticks for them. Enda Murphy was the third nominee in that position and, between the three of us, the goalkeepers' union had a mighty night of it at the All-Stars banquet.

I'd have loved to have won an All-Star but I'd no complaints about the final decision. What really annoyed me was the way I was treated by the selectors for the Ireland team that would play Australia in the International Rules series. There would be two Test Matches, in Perth and Melbourne, in late October. John O'Keeffe was the Ireland manager. The Kerry goalkeeper at the time was Declan O'Keeffe, but Declan was retiring from intercounty football and he wasn't in the running. There was talk that Declan's successor in Kerry, Diarmuid Murphy, would be parachuted into the squad. But Diarmuid, if I recall, said at the time there was really only one keeper they should bring to Australia. To be honest, I thought it was a no-brainer too. The goalie in International Rules has to operate as a sweeper, an auxiliary defender behind the full-back line; he has to be comfortable coming off his line and launching attacks. And I was the only keeper in Gaelic football who was actually doing that. I'd have loved to have represented Ireland; I'd have loved a team trip to Australia; and I'd have loved to have played in the Subiaco Oval in Perth, and in the Melbourne Cricket Ground. But not only was I not picked – I wasn't even invited to the trial games. O'Keeffe in his wisdom decided I wasn't even worth a trial! He was by all accounts a good football coach: I can't believe he wouldn't have known that International Rules suited my style down to the ground. I thought it was an indefensible decision; it really disappointed me. And I can't believe that it was made for footballing reasons. Sometimes your face just doesn't fit. In the end O'Keeffe brought Enda Murphy. I'd say he'd have brought Johnny Culloty before he'd have brought me.

But the player who suffered the worst injustice that year was Frankie Dolan. It was a disgraceful decision by the All-Star selectors to overlook him that year. Frankie was nominated all right, but that was as far as it went. It was wrong; it was unfair. Frankie had kicked twenty-five points in two games alone that summer, against Offaly and Kildare. He was scoring points that were in Maurice Fitzgerald's class. He was unmarkable. He was as good as any forward in the country that summer of '03. Declan Browne from Tipperary got his second All-Star that year. Declan Browne was a class player, but he did not have the championship that Dolan had that year. He just didn't. But Declan was a bit of a darling with the GAA media and Frankie wasn't. Frankie had a bit of attitude; he was intense; he was confrontational. He wasn't a biddable sort of fella. And these things matter with certain journalists.

I often wonder if there isn't a bit of good old-fashioned snobbery at work here, too. The GAA culture likes its players to be humble and biddable, and even subservient, at all times. It also likes players who will make for good pillars of the community, teachers, civil servants, bankers, accountants, solicitors and the like. It likes a fella who comes across as an officer-and-a-gentleman type. Indeed there are numerous examples of these plausible professional types getting soft All-Stars for looking well and sounding well, rather than performing well. The GAA culture doesn't necessarily embrace fellas from working-class backgrounds like myself and Frankie, ordinary five-eighths who are a bit lippy and a bit chippy and who are prepared to speak our minds. No, they prefer you to know your place and keep your mouth shut. And if you don't, someone somewhere in that vast organization will give you your comeuppance some place along the line.

It goes without saying that it's a very political organization, and I've no doubt that politics plays its part from time to time in the All-Stars process. Some GAA journalists have their own favourites among the players; they have their own prejudices and their own tribal connections. It's not unknown for All-Star selectors to act as cheerleaders for their own buddies among the players when it comes to handing out the awards. And if you're not from one of the major counties, and you're not on television every Sunday, that affects your chances too. Out of sight is out of mind. But any journo who was doing their homework that summer, and who was assessing the merits of each player scrupulously, would have given Dolan the nod.

There wasn't a whisper out of Roscommon when he didn't get it. As usual, we just took it lying down. I don't recall even the local journos making much of a fuss about it. In other counties with bigger egos than ours, there'd have been a furore. Could you imagine today someone like Bernard Brogan or the Gooch kicking twenty-five points in two games and not getting an All-Star? There'd be fuckn uproar. But in this case no one kicked up. Dolan was left without the All-Star award that would've crowned his season. And I think it knocked the stuffing out of him; he felt wronged, and it went hard on him. It shook up his confidence and you could argue that his intercounty career never fully recovered thereafter.

15.   A Chip Shop in Kinnegad

I'd like to think I was a pioneer, the original of the species, the man to boldly go where no man had gone before.

Now, I'm sure there were a few goalkeepers somewhere in the club game who were kicking long-range frees long before it became the trend it is today. But at county level, to the best of my knowledge, I was the first.

Stephen Cluxton is widely credited with pioneering this development when he began taking them in 2010. And he deserves a lot of credit because he turned it into a popular feature in Gaelic football. He has singlehandedly had a big influence on the modern game, obviously not just with his scores but in his kickout strategy too, which has changed how the game is played. Now it's almost a mandatory part of the keeper's job to be coming upfield and knocking placed balls over the bar.

Of course, everyone is saying now that it makes sense: that the player who spends more time taking kicks off the ground than any other should be the one best equipped to take long-range frees off the ground too. I'd been saying it for years but it just wasn't the done thing and, if it wasn't the done thing, then why would you do it?! It's only a small example of a big problem in this country, not just in GAA but in society in general: the stubborn resistance to new ideas or original thinking. It seems we only accept innovation when it's worked somewhere else first, and then we just copy it.

Anyway, six years before Cluxton popularized the habit, I scored 1-1 from placed balls in a Connacht championship match against Sligo at Markievicz Park. It wasn't shown live and it only got a few minutes on the *Sunday Game* highlights round-up the next night, so it's a match that has more or less disappeared from the annals. But I think anyone present in the 15,000-capacity crowd that Saturday evening in May will tell you it was one of the best games of football they ever saw. It was a fantastic match that went all the way to extra time. And this was after the sides had drawn in Dr Hyde Park the previous weekend.

The referee awarded three penalties in the replay. Ger Heneghan scored one for us after about twenty minutes, and Paul Taylor buried one for them on the stroke of half time. Taylor was an absolutely class forward and a sound fella into the bargain. Heneghan was replaced at the interval by Jonathan Dunning, who went on to have a major bearing on the game. About fifteen minutes into the second half we got another penalty. With Ger off the field, I volunteered. I'd often taken penalties during my days as a forward, and I still practised taking them, as well as saving them, when I became a full-time keeper. And of course my controversial penalty in the Connacht minor final of 1989 was still remembered. Up the field I went, with lots of Sligo players giving me plenty of 'advice' along the way. I was confident I'd bag it. And I decided to do a bit of a stutter step on my run-up – the Aldo shuffle, as in Liverpool and Ireland legend, John Aldridge. No problem, back of the net. To this day I think I'm the only keeper to have scored a goal in intercounty championship football.

Frankie got sent off a few minutes later and Gary Cox took over on the frees. The match ebbed and flowed, with Sligo picking off some great scores too. A lot of players on both sides were turning in storming performances. Francie Grehan moved from centre half back to centre half forward after Dolan went off, and he showed serious leadership when it was needed – not for the first time either. We had great defensive performances too from the likes of John Whyte and Mickser Ryan. David Casey was carrying a head wound, picked up in the drawn game, that had needed seventeen stitches. He came on late in normal time when he probably shouldn't have been playing at all.

The match was still nip and tuck as it ticked into injury time. Then we got a free, way out on the left. Immediately I came racing out of goals. I figured it was probably out of Gary Cox's range and that I might as well have a pot at it so. Now, the place was frantic at this stage. Both sets of supporters, subs and managements were raw with nerves and anxiety. Tom Carr and Jimmy Deane were shouting at me to get back to fuck into goals. But I came down to where the ball was. Gary was there having a look at the angle and the distance. It was about five metres behind the 45-metre line, and about five metres in from the left sideline. We were looking down into the Boyle end goals, and there was a fresh wind blowing into our faces. It was a mammoth kick in terms of distance and direction. I said to Gary that I was as well to have a go at it. Once the lads in the Sligo dugout saw me placing the ball they started heckling and barracking me, which they were well entitled to do.

Then who should materialize in front of me but the great Eamonn O'Hara – Mr Movie Star himself. O'Hara was a tremendous footballer and Sligo's talisman for the guts of fifteen years. He had power and pace and footballing ability the equal of any midfielder in the country. But Jesus, he didn't half know it. He loved strutting about the field and giving orders and acting the big shot. Mind you, there wasn't much talk out of him after fifteen minutes when John Whyte pulverized him with an almighty body shot. Whytey was a totally committed, wholehearted corner back who never got the credit he deserved. He'd be in my best Roscommon XV of the last twenty-five years without a doubt.

I never saw anyone hit as hard before or since. O'Hara was thundering through the middle and about to unleash a shot when Whytey appeared out of nowhere and lifted him, literally lifted him, with a tackle that would've put a lesser man in hospital. It was clean and perfectly timed. You could hear O'Hara's bones rattle with the impact. Oh he melted him, absolutely melted him. It was a magnificent hit. And in fairness to O'Hara, he got up. He got up and soldiered on.

And by the time I was lining up to take my free, he'd found his voice again too. I doubt he'd lost it for long, anyway. So he comes over and stands in front of me as I'm preparing the free and says to me, 'What the fuck do you think you're doing, you fuckn muppet? D'you think you're gonna put this over the bar?'

And I said back to him, 'I fuckn am, you prick, just watch it going over your fuckn head.'

O'Hara stood back from me with his arms in the air and I realized he was giving me the perfect line of sight for the two uprights way in the distance. His arms were framing them for me. I figured if I could get it up between his arms, it'd have the accuracy anyway. I struck it sweet, made a lovely contact with the ball, and over she sailed, all the way, with room to spare.

The roar that greeted it was massive. The Rossies in the crowd erupted. Jimmy Gacquin, a former Brigid's club mate and now a Sligo selector, dropped to his knees, I don't think he could believe it had gone over. It looked like we were home and dried. But Sligo showed massive spirit and launched a couple of major rallies in injury time. And it finished with one of their late substitutes, Jonathan Davey, firing a superb equalizer with virtually the last kick of normal time. It was a stunning score, every bit as good as mine.

In the second half of extra time we finally pulled away for a 2-16 to 1-15 victory. I think we had an edge in fitness that counted in extra time. Our strength and conditioning coach back then was Des Ryan, a top-class practitioner from Galway who went on to work for the IRFU and is now a member of the fitness staff at my beloved Arsenal FC.

Years later I met that great GAA man Brian McEniff, the manager who famously led Donegal to their first All-Ireland title in 1992. Brian has seen a lot of games over the years and he told me that that match in Markievicz was one of the best he'd ever witnessed.

My 1-1 that day generated plenty of headlines; the *Irish Independent* gave me their sport star of the week award, and the Connacht GAA writers presented me with an award that month too.

It didn't count for much when the provincial final came around: Mayo trounced us 2-13 to 0-9. We had two clear goal chances in the first quarter of that game and took neither of them, and I think it knocked the stuffing out of us. The feeling of dread came into our psyches. It's a familiar feeling, I think, in counties that haven't much of a track record in winning the game's big prizes. Generations of players inherit the inferiority complex that comes with that losing heritage. It just drip-feeds into the psyche from a young age when you first start going to matches with your father, and the team has lost again, and it's all doom and gloom in the car going home. It is a desperate, terrible affliction in so many counties and I hate the way it infects every new generation that comes through, even though obviously they had nothing to do with all the failures of the past. But when it's ingrained like that, it just gets passed on like a virus and no one seemingly can do anything to stop it.

And I think that Roscommon in the first half of the 2000s were a prime example of a team that had far more ability than we in the dressing room knew or realized. Well, a few of us realized it: I was convinced we had the talent to win a series of Connacht titles and push on to All-Ireland quarter-finals, semi-finals and even finals. But the lack of belief ran deep. We had a certain amount of confidence but it didn't go down far enough. It didn't go down into our guts and soul, where the inferiority complex had long ago taken root.

Not enough players in our panel believed they were good enough to perform at the top national level. They didn't believe how good they themselves were. Put a lot of them into a Kerry, Tyrone, Dublin or Armagh set-up, and they'd have been good enough to make those teams and win All-Irelands. But as the collective known as Roscommon, no, they just didn't see themselves in that light.

So two early setbacks, like those missed goal chances against Mayo, would be enough to let the doubts back into their heads. They might have suppressed them in the build-up to the game; but then, in the pressure of a provincial final, we miss those chances, and the belief immediately starts drifting away like the air out of a punctured tyre. I tried hard as captain to cultivate more confidence and raise our ambitions; Carr tried mightily hard too. But it seems to be almost impossible to root out of the system. It would probably take years of sustained success.

It was the same story against Dublin in Round 4 of the qualifiers. We turned up in Croke Park, not believing deep down that we could beat them. And we should have beaten them. Again we missed chance after chance for goals, and the reason we missed them is that we didn't believe we could take them in the first place. We lost 1-14 to 0-13 on a day that Jason Sherlock caused havoc against us. It was one of the most sickening defeats of my career because that match was there for the taking if only we had had the conviction and confidence to take it. We could've used it as a springboard to greater things the follow-ing season, but instead it was a watershed that sent us in the opposite direction.

In 2005, things fell apart. Our league got off to a woeful start with draws against Clare and Carlow. Then, in February, Frankie Dolan quit the panel. After the highs of 2003, Frankie's form came down with a bang in 2004. He just wasn't the same player and I do believe that being overlooked for the All-Star he richly deserved in '03 had really hurt him. Whatever the reasons, his form went into a tailspin, and it all culminated with Carr dropping him to the bench for the Dublin game. Later that winter I had a meeting with Carr. He was in two minds about continuing for another season, but I was unequivo-cal: Carr was the best thing to happen to Roscommon during my time playing with them, and I told him he was taking us very much in the right direction. Anyway, he decided to continue, but I stepped down as captain. I'd poured myself into the job for two years and I was drained. I just wanted to concentrate on my primary duties as goalkeeper.

David Casey took over as captain for '05. Tom brought in Val Daly, the former Galway player, to have a new coaching voice on the training field. Management were looking at a lot of new players dur-ing that league while a fair few regulars, myself included, were nursing injuries. It was one reason why we could only manage draws with Clare and Carlow. And it was a major factor in the drubbing we received from Fermanagh in March, beaten by ten points. This was the cue for an underground whispering campaign against Carr in the dressing room to come to the surface. It was only one or two players at first; they had their own agenda. They were undermining him by drip-feeding negativity into the conversation whenever they got a chance. It could be on the phone, or in a group car on the way to training, on the way home from training, in the dressing room, in the pub – wherever. But with a major player like Frankie leaving the panel, and poor results in the league, it quickly mutated into a virus. Suddenly you had a rump of people saying, 'He has to go, he has to go.' A few players, their family connections and a knot of supporters were moving against him. I heard the talk on the bus home from

Enniskillen. Carr must've heard the rumours too, because on the Tuesday after the Fermanagh game he held a meeting with the players to let them air their grievances.

But the rot continued the following Sunday with a nine-point defeat to Monaghan. A players' meeting was called for the next day in the dressing rooms in Hyde Park. There was only one item on the agenda: getting rid of Carr. A lot of fellas disappointed me that night: senior players, who knew how much Carr had done for the team, spoke against him. And a lot of young lads who'd gotten a chance under him just followed the herd and went with the flow. I thought it was wrong and I said as much. I said we'd never been looked after better as a team: we'd gone on two training trips to La Manga, we'd gone on a team holiday to Thailand in '03, two of us had got All-Star nominations, we'd played in Croke Park two years in a row, and we'd played some of the best football seen from a Roscommon team in years. He'd been good to us as individuals and as a team, and his loyalty should be reciprocated. Apart from showing him some loyalty, it would be a disaster to lose a manager of his calibre as well.

I made the argument, but it went down like a lead balloon. Only a few of us defended him. The dressing room had turned against him – or, rather, it had been turned against him. Once a heave like that picks up momentum, it's very hard to change course; fellas aren't in a mood to listen to reason or see the broader picture.

Naturally Carr had got wind of the meeting, because it would be impossible to keep a thing like that secret. He saw the writing on the wall and announced his resignation before the players had a chance to call for his head. He was entitled to that, he was entitled to leave with his dignity intact.

Val Daly took over. He'd come in as forwards coach and had been a breath of fresh air. But the upheaval had fragmented the spirit and harmony we'd built up over the previous two seasons. We were absolutely blessed to beat London by a point in the first round of the Connacht championship that May. They should've beaten us; they had the chances to do it; and we were dismally bad. I actually ended up getting the man-of-the-match award, which only goes to show

how much pressure we'd been under. Anyway, Mayo put us out of our misery in the semi-final, beating us by eight points in Hyde Park. We weren't going to do anything in the qualifiers either, and Louth duly beat us by a point in Drogheda.

I had a chance in injury time to save our bacon. I'd made a desperate rally upfield with the ball, coming about sixty yards before being fouled. The subsequent free was a long-range effort and I volunteered to take it. For some reason I whipped off my jersey during the preamble. I always wore a couple of layers to keep warm, but it wasn't because I was suddenly feeling too hot. It was just another of my brainwaves: I figured if I landed the free I'd run to the Rossie supporters in the crowd and throw the jersey in to them to try and galvanize us all for extra time. Anyway, this wasn't like Markievicz Park the year before. Everything had changed. I missed the free and our season was over.

I remember driving home that evening with John Whyte in the car, and we decided to pull in to a chip shop in Kinnegad on the way back. We ordered our burgers and chips and, next thing, a load of Roscommon supporters also on their way back from Drogheda landed in beside us. And they were wondering why the county board hadn't arranged a meal for us after the match. One fella said, 'Jaysus it's bad when they're not even feeding ye after a game now.'

And I said back to him, 'To be honest we don't deserve feeding after that fuckn shambles today.'

I wasn't to know it that night in Kinnegad, but I'd played my last game for Roscommon. The long-range free that could've saved us, but didn't, was my last kick in a Roscommon jersey. I did not want to leave it all behind me on such a horrible note as that. But the decision was taken away from me later that winter in '05 when the new manager took over.

John Maughan replaced Daly, and one of his first actions was to axe myself, Dineen, Dolan, Grehan and Mick Ryan from the panel. The perception at the time, and the way it was spun, was that a new broom was getting rid of the so-called 'trouble-makers' in the panel. Carr and Maughan were close friends and it was seen as Maughan getting rid of the lads who'd mobilized against Carr. The irony of course being that I was one of the few who'd backed Carr in the first place. But we were all seen as fellas with big egos and big personalities, and maybe Maughan figured that a fresh start was needed. It would certainly make life easier for him, not having us in the dressing room. We were also associated with a drinking culture that had become known as 'the Monday club' – a group of fellas who'd go drinking on the Monday after a big game. And yes, I enjoyed a drink after a game; so did a lot of other fellas on the team – so do a lot of players on a lot of teams up and down the country. But the rumour mill in the GAA is a major industry in its own right. If you could give GAA supporters jobs just for gossiping about their county team, we'd have no unemployment in this country. Honest to God, if one fella is seen having a glass of orange in a pub, within the week it's twenty lads who were seen skulling porter for two days and two nights. The gossip is absolutely ridiculous. We had our social life, but every one of us was totally committed to the training, and totally committed on the field of play, too. I don't think anyone could accuse us of lacking heart and soul on the pitch.

But we were singled out as the bad boys and set up as the scapegoats for the upheaval that season. The week Maughan announced his new panel, one of the local papers ran a headline referring to the 'gang of five' being axed. It was on the front page. I remember Sharon coming into the house with the paper that evening and showing me the headline. She was upset and I was furious. The manager was entitled to pick whoever he wanted, but the perception surrounding it tarnished the reputation of players who'd given a huge amount to Roscommon football. The county board made no secret of the fact that it wasn't sorry to see the back of us. I remember meeting a senior board officer in the St Brigid's clubhouse a few days after the story broke. We'd just played a match in the Connacht club championship that afternoon. Myself and Frankie were in the clubhouse when this guy walked by us and turned his head the other way; just blanked us completely. There was no mistaking the look of guilt on his face.

Maughan didn't bother ringing me to personally inform me of his decision. I suppose he didn't have to because we'd no prior history and he didn't know me from Adam. And it's how careers end all the time, in all codes, no matter how long or distinguished the player's service. He reads in the paper that he's been dropped, or he hears it on the radio, and nobody thinks to give him a courtesy call. I'd made my debut for Roscommon fifteen years earlier, and that's how it ended for me too, with a derogatory headline in a newspaper and people running the show happy to see the back of you.

In fairness, one man had the decency to pick up the phone, and that was Gerry Fitzmaurice, the former Roscommon great who was now a selector with the new management team. He just rang to wish me the best and thank me for my contribution to football in the county. It was a manly, decent thing to do and I always appreciated it.

I'm not sure he agreed with the decision to get rid of us either. Gerry was close to the football scene in Roscommon and he must've known there wasn't a huge amount of talent coming through. Maughan was getting rid of five of the best players in the county, and he didn't have fellas of a similar calibre to take over the jerseys. I think the decision undermined him from the start. It was the macho thing to do, making a big statement like that, but it wasn't the cleverest thing to do. In one fell swoop he'd cleaned out a lot of experience and a fair amount of class; he was left short of players who were proven performers in the county arena. It didn't buy him any popularity with the supporters either, and I think ultimately it ended up costing him his job, a little over two years later.

It's all water under the bridge now. But at the time it made me more determined than ever to carry on playing. I was thirty-four, pushing thirty-five, when I parted ways with county football. But I had years left in me as a keeper, and I felt it in my bones that we were going places with the club. There was a new adventure up ahead and, as the old man said to me at the time, God doesn't close one door but he opens another. Lots of people might've been writing me off, but I had a few miles left on the body clock; I knew in my heart I was far from finished.

16.   Boom and Bust

In the spring of 2006 I handed in my notice to Capco.

The construction industry was in overdrive; the boom had gone ballistic; the party was roaring. The gravy train was packed, but there was still plenty of room on it and more and more people were climbing onboard. Pearse Gately and I decided it was time to climb on board too.

We had done our market research. In August 2006 we opened 1 Base 4 Building in Athlone. We'd found an ideal premises for a builders' providers, a former farm feed business on a one-and-a-half-acre site on the edge of the town. It had a shed and a warehouse and a shop, so we didn't incur a lot of debt investing in a new-build premises. We took a three-year lease on the property. I had a forty per cent shareholding, Pearse had forty per cent and another partner had twenty per cent. The plan was to grow the business over maybe five years and then sell it on to one of the major trade chains.

Pearse had a strong relationship with Bank of Ireland and the bank supported our business model. One initial problem was with suppliers. They all had longstanding relationships with existing businesses like Ganly's and Chadwicks, and they didn't want to rattle any cages. They were reluctant to do business with us in case it would damage relationships with their existing clients. But I had built up a lot of relationships too over the previous ten years, and eventually most of the suppliers came on board. We had the stock to supply everything a builder would need from the ground to the roof – flooring, bathrooms, timber, electrical, plumbing, second fixings, the whole gamut.

The other problem was getting good staff. This was the era of full employment. Anyone who had the experience we needed was already on a generous salary elsewhere. But we started off with a staff of fourteen, we had two trucks on the go, and we pretty much hit the ground running.

To avoid cash-flow problems we had an invoice-discounting arrangement with the bank. Basically, as soon as we invoiced a customer, the bank would pay us immediately, less a percentage. A customer might have sixty days' credit. If the invoice was for €50,000, the bank would pay us something like €45,000 straight up. The bank would then get paid the full fifty grand sixty days later.

In our first year, turnover exceeded €4 million. It was a fast start. We more or less broke even that first year, which was a good achievement for a new business. But in August '07, about a year in, we noticed the first signs that something was wrong. After the traditional builders' holidays that year, a number of developments in the Athlone area that we were supplying didn't resume. The gates on these building sites stayed closed. The cement mixers stood silent. Some builders just downed tools and never came back. Another building site in Roscommon also ground to a halt. And I personally had two or three properties that I was trying to offload that summer, but my auctioneer was struggling to shift them. This was unheard of at the time. The auctioneer reckoned it was just a summer hiatus and it would be business as usual in September.

We were owed money in relation to a number of developments that had closed down, and we tried to chase up payment. The developers in question were decent, honest lads and they told us upfront that their banks had turned off the tap: they were suddenly refusing any further credit.

It was worrying, but there was no need for panic just yet, we reckoned. The Government had introduced a big grant scheme for farmers to build new slatted tanks on their farms, and the farming community duly went on a building spree in terms of sheds and septic tanks. This demanded a lot of steel, and in '07–'08 we sold a phenomenal amount of steel. It became a life support for our business in its second year of operating. In fact we did €5 million turnover in our second year. But profit margins on steel were tight, so our overall profits were dropping alarmingly. As the old saying has it,

turnover is vanity and profit is sanity. Sales of other building products were also way down. And compounding these problems was
cash flow: we were struggling badly to collect what we were owed by
clients.

It turned out that about a third of that €5 million turnover was
ultimately uncollectable, because in or around August '08 the entire
construction economy fell off a cliff. By then, everyone knew that
the game was up. Builder after builder and developer after developer
was closing down his operation. There was just no action on the sites
at all. Estates were abandoned, half built. There was a lot of shoddy
work left unfinished. They all had the same story: they had run out
of fuel because the banks had stopped lending it. On the other side,
demand had dried up: the banks had cut off the fuel supply here, too.
It became a vicious circle: there was nobody to buy the apartments or
the houses any more. Without the down payments, the developers
couldn't get the credit from the banks to finish their projects.

We were caught in the vortex. Our life support was invoice dis-
counting, but the banks stopped paying us because they knew the
developers no longer had the cash flow to pay them. Everyone was
going round in this ever-decreasing circle until we all started to choke
for the want of oxygen, for the want of cash flow. You'd go to a
developer who owed you forty or fifty grand, but you knew he didn't
have it because his apartments weren't selling. He'd have hundreds of
his glossy brochures in his office, promising a beautiful lifestyle to
anyone lucky enough to buy one of his fabulous state-of-the-art
properties. But by now they were just gathering dust. He was fucked;
we all were. Pearse's development business was taken over by the
banks in due course.

In about March '09 I realized we were doomed. We owed about
€750,000 to creditors. One of these was Capco. We owed them about
a quarter of a million. I approached them with a proposal for a management buyout or some sort of takeover, in which they'd take on
the debt and leave us in charge to work our way out of the quagmire.
They knew my track record, they knew my ability to bring in business. I figured that we might be able to ride out the storm and get
back on a stable footing. But really I was whistling into the wind.

There was no appetite for expansion any more, or any sort of risk investment. The whole climate had changed. Everyone was trying to batten down the hatches and just survive.

On the other hand we were owed about €1.4 million in outstanding debts. A couple of unscrupulous opportunists had bought big from us, knowing full well that they'd never be able to pay us back. They used us and they screwed us. But by and large most of our customers were decent people who, like ourselves, hadn't seen the crash coming. They had no idea it would be so sudden or ferocious. Many of them were left shattered by the new reality. They didn't want to leave us high and dry, but there was no way out. At one of our meetings with the bank, a manager said to us: 'We can't advance you money when you're not selling, and we can't advance you money when you're not collecting.' And there was no argument against that. The arse had fallen out of the bottom of it; the game was up.

All that was left for me to do was to wind up the operation. The only people I had coming into the car park by then were people looking to get paid. I tried to do my best, with the small suppliers in particular. I followed our obligations under company law to the letter, and I followed my own moral conscience too in trying to deal as fairly with everyone as I could. A liquidator was appointed and he gave me the keys to the shop for three days to finalize arrangements.

When you're the public face of a business that's going into liquidation, it can be a very demoralizing time. You've spent three or four hard years, often working seven days a week, to build it up. You've endured an awful amount of stress and anxiety, trying to make it work. And now suddenly it's all falling apart around you. All your hopes and dreams, all the zest and enthusiasm you brought to the project, has gone down the drain. A crisis like that just saps your energy and optimism. It's not unlike spending a whole season, or many seasons, working like a Trojan to land a big championship of whatever kind, only to lose it all in the final, your dream shattered, years of work gone down the Swanee. It's a bloody awful feeling.

So when you're facing this situation in business, you're hoping that people you've been good to, be they staff or customers, won't be found wanting when you need support yourself. And some of my staff and customers were unbelievably loyal to me. We had good times together, and they weren't going to abandon me now that the tide had turned. I will be eternally grateful for their decency at that time. Outside of business, family and friends came to my rescue too – none more so than my great neighbours, Paddy Harrison and his wife Carmel. They live a mile from our house in Brideswell and their door was always open. I could call in any time of the day or night and tell them all my woes. Paddy would produce a bottle, pour a drink and listen. Then he'd give me the advice of someone who himself has been in business very successfully for forty years. I will never forget their kindness and generosity to us at that time. And indeed we've had many a bottle and laugh since, too.

But, on the other hand, there's always a few who'll let you down. And very often they're the ones you've gone out of your way to help at other times. I think I've done my share of good turns for people over the years. But it's funny that the people you expect loyalty back from are the ones who'll desert the sinking ship. They won't do it when they're depending on your support. And in my experience, there are employees who will always try to use you as an employer. You pay them a wage, give them an opportunity, and go the extra mile for them if they're in trouble. But once you're no longer able to bail them out, they won't be long turning on you. Eaten bread is soon forgotten. Needless to say, that particular episode taught me a very valuable lesson in human nature and how people behave in times of crisis. The biggest lesson of all was to try to surround yourself at all times with good people, really positive people, who share your values, philosophies and attitude to life.

Anyway, I tried to do everything by the book. All the staff were laid off and got their redundancy entitlements. I called up all the suppliers who had stock in the yard and in the warehouse and in the shop and told them to come and collect it. They arrived in their lorries and took away what they could. On a Friday in July I turned off the lights and locked the gates. The struggle was over; I was actually relieved to walk away.

Meanwhile I'd had another business up and running for a couple of years by then, albeit on a much more modest scale, and in a very different line of work. In 2005 the GAA had commissioned me to invent a kicking tee for the commercial market. The project had its origins in my own issues with kickouts, going back several years. I found it very frustrating to take kickouts, especially on hard ground in the middle of summer. The ball would just be sitting on short-cut grass with no elevation on it at all. So getting under it, getting purchase on your contact, was difficult to do. But it was also very hard on your groin, your back and your quad muscles. A lot of goalkeepers, myself included, were suffering with injuries in these areas. There was far too much wear and tear going on. So I'd resorted to designing my own DIY kicking tees. I'd cut off the bottoms of one-litre plastic bottles and use them as improvised tees. Just to have a perch, basically, to give you better grip on your kickouts, and to take the pressure off your groin and back. Some referees ignored it and some didn't. I remember Seán Mullaney saying to me during one club game that I couldn't use it.

And I said, 'Sure what harm is it doing?'

And he said, 'There's no rule for it!' Naturally I told Seán where to stick his rules.

But then a medical report came out around 2005, stating that the kickout was causing an excessive amount of injuries to goalkeepers. So I went to the Roscommon county board chairman, Stephen Banahan, and told him about my own home grown invention. I asked him to contact Croke Park about it. Stephen called Pat Daly, the GAA's Head of Games Development and Research, and Pat in fairness was curious about the idea from the start. I had a meeting with him, and he commissioned me to come up with a prototype kicking tee that would meet all necessary industry standards and that could be officially approved by the association.

So I got in touch with my friend and neighbour, Ronnie Byrne, an engineer with a flair for design. Ronnie went to work on a variety of prototypes, which we tested at a laboratory in Germany. The best version was a round plastic or PVC base with a circle of bristles protruding from it. The ball would sit on the bristles, two or two and a half inches off the ground. The bristles were ideal because there'd be no resistance as you put your foot through them. If the ball was sitting just on a rigid base, it could act as a barrier to your foot and affect the trajectory of your kickout. With bristles, there would be very little risk of injury to your foot and a much diminished chance of damage to groin and back. Also, the ball flight on your kickouts would be more reliable; your accuracy in terms of targeting team-mates would be enhanced.

The prototype was manufactured in Germany. It was thoroughly tested, and Pat Daly gave it the green light. The GAA introduced a regulation allowing goalkeepers to use this tool and in 2006 the prod-uct, known as the Puntee, went to market. The GAA officially licensed the Puntee and it's now sold in sports shops nationwide. The Puntee company is owned by myself and Ronnie Byrne. The GAA gets its commission off every sale, the retailers of course take theirs, and there's a bit left over for Ronnie and myself. Most goalkeepers are using it now and the feedback on it has generally been very favour-able. It will never make a fortune for us, but we are designing other sports products and adapting the Puntee for other sports such as rugby.

I enjoyed working on the project because I'm into innovation and design anyway. Getting Croke Park to commission me was a great boost to my confidence and it was a welcome diversion from the pressures of starting up my other business at the time.

I was thirty-eight when the business closed. It was the first time in my life I was unemployed. It was the first time I wasn't taking in a weekly wage of some sort since the age of twelve. Lauren was now eight, going on nine, Abby was six, and the pressures of providing for my family had never loomed larger. Up until then I was always confident that I could provide everything we needed, but now I was facing into a very uncertain future in the depths of the worst reces-sion in living memory. Sharon was working as a nurse and this was keeping the wolf from the door. She was a brilliant support through all of this. Sharon is a rock-solid woman and she made sure the chil-dren never felt the insecurities and worries that we were dealing with at the time. We protected them as best we could and got on with our day-to-day lives as if nothing was happening.

But I had a choice to make: try to find a steady job somewhere or continue on the fraught road that is the lot of the entrepreneur and the self-employed. I have to say I never panicked or despaired or beat myself up over what had happened. It's at times like this that the resilience you acquire from all the knocks and setbacks you get in the sporting arena becomes a priceless asset in other walks of life. And business *is* like sport: you win some games, you lose some games; you move on, you keep going. And the eternal optimist in me kicked in pretty quickly. I figured something would turn up. When I closed the door of my premises for the last time that day in July, I figured another one would open, sooner rather than later.

17.   An Emergency, a Brainwave, a Business

It was on a Saturday in November of 2009 that Ger Brennan and I had our Eureka moment. He and I had set out that morning to help a good friend of ours in Galway whose home was surrounded by flood water. The house was on a country road outside the town of Craughwell. We spent hours in the pouring rain, filling sandbags from a transport box on the back of a tractor and piling them up around the doors and walls. The water was sitting in the garden path and lapping at the front door. Eventually someone alleviated the flood pressure further up the road and finally the water subsided. But it was a really stressful, frightening day for our friend and his young family.

Coming back in the car that night, the idea dropped out of the sky. Entire swathes of the country were under water. Towns and cities were being flooded. It was a national crisis and a hot political topic. Why couldn't we design a better flood-barrier system than just a wall of bloody sandbags? Here was an opportunity right in front of our noses. If there wasn't already a better way of tackling floods than sandbags, then we'd develop one.

Ger and I had been good friends for the guts of ten years. We'd done a lot of business together in the construction game. But in November 2009 we were both in desperate straits. My business had been liquidated. Ger's business as a civil engineer and project manager had fallen off a cliff. The worst recession in living memory was getting worse by the week. Our backs were to the wall. We both had young families to support. Ger, a fellow Roscommon man, had emigrated to Scotland with his wife and young daughter in the summer of 2008 to find work. I hadn't seen him for twelve months when he walked into my house one day in the summer of '09 and said, more or less, 'How're you fixed?' It was a bit of gallows humour on his part. He knew well how I was fixed, and vice versa too.

I'll let Ger pick up the story from here:

There was an awful lot of doom and gloom about the place. A lot of
fellas had their tale of woe that they were telling everyone who'd listen. I had my own story too but I wasn't interested in telling it. It was
pointless going round blaming the banks and the government as far as
I was concerned. I wanted to be around positive people and I had a
few ideas that I wanted to explore. And I was thinking, 'Who's the
most positive person I know? Someone that might be interested in
getting a business off the ground and who'd bring a lot of enthusiasm
and drive to it.' Almost immediately I thought of Shane Curran. I
never knew the man to be in bad humour. And sure enough, when I
walked into his office that day he was the same as ever. Laughing and
joking and not down in himself at all. And this was a fella going
through the middle of a liquidation at the time!

Ger and I spent the next few months brainstorming and researching
various business ideas. Ger moved his family back from Scotland.
He'd got an engineering job with a big construction company in
Edinburgh and he gave that up to come back. I could have got a job
of some description, given my track record in business and sales. But
we were both committed to the dream of setting up our own business. We had no safety net, no pile of cash to fall back on, none of the
security that comes with a full-time job. We had whatever creativity
we could muster between us to rely on and, I suppose, the entrepreneurial spirit to take risks and keep going.

We had explored a few other ideas before our light-bulb moment
that day on the road back from Craughwell. One of them, a specialized website for tradesmen, was well down the track. But once we
started investigating flood protection systems, we parked everything
else. We invested all our energy into it. When you've nowhere left to
turn to, it fairly concentrates the mind. We had to make this work
because we had no other choice but to make it work. We spent weeks
and months designing prototypes, researching industry specifications, wading through hundreds of websites looking for some sort of
innovative solution already in existence. The more we investigated
the flood-defence market, the more we realized how little was out

there to address a problem that was worldwide, affecting rich countries and poor countries alike.

One night in particular I couldn't sleep with the ideas that were tossing and turning in my head. So, at about five in the morning I got up and went down to the office and switched on the computer. I went clicking again through dozens of websites. There was a link that kept popping up on the right-hand side of the screen, not on the normal search-engine side on the left. The writing on it was in German, and for a long time I ignored it. Eventually I clicked on it and found myself on the website of a German company, Big Bag Harbeck, that specialized in manufacturing all sorts of heavy-duty fabrics for industrial and agricultural uses. Lo and behold, I saw something that resembled what we'd been looking for: a large polypropylene system which they said could be used in flood situations. Bingo!

A few hours later I was in Ger's house. As we scrutinized this particular system, we realized its design had some similarities to our idea, but it needed a large amount of modification.

I rang Big Bag Harbeck that same day. It was based in a Bavarian town called Bad Birnbach. I was put through to a Mr Rudolf Harbeck, the owner of the company, but he spoke no English and I spoke no German so he transferred me to Mr Ulrich Dworznik, the managing director. I told him who we were and that we were interested in discussing our ideas with them. I asked if we could come over and meet them. This was a Thursday. He said when, and I said next Monday. He liked that – he liked the fact that we weren't hanging around. We booked flights for Munich that day and landed on the Saturday. This was February 2010. We weren't to know it at the time, but it was the beginning of a whole new adventure.

On Monday morning Ulrich picked us up at Munich Central Station in his beautiful black Mercedes estate, a top-of-the-range job with a lovely cream leather interior. We were looking fairly rough in our cheap suits, especially after two nights on the German beer before that. And when we were introducing ourselves, nearly the first thing he said to me was: 'Yes, you look like a goalkeeper all right!' He'd Googled my name after our phone call the previous Thursday and was intrigued to find photos of me online playing in goals. He'd been a goalie himself, back in the day. He'd actually played for one of Bayern Munich's youth teams. Once we started talking about goalkeeping, I got a good feeling about how this trip was going to go. For me it was a good omen.

Bad Birnbach is a spa town in a very scenic part of southern Bavaria, close to the Austrian border. We went straight to the factory in the town's industrial zone, a premises of about 20,000 square feet.

Rudolf and his wife Elisabeth were there to greet us. Now, Ulrich is a big man. But Rudolf was enormous in height and girth; about seven foot tall, I'd say. Elisabeth was the company accountant. They'd built their business up over thirty years; very nice people who were obviously hard-working and successful.

Back in their office Ulrich produced the prototype flood system we'd seen on their website. Essentially what Harbeck had here was a heavy-duty geotextile cell commonly used to carry and store bulk materials. For our purposes it was crucial that the cells should be self-standing when empty, for ease of filling. Our vision was of a stack of cells that could be loaded flat on to a pallet, taken off the back of a truck and pulled out, almost like a concertina or accordion, into a standing row. Then you'd have a lorry-load of fill come along, probably sand, slide the sand down the lorry's chute into one bag, and move down the line filling the bags in this way. Ger's idea was that the cells would be self-standing by virtue of a wooden frame fixed inside the top of the cell and down the sides. These wooden frames would be screwed together so you'd be joining one cell with the next, and the next and the next. But the frame would be collapsible, so you could stack the cells flat and transport big quantities of them in containers and lorries. Transport and storage were critical priorities in our design strategy.

Ger told our Bavarian friends we had a design that would make the cells stand up freely, using a wooden frame. We took them through it, using words and sign language when necessary. They were intrigued; I think they were probably still sceptical as well.

We moved on to discuss a possible joint venture on an international scale, whereby we would do the marketing and distribution and they would be our manufacturing partner. We were there for about three hours before Ulrich dropped us back to our hotel. That night they took us to a beautiful Bavarian restaurant where they wined and dined us royally. I've always found that the social part of any business relationship is crucial for building up trust and friendship. Ulrich and the Harbecks couldn't have been more hospitable. Over copious glasses of splendid Bavarian weissbier, we hatched plans to develop the prototype and work out a business arrangement. The next day we headed for home.

A week later Ger went back and stayed in Bad Birnbach for three weeks. I'll let him pick up the story again:

> We wanted to do a thorough design on the prototype and cover every angle. I asked them to have a few laths of wood ready and a Skilsaw and a tape. Ulrich had it all waiting for me in one corner of the factory floor. I said I'd work on it on my own for a while and I'd call him when I had something made. The main thing for me was proving to them I could get the cells to stand freely. So I measured the width and depth of the bag they were intending to use. I sawed off a few lengths of the wood, made a three-part frame, more or less in the shape of the letter 'N', and fitted it into one side of the cell. I made another frame and fitted it into the next cell. I joined the two cells together by screwing the frames together, across the top and down the sides. And straight away I could see that they were more or less standing on their own. Then I added three more cells to give it a lot more stability.
>
> Now we had a unit of five cells standing solid on the floor. So I collapsed the unit flat and sent for Ulrich. When he came down I asked him to hold one end and I'd hold the other. And he did and we had a row of standing cells there in a second. Ulrich said nothing. He just looked at it for a while and then collapsed it and said he was going off to get Mr Harbeck. We did a demonstration when Rudolf arrived. And he just looked at it for a while. And then he came over and shook my hand and shook Ulrich's hand and the two of them started talking together in German. Rudolf went away and Ulrich turned to me and said, 'I think we have achieved something today.' And I said to him we had, but I thought we could make it better. It needed more refinement.
>
> An issue for us was the weight-bearing capacity of the material. We were concerned also about seepage. If you had a wall of these cells

aligned along a sea front, for example, how much water could seep through the polypropylene and through the sand? We also needed to ensure that when the cells were standing side by side, they'd be so tightly aligned that no water could get through any space between the cells. Basically, you couldn't have any chink of daylight between one cell and the next.

Ulrich was very well up on geotextiles and plastics and polymers. I asked him about using some sort of waterproof sealant on the side of the cells that would be exposed, for extra reinforcement against water penetration. He said it could be easily done and we immediately agreed it should be a feature of the product. Other design features included lifting straps that would comply with best international safety standards. This would enable pre-filled systems to be lifted by crane or other plant machinery in modular segments and deployed into position.

We then proceeded to practical experiments. We filled a five-cell system with sand on the factory grounds and got a forklift to lift it up off the ground. The straps held, the system itself held, there were no apparent problems at this stage.

We knew we had something solid and innovative on our hands. But it needed scientific testing to comply with industry standards. Ulrich later sent the system to a lab in Munich that would thoroughly test its weight-bearing capacity. The industry standard was a 5:1 safety factor. In other words, it was tested to see if it could take five times the weight of a bag filled with wet sand, which was a massive margin. The lab proved it could and the necessary paperwork was approved.

Ger came home and then went back out to Bavaria for another three weeks. They had worked on the prototype in the meantime, with all the additional modifications built into it. Then they conducted a series of experiments to test its water resistance. One of these was in the town of Brno in the Czech Republic, where they have a purpose-built facility for testing flood-defence products. Our system came through with flying colours; it was awarded a gold certificate for excellence in meeting their environmental, flooding, and health-and-safety criteria.

I went out for the last ten days of Ger's second three-week visit and was hugely impressed by the progress they'd made. I was really excited. We had a top-class product that would do exactly what it said on the tin. Ulrich and Mr and Mrs Harbeck were excited about it too. So we moved on from testing to talking about the business partnership and strategy: manufacturing, distribution and marketing.

We now had the specifications for the product: each cell would be a uniform 900mm in height and 900mm square. We would sell them in five-cell systems; each system would be 4.5 metres in length when fully extended. We calculated that each system would do the job of 670 to 700 sandbags stacked to the same height and same length. It would be fifty times faster to deploy. And the clean-up operation would be immeasurably faster: our system could be removed in an instant by forklifts or cranes. Environmentally, it would be much cleaner than sandbags. Our product would have a much lower carbon footprint than sandbags in terms of manufacturing and transportation. Flood water is filthy, and sandbags get infested with all the hazardous filth. After a while they get torn so the water breaches the barrier and carries the sand with it, making an unsightly mess that is also laden with bacteria. Our product would circumvent all these flaws and side effects. And the systems could also be stacked on top of each other to form a solid wall, which made it applicable in military and humanitarian theatres. We envisaged applications in conventional construction, maritime construction, the oil and gas industry, and environmental protection – for example, in the case of oil spills.

When we wrote it all down and totted it all up, we figured we had a product that ticked just about every box you could wish for in this field. It was a quantum leap forward from the old sandbag solution. The next challenge now was to bring it to market. So we came up with a name for it: the Big Bag Defence System. Our company would be called Global Flood Solutions. It would form a joint venture with Big Bag Harbeck. The negotiations went very smoothly. We found our new German friends to be very amicable, humble, fair-minded people. There was trust and common sense on both sides. We signed the contracts, and Global Flood Solutions was incorporated as a company on my thirty-ninth birthday, 8 April 2010. Ger and I were already developing plans to have a major launch of our product at the end of May.

Back in Roscommon, the local Enterprise Board rowed in behind us and proved to be invaluable. They put up a few thousand euro initially to help us do a feasibility study and set up a website. They mentored us on marketing and branding and many of the other challenges you have in starting a new business.

A few weeks before the launch, Ulrich rang us with terrible news. Mr Harbeck had died suddenly in hospital in Munich. We got an awful jolt because we had come to like and admire him so much in a short space of time. Poor Ulrich was devastated. He said we'd have to make Mr Harbeck proud with the launch of our product, and we were certainly determined to do that. We sent out 600 invitations across a whole spectrum of potential customers, from county council managers and engineers to construction companies, general industry, the army, fire services, politicians and first responders in flood situations. Ulrich would be our guest of honour.

It took place in the Hodson Bay Hotel in Athlone. We organized a demonstration in the car park to show the guests how our product worked. We set up two separate barriers, one using sandbags, the other using our system. We had two tankers of water come in and pour it into the two rectangular formations. Ours held firm, whereas water could be seen leaking through the sandbags. We hired a professional camera crew to film the operation and we uploaded the video to our website. It became a great marketing tool in its own right.

Ulrich was hugely impressed by how professionally the launch was organized, the number of people who turned up and the reaction to our product. It came at a time when flooding had become a hot issue in Irish life: everyone had recently witnessed distressing scenes on television of thousands of householders whose homes were destroyed by flooding in various parts of the country. We had designed a product that could be deployed quickly and cheaply in virtually every place threatened by flood water.

We thought it was a no-brainer; we thought that every city and county council in the country would come knocking on our door. Our product was ready to roll, our company was preparing for lift-off.

18.   Gangbusters!

In the summer of 2012, I went to Montreal for three months to set up a hub for our business operation there. I kept in touch with the club's results, but really I was too busy to be concerned with the comings and goings at St Brigid's.

But thankfully they hadn't forgotten about me: out of sight wasn't out of mind. The management team had stepped down after our defeat to Garrycastle in the All-Ireland semi-final and a new crew had taken over. Kevin McStay was now the manager in charge, with his friend and brother-in-law, Liam McHale, as coach; Benny O'Brien, a Brigid's man through and through, would complete the line-up.

I wasn't long back from Canada when I got a phone call from McStay. I didn't know him very well at the time. Kevin had a high profile as a GAA pundit on *The Sunday Game*. He'd been a stylish corner forward for Mayo in the 1980s, and I knew he'd also managed Roscommon Gaels to a county title in 2004.

I met him and Benny in Athlone in August of that year. The season was well advanced at this stage and St Brigid's were on course to retain their county title. Long story short, McStay wanted me back in the squad. He told me that a lot of the senior players had talked to him about getting me back. They felt I could make a difference. I was flattered to hear it, I was delighted to hear it. And McStay said he felt I could make a difference too. He just wanted to know if I could commit one hundred per cent. He knew I'd had injury issues in recent years and that I had a demanding business schedule too. But there was no point coming back if I couldn't commit a hundred per cent.

The meeting went on for two hours, and by the end of it he'd sold me completely on his vision. Winning the All-Ireland was the project and he mapped out his ideas on how we needed to improve to go the extra mile. I was immediately impressed. He was singing off the same hymn sheet as I was in nearly every aspect of what needed to be done. It was obvious to me that he had the knowledge and intelligence to do the job. He was going to bring a structure and methodology to our play. He was thoughtful and articulate, so he would have the communication skills and dressing-room diplomacy needed to handle players and unite a squad. This was a manager who was going to bring an extra layer of class in how he organized things and how he would communicate with us. I was hugely excited by the end of that meeting. I told him I was ready to give two hundred per cent. I came home to Sharon that evening and told her that this guy was going to give us a great chance of winning the All-Ireland.

I got another great boost to my confidence the night of the All-Ireland final between Donegal and Mayo that September. *The Sunday Game* had been running a feature that summer, where various high-profile players were interviewed about their boyhood GAA heroes. The guest this night was a bit off the beaten track: it was the former Roscommon minor goalkeeper, Chris O'Dowd, now better known as a star of television, stage and screen. Chris grew up in Boyle. He'd been minor keeper when I was Ros's senior keeper, and apparently he'd been a fan all along.

Being a famous comic actor, he was suitably hilarious on the show. Shane Curran, he said, 'comes from that great dramatic tradition of out-of-your-box crazy goalkeepers. And he could save a penalty and score a 45, but at the same time he'd be just as happy to ride a bull into a church. And he could do all those things in the space of two hours. He was gangbusters.' Asked if he'd ever taken advice from me about goalkeeping, he demurred. 'I would take advice from him like I would take advice from a drunk clown! But you know, he was a law unto himself, he was the Bruce Grobbelaar of Gaelic footballers at the time.' Going out on *The Sunday Game* the night of the All-Ireland final, it seemed the whole world saw that interview. The reaction was unbelievable. I got some slagging over Chris's remarks, but at the same time it was a lovely, affectionate tribute and I was walking ten feet tall when I heard it. To me it was just another little omen that things might finally all come together for us that season.

Meanwhile my first impressions of our new management set-up were subsequently confirmed by a training weekend in the Johnstown

House Hotel in Enfield. It was superbly organized from start to finish: McStay spoke to every player individually; and the training drills, skills work and coaching insights from McHale were top class. We took real momentum out of that weekend and subsequently breezed through the later stages of the local championship. My old quad muscle injury flared up in the quarter-final and I wasn't able to take any kickouts in the semi-final. So McStay gambled on leaving me out of the team for the final, in the hope that I'd be ready for the Connacht championship. Cormac Sheehy stepped in and did a sound job, despite not having much experience in the position.

We beat Padraig Pearses by five points in the county final but it wasn't as comfortable as the scoreline suggested. Peter Domican made a magnificent block on a goal-bound shot late in the game; we swept downfield and Frankie Dolan finished off a brilliant move with the goal that sealed the game and completed our second Roscommon three-in-a-row. Domican was a defensive rock for us in those years. A natural leader and quality footballer, I rate him among the top defenders in the country.

Another part of the management strategy was to build up a panel of twenty-two or twenty-three players who would all be viable contenders for the first team. The only downside was that they had to deal with a lot of players who felt they should be starting. It was a delicate enough balancing act but they managed it shrewdly; everyone bought into this new mindset and accepted that old attitudes had to change if we weren't going to be perennial also-rans. The payoff was depth on the bench and hot competition for places on the starting fifteen. When we were bringing on subs we now had square pegs for square holes and round pegs for round holes. We got a bounce in youthful energy too with the arrival of talented rookies like Ronan Stack, Johnny Murray and Richie Blaine into the team.

We sailed through Connacht. In 2005, the Galway champions Salthill/Knocknacarra had beaten us handy. We were novices back then, they were well seasoned. Seven years later the roles were reversed. The same applied with the Mayo champions, Ballaghaderreen, in the provincial final. We were never really in trouble, but at half time McHale took the opportunity to have a proper rant at us.

And it was none other than Karol Mannion who got the brunt of it. This startled everyone because Chutty was one of these fellas who usually performed well and was a county player into the bargain. But management were laying down a marker: no one was sacred, no one's reputation was too big, everyone was fair game for a bollocking. It sent out a message to the county stars and senior players that the management weren't afraid of them; it sent out a message to the lesser lights that everyone was being treated equally in this regime. They weren't going to tolerate any hierarchies within the dressing room. My injury meanwhile had healed and I played in the provincial campaign; it was my first Connacht title won on the field of play. My father had won a Connacht club title back in 1969 with Castlerea, albeit that it was an unofficial championship, so it meant we were one of the rare father–son combinations to win provincial club medals.

McStay and McHale had also engineered a major shift in emphasis on the training ground. Virtually everything was done with the ball; there was a heavy concentration on ball skills. And they instilled a structure to our play where previously we'd tended to perform off the cuff. There was an emphasis on moving the ball quickly out of defence, through the hands, until you got into a certain zone on the pitch. Once you reached that zone, players on the ball and off the ball were supposed to know how to react and where to go. It was all about moving the ball quickly into the right areas and, from there, targeting the full-forward line with long, early kicks. No hanging around with it out the field.

Management wanted us to lengthen our game, too: keep the full-forward line high up the pitch, and get the ball into them there, rather than have them drifting out to the half-forward line and beyond, looking for possession. Frankie in particular had developed a habit of doing this over the years, usually out of frustration with the poor service he was getting. The emphasis this season was on keeping him much closer to goal, where he could play off Senan Kilbride and Cathal McHugh in the full-forward line, and do a lot more damage on the scoreboard. This was the methodology that was drilled into us that season, and it gave us more confidence because everyone knew what he had to do in a given situation. There was scope within this structure to improvise and play off the cuff, but it gave us security and a reliable platform.

On 16 February 2013 we faced Crossmaglen Rangers in the All-Ireland semi-final. Not only were they the two-time-defending All-Ireland champions; they were probably the best club team ever assembled. In terms of skills, experience, physical strength and mental toughness they were a truly formidable outfit.

A bunch of us had travelled up to the Athletic Grounds in Armagh to watch their Ulster final against the Down champions, Kilcoo. They trampled all over the challengers in the first half and led by eleven points at one stage. But when Kilcoo staged a comeback in the second half, they were badly rattled. They had two players sent off and lost their cool. All of a sudden they looked like mere mortals. As far as I was concerned, the key to it was that Kilcoo had stood up to them. Equally there was a feeling in our club that Cross had bullied us in the 2007 semi-final and the 2011 final.

The reality was that Cross could play you any way you wanted: they had the requisite style and class to put you away through sheer ability. But we felt it was imperative that we harass them every bit as much as they would us. They weren't behind the door when it came to the verbals, and we decided we'd have to give as good as we got here too. We reckoned that if we didn't do something different this time, we'd be lambs to the slaughter again. So a few of the senior players took it upon ourselves to get into their faces with the verbals every chance we got. It would just let them know that we weren't going to give ground anywhere. They would test our mettle, so we were going to test theirs, on every front.

Frankie got us off to a great start with an early goal, but we squandered a load of handy chances in the second quarter as nerves took over. Cross lost the legend that is Oisín McConville after twenty minutes, but they still led by two at the break. And they had a great chance to really hurt us just after half time. We coughed the ball up in defence and I was left totally exposed. Jamie Clarke was completely free about fourteen yards from goal and he had Kyle Brennan, the sub who'd replaced McConville, available to take the pass from him. The only weapon I had in my armoury here was pure experience. I knew if I dashed out to tackle Clarke he'd just slip it off to Brennan, who would walk it into an empty net. Clarke had his back to me as he waited for the ball to come into him. So I came off my line about eight yards and let out this almighty roar. 'Keeper's ball!' And it frightened him into thinking I was right behind him. So he didn't even turn with the ball to see where I was. He offloaded it to Brennan instantly, thinking that I was already out of the equation. But I wasn't. And as Brennan took aim from point-blank range I scrambled and spread myself best I could, made myself as big as possible, and he snatched at the shot, rushed it completely and drilled it wide. I think he just shit himself basically. I remember McStay saying to me afterwards it was the greatest save he'd ever seen me make – and I never even had to make it. It was just vast experience making a difference in a crunch situation. And we got lucky too.

That miss really rattled them. We had gotten under their skin bigtime, and with ten minutes to play we were leading by two. Cross are famous for their nerves of steel going down the stretch, and sure enough they reeled off three points in four minutes. But, just like ourselves, they were still feeling the pressure, and we panicked them into making a critical error in their own defence. Senan sent in a sideline delivery, Frankie latched on to the loose ball and squared it to our sub, Conor McHugh, who poked it into an empty net. We were two up with a few minutes left.

At the other end, I decided to do a bit of baiting. I'd been peppering their young corner forward, Kyle Carragher, with verbals all afternoon. He was a ginger lad, like myself, and, having been on the receiving end of a few ginger insults over the years, I had a few lines to aim at him, especially now that I wasn't so much carrot-topped any more as strawberry blond. When Conor's goal went in, I ran off on a celebration that included a sort of a handbrake turn around young Carragher. I took a conscious decision to goad him, running a circle round him, knowing full well I was going to get a smack. It was just a matter of how hard the smack was going to be. And he got me with a right shot on the nose; in fairness he couldn't miss it, and in all honesty it was well deserved. I went down and stayed down. I wanted to kill time. I wanted to get yer man in trouble. I'll make no bones about it. We were two up and I knew they would be frantic to get the game started again. So I wanted to break up the game now and leave them stewing in their own anxiety for as long as I could. And if Carragher could get sent off, so much the better.

I got a lot of stick afterwards for this behaviour. But first of all, the lad hit me. I wasn't injured, but he did strike and he did connect; it was a sending off. The umpire duly notified the referee, and Maurice Deegan had no option but to show him a red card. Once he did, I jumped up off the ground like a rabbit. Apparently the Crossmaglen crowd in the stand were baying for my blood by then. Frankie was getting it too every time he touched the ball. But me and Frankie were going to be getting stick anyway; I reckoned if we were going to be getting it one way or the other, we might as well earn it. A few of their supporters tried to get to me on the pitch afterwards. It was a highly charged atmosphere and they were coming for me. In fairness to Aaron Kernan, an outstanding player with Cross and Armagh for over a decade, he kept them at bay and told them to disappear.

I had no regrets about using all my experience that day because by then northern teams had made an art form out of this sort of provocation, both verbal and physical. And they knew how to break up a game with all sorts of bogus injuries when they were leading, just to frustrate the hell out of their opponents. They were masters at it, and Crossmaglen were just getting a dose of their own medicine. All is fair in love and war.

The amount of criticism I got from football people in Roscommon surprised me. None of it to my face, of course. And some of these were former players who'd lost a fair few big club games themselves in previous eras. All I was doing was using the cynical sort of knowledge you pick up in the GAA playing culture. Experience isn't much value to you if you don't use it. The people who criticized me had picked up plenty of experience in losing major matches, as we had, but were never able to turn it into a winning formula.

We held on to win by a point, 2-7 to 1-9. We had immense performances all over the field: Domican, Mannion, Dolan, Kilbride, Stack and a host of others. It had been a war of attrition and we'd come through it. We'd survived; we'd beaten the best in the business.

The drama and the nature of the win overwhelmed me completely. I lost my breath on the pitch afterwards, my heart was palpitating, I had to go down on one knee to steady myself.

The funny thing was, although I was surrounded by Dolans, from Frankie to Garvan to Darren, there'd been another Dolan on my mind. The match was played in Mullingar and it had put me in my mind of that great showbiz legend, the one and only Mullingar maestro, Joe Dolan. And for some reason his songs were ringing around in my head in the build-up all that week. *Make Me an Island* and *It's You It's You It's You* and *Goodbye Venice Goodbye*: I was humming them and singing them to myself every time I thought of the game. And in the dressing room afterwards I was singing *Goodbye Venice Goodbye* to anyone who'd listen! We bailed out of town that night after a few jars and headed for Athlone. It was a case of Goodbye Mullingar and Good Night Irene.

Beating Crossmaglen felt like we had climbed the mountain, but of course we were still one game away from planting the flag. Our opponents would be Ballymun Kickhams, one of the Dublin super-clubs with a massive population base and resources.

The referee would be Pádraig Hughes – from Crossmaglen. This worried us. There'd been bad blood between ourselves and Cross in the semi-final; it had been a heated battle. So to give a man from Crossmaglen the job of refereeing a final, involving a team that had dumped your own club out of the competition in acrimonious circumstances, was a poor call by the referees appointment committee. Hughes was bound to have heard some amount of criticism of our behaviour back in Crossmaglen. We didn't doubt his impartiality or competence, but there was a chance that even subconsciously he might be inclined to make 50/50 calls one way rather than another. It's just human nature, and it wasn't fair on him either. The optics of it were wrong. Pádraig Hughes, as it turned out, did a solid job. But the GAA community in general is so incestuous that they need to be a lot more careful in how they pick and choose their referees, especially for major fixtures.

Anyway, we couldn't afford to let it distract us. St Patrick's Day fell on a Sunday that year. On the Friday night Kevin McStay stood up in the players' meeting room in the St Brigid's clubhouse and delivered the speech of his life. I've sat in on hundreds of meetings over the years, and meetings about meetings, and listened to a lot of boring talk and empty rhetoric. But McStay's speech will live long in the memory. It was confessional, personal, emotional. He opened himself up. He spoke deeply and from the heart. There was an innocence about it and a humanity that made it completely authentic. He made himself more vulnerable than any manager I've ever seen, and it touched everybody in that room. He announced the first fifteen that night, but his own policy of building a panel came back to haunt him a bit. It was so successful that he had to leave three players off who'd been instrumental in the win against Crossmaglen. On a human level, you could see it was hard for him. He knew it would hurt the players in question and he hated having to do it. But he had that sort of bond with all the players. He talked too of loved ones no longer with us who would be watching over us. There was a definite aura of spirituality in the room that night. It gave me goose pimples. It filled me with energy and conviction. It filled us all with energy and conviction.

And this goes back to a point I made about management in a previous chapter. The best managers are brave enough, and confident enough, to show their own vulnerability, their own human side. Kevin's speech that night was the final piece in the jigsaw of preparations that had been going on all season; they had been going on for several seasons, you could say. I for one left the room that night utterly convinced that we were going to win.

But after ten minutes we were in a crisis: 2-3 to 0-1. I would have to take an element of blame for their first goal: a high ball, Dean Rock beats me to the jump and swipes it to the back of the net. A minute or so later I block a shot, but Philly McMahon arrives to knock the rebound home. Eight points down but there's no panic. This is where experience is crucial. I used to be sceptical about all this talk of the importance of experience. And I still am to some degree, because as you get older your 'experience' can often be used against you by supporters and commentators. It becomes a form of ageism. You make an intervention of the kind I did against Clarke and Brennan in the Crossmaglen game, and it's experience. You're beaten to the punch by Dean Rock in the next game, and it's because you're too old.

But this is exactly the kind of situation where an experienced team can call on it: you're battle-hardened, so you're better able to keep your nerve. You've been in crisis situations before, so you've acquired a sort of emotional resilience along the way. You have picked up knowledge and developed calmness. And it all buttresses you against the shockwaves of conceding two early goals.

Three minutes after their second, we got our first. Senan did brilliantly to finish it to the net, and finally we had a foothold in the game. By half time we'd reduced their eight-point lead to four. Back in the dressing room we got amazing contributions from a variety of people. Frankie spoke superbly and Mark O'Carroll pitched in with a fantastic rallying speech. Mark played midfield on the three-in-a-row team of 2005–7, he was captain in '06. A terrible injury in 2010 cruelly cut short his career. But he remained a valuable part of the set-up, respected by everyone, and he really galvanized us with his words. Pat Regan, our physio, was another non-playing member of our group who was very important to the overall dynamic. Pat was one of the best speakers in our dressing room.

Meanwhile our brains trust were hatching a series of tactical changes. I felt very sorry for Garvan Dolan, one of the trio that Kevin had left on the bench. Garvan had been great for us all season, and likewise Ger Ahern and Eoin Sheehy. But now Garvan was getting his chance: he came on at half time for Damien Kelleher, who'd played at wing forward. Garvan was installed in midfield, Ian Kilbride was moved from midfield to centre half back, and our centre half back Darragh Donnelly was moved to centre half forward. McStay and his selectors weren't tinkering around the edges here; these were structural changes to the spine of the team. It took courage and it took tactical intelligence, but it was in keeping with their fearless attitude all season. The switches paid off handsomely: Garvan roared into the match at midfield, he creased one of their players with an unmerciful shoulder shot, and it gave the team an electric jolt.

About seven minutes after the re-start we pulled level. Senan drove a sideline ball in around the house, the ball broke and Karol, arriving late from midfield, fisted it to the back of the net. It was a handball-style finish, underarm, a kill shot with his fist that Ducksy Walsh would've been proud of. People might've thought we just got lucky here with a random break of the ball from a lob into the square – but this was a rehearsed move. Conor McHugh's decisive goal against Crossmaglen had come from the same pre-planned set piece, only from the opposite sideline. Basically, if we got a sideline ball high up the pitch, the ball had to go in around the square first time, as early as possible, before the defence had time to settle. But it had to be delivered properly, at the right trajectory and pace, which meant that only Senan and Frankie were allowed to take them. On both occasions Senan took them and on both occasions we got vital goals.

The game was nip and tuck from there till the finish. It was absolutely frantic stuff. Ballymun missed two frees late on, and even later still we missed some simple chances to edge our noses in front. It was up and down the field, perfectly balanced on a knife edge. They came raiding downfield as it ticked into injury time. Any sort of a slip now or a rash tackle could have been disastrous. But Niall Grehan came up with a brilliant steal for us, and from there we launched the counter-attack that brought us home. The move culminated with Frankie latching on to the ball, hurdling a Ballymun player and clipping the ball over the bar. The right man in the right place at the right time.

As the game reached its climax you could feel the electricity from the crowd coming down on top of you. There were about 30,000 in Croke Park that day. Every pass, every score, every wide, every turn-over was cheered; the anxiety in the stands was palpable on the field. When Frankie notched that point, our supporters let out this massive roar; it was a release of pent-up fear and joy. One of the umpires said to me then, 'Ye're All-Ireland champions!' Seconds later, we were: 2-11 to 2-10. When the final whistle went, the noise was just like an explosion. And having blown up the fuckn science lab in school all those years earlier, I think I know what I'm talking about here. It was just an earth-shattering tremor of noise, colour and emotion.

We had done it. We were All-Ireland club champions, the first team ever from Roscommon to do it. I hope in future there'll be many other winners from Roscommon, but we were the first and there'll never be another first. On the cusp of my forty-second birthday, I was an All-Ireland champion. It was incredibly fulfilling for me personally, a bit of a fairytale really, because when I'd had my back operation in 2010 it looked like curtains. I was thirty-nine at the time and was being written off. You couldn't blame people for writing me off either, given my age and the serious nature of the injury I was dealing with.

And now here I was, on the steps of the Hogan Stand with my teammates, family and friends. And having three generations of the family there made it extra special: Dad, Sharon, Lauren and Abby. The two girls rarely missed even a training session back in St Brigid's, and seeing the delight on their faces was an unforgettable feeling. Conor 'Stinky' Martin was our kit manager that year and an integral part of the set-up too. Lauren and Abby were his trusted lieutenants when it came to collecting footballs at training and dishing out the energy drinks to the players.

Seeing Dad there was emotional for me too because he and Mam had been with me all the way from when I was a kid in shorts. My first pair of boots, first football, first Arsenal kit, first everything: when it came to sport, they never said no to me for anything. Mam was always too nervous to go to games but would be tuning in to the bould Willie Hegarty on Shannonside radio at home and chewing her fingernails at the same time. Dad rarely missed a game I played, from the age of eight to thirty-eight and beyond. One of my personal highlights afterwards was seeing himself and his great friend, the legendary Gerry O'Malley, shuffle into the dressing room to take part in the celebrations. It was brilliant to have these old veterans of many a battle back in the day finally witness an All-Ireland triumph among their own people. It was one of those days when everything was perfect and all was right with the world.

We met the Ballymun boys under the bowels of the Hogan Stand after the game and before having a bit to eat in the dining room. I had a brief chat with Ted Furman and you could only feel extremely sorry for their plight in defeat. They are a very honourable bunch of lads and were managed by one of the game's real gentlemen in Paul Curran. Their time will come, I hope. We were very conscious about being gracious in victory because we all knew how they felt. A defeat like this is a sort of bereavement; it is a desperately shocking thing to have to come to terms with, and we understood that only too well. A win like this is all the richer and more satisfying if you've experienced the other side of the coin. And the margins between one place and the other are frighteningly thin. This time we just happened to end up on the right side. But we'd earned it; we'd earned the right to win it. Not just that day but because of hundreds and thousands of other days, stretching back over a decade and more. We all knew how hard we'd fought, and how long we'd worked, to reach this golden moment. And when you reach it, everything is forgiven and forgotten: all the arguments and bitching and stupid shit that goes on in teams. It all disappears. There's a golden halo around every one of your teammates in these golden moments.

We had a couple of drinks in Croke Park and a quick meal, before hitting the road for Kiltoom. It was the fourth decade in which I'd played in the iconic stadium: 1989 as a minor; the senior league game in '91 when Mick Kennedy kindly decided not to give me a slap; the championship matches against Kerry and Dublin in '03 and '04; and now St Patrick's Day 2013. Twenty-four years between my first and last appearance: a lot of water under the bridge, a lot of kickouts, a lot of ups and downs.

In Athlone we got off the bus and carried the cup over the bridge, over the Shannon, and into Roscommon – into the west. It had been fifty-nine years since Jimmy Murray carried the Sam Maguire Cup over that same bridge, the last time a team from Roscommon had won a senior All-Ireland. The raw emotion of the moment was, for me, almost overwhelming. Thousands upon thousands of people turned out to cheer and applaud our symbolic walk. I met our former manager, Noel O'Brien, on the bridge and we shook hands: we accomplished so much under him. It could easily have been his team that was walking across that bridge. He played a significant part in our achievement and it was great to see him celebrating with us. We headed for our unofficial headquarters, the Hodson Bay Hotel, where hundreds more were waiting for us. From there we headed for the St Brigid's clubhouse and saw the dawn rising. My brother Jason is a gigging musician, and he and his band provided the entertainment to a packed crowd in the club's gymnasium. My other brother, Evan, and his wife, Catherine, had also been on the steps of the Hogan Stand that afternoon with the rest of our extended family, so all in all it was a fantastic occasion.

I didn't drink much that night because I wasn't interested in drinking; I was too elated and too exhausted. Once again I heard so many stories from our supporters who'd been in the stands, and once again I was half envious that I wasn't up there with them to enjoy the atmosphere from their point of view. When I eventually got to bed I couldn't sleep a wink; the adrenalin, the happy hormones, were just bouncing round my body.

Not long after the break of dawn, Benny O'Brien phoned – like me, he hadn't been able to sleep. I drove out to collect him from Kiltoom, and the two of us were purring with excitement on the drive back. Sharon put on a beautiful continental breakfast with champagne for the twenty-odd family and friends who had spent the night in the house. We were all buzzing, and there was a day of celebration ahead of us.

A bit later I called round to Paddy and Carmel Harrison. And Paddy, being a connoisseur in these matters, decided it was time to break out his bottle of Jameson 18-Year-Old Limited Reserve. Next stop was the Snug pub in Athlone, where it seemed all of Roscommon and Westmeath had gathered to celebrate. It was a massive party that went on all day and late into the night. And, may I add, a night or two more.

I don't like the idea that careers should only be measured in medals. But there is a profound feeling of security too in knowing that you have left something behind you in the record books. As a kid I used to look up to the likes of Gerry O'Malley and Jimmy Murray and Larry Cummins as if they were gods. And nowadays I suppose you get kids looking up to you in a somewhat similar way. I'm not for one minute saying I was as good as them, or achieved remotely as much. But somewhere along the way you find young people asking for your autograph and a photograph; and I can see in their faces how I must've looked when I was beaming up as a boy at the great figureheads of previous generations. It's how the wheel turns, I suppose. And it gives me a deep sense of fulfilment that we have added something to the legacy for future generations; that we have left something behind which can never be taken away.

19.   Age of Challenge and Change

I've been an amateur sportsman all my life. A good amateur, I hope, but an amateur all the same. Even when I played in a professional sports league with Athlone Town and was getting paid a few quid, I was still an amateur. I was part time. I had a day job. Athlone Town was evenings and weekends. Likewise, obviously, when I was a county player with Roscommon or a club player with Castlerea and St Brigid's.

But in the last five years or so a new phrase has entered the vocabulary of GAA jargon. You're hearing it more and more. The Gaelic Players Association routinely refers to its members now as 'elite players'. The players themselves do it without thinking; the corporate end of the GAA frequently refers to them as such; and it's becoming commonplace among the GAA media too.

I don't know whether it's a bit of vanity or insecurity or self-importance, but suddenly now we apparently have a corps of 'elite' players in Gaelic games. The irony is that you don't hear the soccer community in this country referring to their players as elite players, even though many of them are getting paid to play. And because they're getting paid they are therefore closer to the world of professional sports than their GAA brethren. (Although the financial clout and organizational ability in the 'amateur' GAA made it a much more professional outfit in my experience than the League of Ireland.)

Maybe this 'elite' buzzword has something to do with the ongoing commercialization of the GAA. Gaelic games, like almost every sport, are a 'product' now. They have a commercial value, they come with a price to advertisers, sponsors and broadcasters. And maybe by trying to elevate themselves on to an equal footing with professional sports, they can wring more revenue out of their product. If they promote Gaelic players as 'elite' players, it raises their profile and prestige and makes them more attractive to the corporate world. It helps to somehow transcend the boundary between amateurism and professionalism. The GPA has probably accelerated this process over the last ten years or so because part of its remit is to generate more revenue for players. That's not a criticism by any means of the GPA. I think it has done wonderful work for players in terms of welfare, education and holistic support; and also in terms of getting more money into players' pockets. That's all good and important work as far as I'm concerned.

But I get a bee in my bonnet when I hear this word 'elite' being bandied about, as if they're on par with feckn LeBron James or Wayne Rooney or Usain Bolt. The GAA is a major organization in this country, but in the worldwide spectrum of sport it is tiny. It is not even on the radar. It is a pimple on an elephant's arse. And within this tiny bubble you have a handful of players who can make a small bit of money on the side from doing endorsements and making personal appearances and wearing branded sports gear. These few stars are a microscopic bubble within this tiny bubble. And none of them are giving up the day job either. So let's keep a bit of perspective here.

This change in how we see ourselves has probably also been triggered by the knowledge revolution in team preparation over the last decade and more. I have lived through this sea change, and it is now light years away from what it was when I started out in senior football, nearly twenty-five years ago. The whole approach has been transformed into a scientific, evidence-based process. It is informed now by an expertise in physiology that makes the old-school twenty-laps-of-the-field attitude look like the dark ages. The whole area of performance psychology has blossomed, too. Where once it was seen almost as a taboo subject, it is now viewed as integral to any team's development. And match analysis has been transformed by statistics and data that provide hard evidence of a team's performance on any given day.

The GAA has embraced these changes with enthusiasm, and in some cases has actually stolen a march on professional sports like soccer and rugby union. And because players are taking on board all this information and very often living the regimented lifestyle of professionals, they maybe feel entitled to call themselves 'elite' sportsmen.

But in reality they are not elite sportsmen. They can't be, not as long as there's an amateur cloak around their head. Unless you are living the lifestyle full time, without the massive inconvenience that is a day job, you are not an elite sportsman. It's just a different level of commitment and development. Professionals can train or practise all day every day if they want. The room for growth and development in their fitness and skills and knowledge base is massive. They have the luxury of worrying about nothing else. Gaelic players have to grapple with the basic struggle of trying to make their way in the world: points in their Leaving Cert, college, finding a job, building a career. And then, at the end of a long day in the office, heading to training for a couple of hours. Professional sportsmen of course have their financial worries and families and relationship issues to deal with too, but they exist in a comfort zone that's way beyond what the serious amateur sportsman has to deal with. For one thing, they get plenty of rest, both physically and mentally, and have lots of downtime to deal with any issues beyond the sporting ones. If you have to spend ten hours a day working and commuting to work, you're always going to be hugely stunted in the levels of sporting excellence you can achieve. It's no wonder that more and more county players are going to college and extending their time at college, just to maximize their chances of being the best they can be at their chosen sport.

Now maybe the very few top counties in football and hurling are edging towards a semi-professional set-up. But even they would be well behind the professional pack in other sports, and overall I think that intercounty footballers and hurlers are codding themselves if they feel they are part of the sporting elite. It's a delusion.

There's an inherent contradiction in this aspiration towards elitism. One fundamental dynamic of elite sport is that the cream rises to the top. The best go to the best teams and make the most money. Of course this can never happen in the GAA because all players, no matter how talented they might be, are destined to play for the county in which they've grown up. There are exceptions to the rule, but they are few and far between. Only in the GAA can a so-called 'elite' talent be barred from reaching the top of his sport. It happens all the time. A brilliant player has to spend his career down in the basement of the game because he happens to be born in a weak county, and he ends up surrounded by teammates who are not in his class.

The GAA is built on an unconditional loyalty to parish, village, town and county. We grow up with this ideal and it becomes so ingrained in us that we don't even question it, never mind challenge it. The GAA is a mammoth propaganda machine for its own agenda, and this blessed principle of loyalty to home, of doing it for the ancient jersey and for the pride of the parish, has been hammered home for more than a century.

For me, there's an awful lot of bollocks talked about this, sentimental old guff about the parish and the jersey. The reality is that we players are doing it for ourselves. The colour of the jersey you're wearing ultimately doesn't matter one iota. You want to achieve things, you want to win championships, and your club facilitates that ambition.

A lot of GAA clubs are the heartbeat of their parish from a social point of view, a community point of view and even a business point of view. A lot of friendships and relationships are formed that are also intertwined with business and family life. You are coached and taught there as a young fella, and when you become a parent yourself, your own kids become absorbed into the life of the club too. They are coached in the games and learn valuable life-lessons along the way. The club becomes part of the fabric of your life over generations, from your parents, to yourself and to your own children in time. It's a wonderful thing.

And yes, it's a great feeling to see the happiness a championship win brings to all the people who are involved in making the club work. There's a powerful sense of fulfilment you get from knowing that you've made a lot of people happy.

But it's a two-way street. The club has coached you from the age of eight in the hope that one day you'll help them win championships. They're not doing it to make you a better person and a better player just for the sake of it. The club needs you as much as you need it. And if you don't come up to scratch at the end of the day, they'll not be too sorry to see the back of you. If you play badly they won't be long letting you know about it. It's not you they're worried about, it's themselves. In their eyes you have let them down, you have frustrated their hopes and dreams. If you're playing badly because you have various problems off the field that are bothering you, they won't want to know about it. They just want you to perform and to win.

It's a complicated relationship. You wouldn't want to romanticize it too much. There's people who like you and people who don't like you. There are rows and bust-ups and politics and agendas. There's a lot of love and support in one way, there's a lot of negativity and criticism and back-biting too.

The bottom line? Every player is ultimately doing it for himself. You've set that target for yourself in your sporting life, to win championships and to go as far as you can in your chosen sport. Players are basically greedy, self-centred people. They want to win things for themselves, they want the glory and the ego trip and the personal fulfilment that comes with winning things. When you're preparing for a big game, the last thing on your mind is doing it for the pride of the parish. The first thing on your mind is you: your own performance. When I go on to a pitch, the most important thing for me is that I represent myself well. That is my fundamental motivation. Now, there are other people within your circle that you have a duty of care to as well: your teammates and the coaching staff who are in the same boat as you and who have been with you every step of the way. And of course your family too, because they're going to be hurt if they see you hurting after a bad performance or an upsetting defeat. You don't want to let any of these people down. But beyond that, I don't really care. If I've played badly, I've let these people down. But I haven't let the parish down, because doing it for the parish and the jersey wasn't my motivation in the first place. Likewise when you're winning, you're not winning for them either. You have a responsibility to your teammates, the coaches and your family, and no further.

And mark my words, a player who transfers to another club or another county will play with the very same level of commitment as he did for his home place. Playing for your home place won't bring out any more heart and soul in you than playing for some other team. If you have courage and honesty in your character, you'll show it on the field, no matter what jersey you are wearing. And if by nature you lack a bit of courage or you're not an honest grafter, those flaws will always be there, whether you're playing for your home place or you've joined a new team. You are what you are, and the ideal of the pride of the parish won't make you braver going for the ball, or more willing to put your body on the line for the cause.

It hasn't happened among the GAA's playing community yet, but nowadays we're seeing managers and coaches switching from county to county and club to club at a rate of knots. The turnover among managers at club level is enormous. Fellas are criss-crossing the country, managing clubs, and basically these fellas are guns for hire. Even at lower levels, fellas with no previous connection to a parish or county are being appointed on a regular basis. The days of only appointing managers from inside your own club are gone, and they're going at county level too.

And it has all happened organically, from the bottom up, without any change in policy from the top in Croke Park. In fact, Croke Park takes a dim view of this trend, or used to anyway, probably because there are undercurrents of professionalism about it. There's a lot of loose talk about managers getting paid under the counter to take over clubs, and I've no doubt that at least some of the rumours are true. Winning championships has become something of an arms race within the GAA, at club as well as county, with every unit looking to find an edge some way or another. They're prepared to spend and they're prepared to recruit an outside manager who they think will make the difference. This is putting pressure on the amateur ethos and the old principle of parish loyalty.

You wonder, is it only going to be a matter of time before we see the same trend happening among players, too? There's plenty of gossip too about players being lured away from their home clubs, especially country players transferring to Dublin clubs, for various financial incentives.

Society is becoming more urbanized, there's a continuing migration for work and study to the cities, big urban centres and large towns. It means small rural clubs are slowly dying and the player base in smaller counties is being eroded. I am very concerned about this pattern of decline. It's not just because it affects the GAA side of things: that's just a symptom of a deeper economic problem. The larger urban centres are hoovering up the jobs in industry and technology, services, retail, tourism and the public sector. The state's education infrastructure is dispersed among these same cities and large towns. Everything seems to be migrating towards these urban strongholds: jobs, money, people, the knowledge economy. And smaller counties are struggling in their shadow. I'm thinking of counties in the BMW region (borders–midlands–west). Our school-leavers are going away to college, and if they're lucky enough not to have to emigrate when they graduate they'll get work in the cities and big towns. A lot of them will still come back to play their GAA with their local clubs, and the modern road network makes that part of it a bit easier. But eventually they'll settle down in places like Dublin, Kildare, Meath, Cork, Limerick and Galway, the big commuter belts and satellite towns, and bring their children up there.

Ironically enough, St Brigid's have been beneficiaries of this expanding urban sprawl. The two parishes in St Brigid's catchment, Kiltoom and Cam, border the outskirts of Athlone on one side, and so we've had a lot of inward migration over the last few decades because people have jobs in the town and it's a handy commute into Athlone from there. In fact, of the team that won the 2013 club All-Ireland final, only four had fathers who were originally from the area. So we're doing okay.

But the point still stands. Country clubs are dying as their populations get older and the young people move away. And I'm not just talking about rural clubs, I'm talking about small-town clubs in rural Ireland too. This is a bigger problem than the GAA's. The state, and government economic policy, has to seriously address this chronic demographic and economic imbalance. It is a massive task that demands innovative thinking and bold initiatives.

The GAA has a big part to play in looking after its struggling outposts, be they clubs or counties. Again, major innovative thinking is required. Their hand may be forced if present trends continue over the following decades. To keep small clubs going, and to keep marginalized counties even vaguely competitive, they might have to relax the rules on native players; they might have to loosen up the old ties that bind. They might just have to give players permission to play for counties other than the county of their birth. I would like to see players who are surplus to requirements in counties with huge population bases freed up to play for one of the marginalized BMW counties.

It would take a bit of planning. Maybe it could be organized along the lines of a player draft. There could be a database of players pooled from all over the country, fellas who want to play county football or hurling but aren't quite good enough to make their own team. You could get Croke Park to distribute them to the weaker counties, factoring in the populations of these counties and their placing in the previous season's league and championship. The players wouldn't have to have any blood ties to these counties; they would be fellas who just want to play county championship and are willing to commit to another county. In many cases it would be giving these fellas a second chance. Players get reputations for one thing or another, and as long as they stay in the same place they don't get a chance to reinvent themselves. A fresh start can do wonders for a player; sport in general is littered with stories of players who were rejected by one team but who blossomed in another environment. It would give everyone a boost: the players themselves, the county squad they're joining and the supporters who follow these teams without ever enjoying much hope of a breakthrough.

And could you imagine the excitement every year if you had a player draft, the sort of buzz and anticipation it would give to a county's supporters as they waited for news of the new faces they were getting in that season? And what if one of the players had been a star, an All-Ireland winner in one of the big counties, but was a bit past his prime? That would get the natives talking in many a marginalized county. You'd have a few more clicks at the turnstiles during the national league, that's for sure. Fresh faces of any description would give a team that sort of a bounce at the start of every season.

And I can guarantee you that if these new players started doing the business on the field for their new county, those supporters wouldn't give a damn where they came from. They wouldn't for one minute question their commitment to the jersey, just because they weren't breastfed from day one within the county boundaries.

Now, something like this would take imagination and courage, and these are qualities in short supply among the GAA's sprawling bureaucracy. I'm not necessarily talking about the head honchos either. I'm also talking about the majority of delegates who turn up at Congress every year to shoot down any initiative that threatens – even mildly – their innate conservatism.

The whole issue of GAA infrastructure also needs a major shift in thinking as far as I'm concerned. The organization is absolutely brilliant at building pitches and running a breezeblock wall around it and putting up a few dressing rooms. There's hardly a parish in Ireland that doesn't have one of these. And nearly every county has its own venue for the big-ticket games. These are a lot bigger than the parish facilities and cost a fortune to build, but they are just bare steel and concrete sheds with three-quarters of the place exposed to the elements and no creature comforts to speak of. The GAA man is traditionally a fairly rough-and-ready sort of fella, and the venues reflect this. They are built with great enthusiasm but little attention to detail. It seems never to dawn on anyone that they might need to make them more attractive for women and children. It seems never to dawn on anyone that people have travelled all over the world and sampled sporting venues that are designed to make it a pleasant day out, a day's entertainment, as opposed to just hosting a sports fixture of some description. The GAA has poured millions upon millions into these shells that don't offer even basic spectator comfort, much less decent food and entertainment and other attractions. And, of course, all these venues are pretty much empty and deserted for 350 days of the year, if not more. The GAA landscape is dotted with white elephants.

The current policy is to build 'centres of excellence' in pretty much every county, where all that county's teams can train and get fed and have their medical treatment and video analysis and all the rest of it. Grand. But these facilities don't interact very much with the wider economy. They don't generate ongoing revenue and jobs.

What I have in mind is a facility that would become an economic engine in a region that is haemorrhaging its young people. I'm talking about a stadium that would be part of a campus with education facilities, entertainment attractions, retail and office space. The whole campus would be the economic heartbeat for the surrounding region. It would pump jobs and money and activity into its satellite communities. Such facilities could be operating in five to seven years with the right planning and investment.

A lot of new stadiums have been built in Europe on greenfield sites in the last decade, and more have had conference facilities, offices, leisure amenities, cafés, restaurants, a hotel, museum and retail park attached – or at least some combination of them. I am proposing something similar but with one massive difference: education would be at the core of this development, and this would make it an attractive proposal for public and private investors. We need something sustainable that creates jobs and generates revenue during the ten months of the year when the stadium itself is not being utilized. Venues like Pearse Park in Longford or Hyde Park in Roscommon are not viable any more. They are ugly relics. There are far too many of these around Ireland that have soaked up far too much money for too little return. The GAA needs to rethink its infrastructural strategy. Pumping millions of euro into stand-alone venues is an archaic strategy.

There are examples out there of new developments which help to revitalize regional communities. The Keepmoat Stadium at Doncaster Rovers FC in England is one such development. The venue has a capacity of 16,000 and was built for around €30 million. It is a mixed-use facility and is leased to the development company on a ninety-nine-year contract. On match days it employs between 600 and 700 people, while 2,000 people work there for concerts – the likes of Robbie Williams has played sell-out shows there to crowds of 40,000. It can host conferences, weddings, corporate parties, all sorts of events. It brings between 300,000 and 400,000 people into the

Greater Leeds area and in just under eight years it has provided 8,500 jobs. Obviously an Irish model would have to be planned and tailored to local criteria in terms of population size, economies and the sporting landscape here, but the Keepmoat is a model which should be studied closely.

I would like to take it one step further and include a post-primary education campus alongside a mixed-use stadium with a capacity of around 20,000. A campus attached to Athlone Institute of Technology, for example, could encompass the very best teaching facilities, science labs and technology rooms. In addition, there would be ancillary courses for adult learners in subjects like IT, sports science, business, nutrition and physiology, languages and sports medicine. It would become a knowledge centre for local business and local clubs from all sports.

A project of this scale would act as a socio-economic regeneration vehicle for a region of some 200,000 people. It would encompass in one place three pillars of any successful strategy: facilities, education and employment. It would act as a core contributor to the economies of two or three surrounding counties. It would generate knock-on investment. It would help to redress the balance of outward migration. It would generate a lot of local employment, revitalize the local economies and help to keep small GAA clubs going in the satellite towns and parishes.

Places like Roscommon are crying out for this kind of investment and imaginative thinking. Back in 1992 there was a big announcement made about a proposed £1 million redevelopment of Dr Hyde Park. It was going to be a flagship development for Connacht. Needless to say, nothing came of it. Tommy Kenoy was chairman of the Roscommon county board at the time, and he said that the GAA needed to show 'positive discrimination' towards Connacht because of the province's disadvantaged economic status. That's twenty-two years ago and we're as disadvantaged now as we were then. It's not just Connacht either, but the whole BMW region that needs massive investment and a meaningful government strategy.

The GAA is a sports organization with a social conscience. It is embedded in the fabric of Irish society. When the economy is suffering, it suffers. When young people emigrate in their thousands, it hits every unit hard. It's in their interests to see the economy thriving, not just in the cities but in the small towns too. But I believe it has to start thinking about projects on this scale if it's going to make a substantial contribution to reversing current demographic trends.

Migration and emigration aren't the only big issues facing young people and the GAA. Like every other sporting organization, it loses a huge number of teenagers who simply give up on Gaelic games after they leave school. A lot of them will continue playing sport for leisure, be it golf or cycling or their weekly five-a-side soccer game. They still enjoy sport but they don't want the pressure and relentless seriousness that playing Gaelic games demands. Even at club level, the commitment demanded is far too much for a lot of young people who just decide to walk away from it because they want an easier life or because they have found better ways of spending their spare time. They've experienced the GAA culture at underage level and know what's in store for them if they decide to continue: far too much training for too few games, a year-round commitment and an obsession with winning that's just a complete turn-off.

For those who decide to stay in the system and continue playing with their club, college or county, the system doesn't make it easy for them. In fact, between the ages of eighteen and twenty-one it becomes downright punitive on them. They have multiple teams calling on their services during these years. The more talented they are, the more teams come calling. And all too often you have the managers of these teams unwilling to make any compromise or to give the young fella a break. They all want him; they all lean on him; they all tell him he has to be there for training, he has to be there for the midweek challenge match, the meeting, the bonding weekend away. These young men could be playing Under 21 and senior for their club and county, plus lining out for a couple of college teams too. They could be on the road, commuting from college to home during the week, and every weekend. It is common for them to be spending hours in the car on weekdays, travelling to a training session down the country and arriving back in Dublin or Galway or wherever well after midnight, wrecked after another gruelling session.

Then it's up for lectures the next morning, all day at college, and tog out again that evening for another team. They're not getting the proper rest periods and proper nutrition which are vital for any hard-training athlete. The professionals in sport science nowadays are emphasizing how critical rest and recuperation are to the body. But in the GAA culture of professional amateurism, they are handling these young people in a very unprofessional and, in my opinion, damaging way.

A lot of the coaches/managers who are pulling these players from pillar to post don't care about their wellbeing. They just want another win on their CV. They don't bother to communicate with the other managers who are looking after his other teams. They just hand the young fella his weekly training programme and match schedule and tell him that he has to be there, no excuses. All of these managers have a duty of care to these young players, but a lot of them don't seem to know the meaning of that phrase. Inevitably, the player starts going down with injuries. And in too many cases, psychological damage isn't far behind. The stress becomes too much. And this is before the lad's academic pressures and financial worries and relationship issues are even factored into the equation.

It's great that Irish society and indeed the GAA are recognizing at last the worrying problem of mental illness among young people. The GPA has been sensitive and proactive in this area; their work here is admirable and badly needed. The prevalence of depression, addiction and suicide is absolutely frightening. And the last thing a talented young school-leaver needs is several managers pressurizing him to commit fully to their teams when he hasn't enough hours in the week to fulfil all his sporting commitments, never mind keep on top of his studies or his job.

Mental health among young people is a massive issue coming down the track for society in general, and the GAA has to look after its responsibilities here in a serious, meaningful way. The GAA needs to create a mechanism to regulate the whole area of player welfare. At a minimum, every county board should have an auditor who monitors closely the schedule of every player in that age bracket between eighteen and twenty-one. If there are too many teams, too many training sessions and too much travelling, he should have the power to step in and order the various managers/coaches to lay off. Each young player should have a set number of games and sessions, and no more. Any county that doesn't follow this template should be fined or seriously reprimanded. Croke Park must insist on a commitment to player welfare, enshrined in a series of regulations and implemented and supervised at local level. The issue is too serious to be left in the hands of managers and coaches who move on after a couple of years and aren't particularly worried about the legacy they leave behind.

The best managers won't abuse players like this because they understand the importance of treating them humanely. They understand that the best way of getting maximum performances from players on the field is to treat them like human beings off it. They have a humanity and an empathy about them that players appreciate. If a manager can prove to players that he cares about them as people, not just as footballers, he will win their trust. They will give more back to him. They will play for him and play for each other. They'll want top-notch skills drills and physical workouts from him too; they'll want him to be good at tactical planning, decision-making and in-game management. But, first and foremost, they will want sincerity and integrity from him. That's your basic building block in any relationship between a manager and his team.

Now we can all name highly successful managers who were chalk and cheese when it came to their own personalities. An example that comes to mind is that duo of legendary Liverpool FC managers, Bill Shankly and Bob Paisley. Shankly was an extrovert, Paisley a quiet, grandfatherly sort of man. Bob took over from Bill, and you couldn't think of more contrasting people, and yet both of them inspired their teams to fantastic achievements. In GAA, great managers of recent times like Ger Loughnane and Mickey Harte and Seán Boylan are all very different people, but able to connect deep down with their players.

The best managers are natural psychologists. They know what makes players tick. They can see the nuances in a dressing room, the difference between one player's mentality and another's. They can spot problems in an individual and not be afraid to make allowances for him. A good manager will know when to make exceptions. He will spot the need for a personal phone call, an email or text message that is confidential between him and the player involved. He will give a player a week off if he feels he needs it. In a room full of testosterone and machismo, he will spot the player who is struggling and look after him in a subtle, sensitive way. Those are the best managers to me, the ones with the humanity and a bit of humility.

The macho guys who come strutting into the dressing room with a big voice and a big attitude, you'll see through these guys sooner rather than later. These fellas are there on a power trip. It's a case of, here's me ego, the rest of me is coming. These are the managers with a barrier around themselves, a shield to maintain a distance between them and their players. For some reason they don't want to let go, they don't want to fully expose themselves. Players cop that pretty quickly and automatically put up their own barriers in return. They'll train hard and they'll play all right, they'll do enough to stay on the team, but they won't give him their full heart and soul. They'll hold something back because he's holding something back. They won't trust him enough to expose themselves completely because he won't reciprocate; he won't have earned the right to their unconditional emotional and psychological commitment.

It's amazing the array of managers and coaches you'll meet in sport, all sorts of personalities and mindsets and ways of doing the job. Brilliant, inspiring men; solid, mediocre operators; shy fellas; loud fellas; fellas who can hardly string a sentence together; bullshitters who can talk for Ireland and say nothing; various chancers and cowboys. The first thing any player will do when a new face walks in the door is to start sussing him out. And you begin from a sceptical, maybe even cynical, position. Because this guy is going to be in charge of your team for the next season at least. That's a year out of your life. Every year is a big commitment on your part and you don't want it compromised by some guy who talks a good game but in the end can't back it up. If you get the feeling that this guy is going to be wasting your time, it's an awful depressing prospect. You'll know from fairly early on that your season isn't going to work out well, but you have to go through the motions with him anyway for the whole year and just hope that maybe the players can get the job done themselves.

There's too much at stake for managers to be getting away with shit that you know is wrong. That's why certain managers have probably found me hard to handle. I would challenge their methodology, voice my own opinions, disagree with them in front of the other players. I was bringing my own football intelligence and experience to bear on the conversation. And I felt I had the right to, because it was my time and my career, and I couldn't stand seeing it being wasted by managers who I knew were making mistakes in various aspects of team selection or preparation.

One day in the not too distant future I hope to be managing teams myself. I know that I'll be involved in GAA life in one form or another for many years to come. Will we have 'elite' players by then? Will we have free player movement between teams? Will we have visionary infrastructure, and will we be looking after our players with the best due care and attention?

Some of these changes will come, and others will take a lot longer to get right. But we have to keep aspiring to be the best and to do the best – and I hope to play my part in that never-ending process.

20. Sweating Bullets in Somalia

After our big product launch we started knocking on doors. Our first port of call was the local authorities. Naturally we targeted every county, town and city that had been plagued by flooding in recent years. We made hundreds of phone calls, sent hundreds of emails. We'd designed a top-notch website. We'd put a lot of time into search-engine optimization to bring Global Flood Solutions high up in the pecking order on Google.

We organized meeting after meeting after meeting. We'd go in and meet the county manager or county engineer or some few senior officials, and we'd show them the system, tell them how it worked, talk them through all the savings they'd accrue in money and man-power. We talked about its speed of deployment and how, for a small financial output now, they'd save a fortune in protecting infrastructure, businesses and homes when the next flood arrived. Usually they were impressed, very impressed, with the product. Many's the time we walked out of a meeting, convinced we'd made a sale. And then, nothing. Not a word. We'd follow up with further calls and emails, and there'd be silence at the other end. Oftentimes you wouldn't get a call back or a reply. Our experiences with the local authorities in this country were downright demoralizing. Everywhere you turned, you were met with inertia, indifference, complacency. No urgency, no one taking responsibility, a lot of the time not even basic manners. They wouldn't have the courtesy, a lot of them, even to return a phone call.

To give but one example. We set up a meeting with Cork city council. Now if ever a local authority needed solutions, you'd have thought it was Cork. The city had been hammered by flooding for decades, homes and businesses destroyed without fail year after year after year. We went down and met their senior officials and made our presentation. They said Ger should hook up with one of their engineers to do a ground survey down by the river Lee.

Ger:

> So I did the survey with the engineer, located the low points where the river would burst its banks, calculated the water levels, showed them where to deploy our product and calculated how much of it they'd need. They were hugely enthusiastic. They said they had a major requirement for the product and they talked to us that day as if there wasn't a doubt that they were going to put in an order. So I did up the drawings, which mapped out exactly what was needed, and sent them to the council. We figured they needed about 600 metres of the system. Sent them the drawings and then never heard a word back. Not a word. Followed up with phone calls and emails, and still not a word back. And this happened regularly with councils. You'd do up the drawings for them and it was nearly like you were doing their job for them. They'd know where they needed the system, they'd know how much of it they'd need and how much it would cost, but that'd be the end of it.

The councils in this country are hamstrung by budgetary constraints and bureaucracy at national level. There is absolutely no leadership from the top down, among either politicians or senior civil servants. The culture is all wrong. No initiative and no accountability. There've been multiple major flood events in this country since we launched our product, and not one other local authority has placed an order with Global Flood Solutions. Not one – despite it being internationally recognized as the best flood-defence product on the market, with gold-medal accreditation from industry specialists.

Local authorities seem to be wary of spending scarce resources on preventative measures. With something like flooding, which doesn't arise on a day-to-day basis, they'll take a chance and hope that they'll escape the next time. But sure enough, you turn on the TV news the next winter, and there you see Cork and several other towns and rural areas under water. And you see the pictures of the council workers in the pouring rain unloading hundreds of sandbags when the floods have already broken through and it's too late anyway.

The one council that took an order from us was Roscommon. That was in about September 2010. Roscommon bought €25,000 worth of product off us and it was badly needed. It kept us going, and we're grateful to Roscommon County Council for supporting one of their own. Neither Ger nor I was taking a salary out of the business at this stage; there was no money coming in. The word 'entrepreneur' gets bandied about a lot in this country, particularly among politicians and quangos and various government departments that are supposed to be promoting business and enterprise. And it conveys this image of prestige and wealth and big cars and fancy houses. But the reality is often the dead opposite. The reality is constant worry, uncertainty, bills piling up on the table and no money coming in to meet them. It's the stress about paying your mortgage and putting food on the table and paying all the expenses of your children going to school. It's a life of anxiety and, for some people, despair. You have no safety net and you don't know from week to week if your business is even going to survive.

Around this time, because there was nothing happening for us in Ireland, we started urgently looking at the UK. We didn't have the money to start our own hub in the UK from which we could distribute directly to the local authorities. So we knew we had to find a big distributor that already had relationships with our potential customers.

One day in that autumn of 2010 I picked up the phone and rang an outfit called SG Baker, a big operator in the packaging business. They started out supplying hessian bags to the potato industry and diversified into bulk bags for animal feeds, cereals, construction, logs, and so on. They also supplied sandbags to the municipal authorities across Britain. They are a Scottish company originally but have a big base in Grantham, Lincolnshire, too. So I referred them to our website and they asked us to send over some samples, which we did. They got back to us within a few days and invited us over to a meeting. They were very impressed with the product, you could tell just by talking to them on the phone. But, honest to God, we didn't have the price of the flights at the time. We had to borrow the money to pay for our flights and expenses to East Midlands airport.

We were picked up at the airport and taken to their premises in Grantham. It was a massive operation with an enormous yard and warehouse. The MD was a very astute Scotsman, Dennis Fearon. We sat in the boardroom, surrounded by Dennis and his management team. He was dying to know how we came up with this product. He was an expert in the packaging game and it was a mystery to him how two Paddies with no experience at all in the bag business had come up with it. So a lot of the meeting was spent trying to suss us out, and we knew well what they were trying to do. They fired dozens of questions at us about everything, from our German connection to our sales to date.

Ger:

Any technical questions, Shane would turn them over to me and I'd answer them best I could. Any financial questions, Shane would handle them. But we were both fairly tense because we had about eight different fellas in that boardroom looking at us and asking us this and that. And the bottom line was, we needed to make a sale here. We had to come away with something because we hadn't a bean. We were in serious need of cash flow.

At the same time, we could tell they were keen to make a deal. Eventually the crunch came. We were retailing a five-cell unit at €325. We said we'd give it to SG Baker for €225. And Dennis was more than happy with that margin. We started talking about a deal to distribute our product into the UK. In the end we negotiated a contract that would give SG Baker exclusive distribution rights for the next three years; it was worth almost €2 million if all agreed targets were achieved. I tried to stay cool, but inside I was dancing. Two million! And they put in an immediate order for €85,000. It was the lifeline we needed.

We finished up, shook hands and headed back to East Midlands airport. We were high as kites. Now, we weren't to know it at the time, but ultimately SG Baker weren't the right fit for us. They just didn't sell the product well, for some reason. But by the time we realized it wasn't working there, we had moved on a bit anyway. In fairness to them, they'd moved fast at the start and given us €85,000 at a time when we could have gone under. It was that close.

And the deal with SG Baker meant we could go back to the Roscommon County Enterprise Board and apply for further funding from them. This was one small arm of the state sector which, in our experience, worked very well and we owe a debt of gratitude to Louise Ward, CEO of the Roscommon County Enterprise Board and her deputy, Anne Browne, for giving us vital financial support and much encouragement at the time. The enterprise board came up with €15,000 for us each in salary grants. That was in early 2011, and again it was a lifeline because we'd made no further sales since the SG Baker deal. Once again we were hanging on by our fingertips.

Then, that spring, another cash injection came our way to keep us going – this time from America. We'd set up a new company in the US, GFS America, through a friend of ours (and former member of the 1989 Roscommon team), Frank McNamara from Oran. Frank has been based in the States for over twenty years and he is basically our point man in America and a valued partner in the business. The Springfield Water and Sewer Commission supplies water and waste treatment services to a large swathe of western Massachusetts. They came across our website, made contact with Frank and, without further ado, put in an order for $95,000.

In April 2011 we got our first major breakthrough. Frank took a call from the municipal authority for Medicine Hat, a city of about 60,000 in the Canadian province of Alberta. Their department of engineering services was in a state of emergency. Situated on the South Saskatchewan River, Medicine Hat is vulnerable to flooding in the spring when the snow melts in the Cypress Hills above the city. A few days earlier, the swollen river had breached the town's main dam. Someone in the local authority came across our website and made contact with Frank. (If we hadn't invested heavily in that website and in search-engine optimization, they might never have found us.) They asked dozens of technical questions, we were over and back to them with specifications and all sorts of data for two or three days. Then without further delay we received a purchase order worth well over $300,000. And they wanted the product fast. It was flown out from Germany within a couple of days and immediately deployed. It was a major milestone for us.

Still, we weren't out of the woods. The company had built up a lot of debt by then, and the Medicine Hat money was eaten up almost as soon as it came in. A few weeks later we went to a huge international trade show in Dubai, organized through a business friend of ours and another Roscommon man, Steve Fahey. Steve told us that at these trade shows people talked in billions rather than millions. There would be serious operators there and we couldn't turn up looking like a pair of navvies in our Sunday suits. We'd need better threads than that! The bills were piling up, but we put our best foot forward and headed for Louis Copeland's in Dublin. A couple of Canali suits later, plus all the trimmings and accessories, and we were ready for our first business trip to the Middle East. We mightn't have a bob to our name out there, but at least we'd look the part. The trip was a brilliant learning curve and paved the way for new opportunities in a massive market.

When we landed back in Dublin from Dubai we went straight to the RDS because a friend of ours, John Gillooly, was exhibiting his beautiful turf craft products at a trade show there. A few weeks earlier, various newspapers had run articles on our Medicine Hat deal and a couple of random fellas in the RDS, who knew me as a footballer, had seen the articles. And they said, 'We have the man for you.' Who's that, said I. And they said, 'Matty Walsh.' Now I didn't know Matty Walsh from fuckn Methuselah. Turned out he was the fella behind the MW Hire Group, an international plant-hire and machinery operation in Kilkenny. So we adjourned to Paddy Cullen's bar in Ballsbridge and the buckos rang Matty from there. He agreed to meet us the next day, so down we went to Kilkenny. Within a few hours Matty was our new distributor in Ireland. And he put in an order there and then for €80,000 worth of product. It was manna from heaven: we were on our knees; it would keep us going for another few months. We had the Canali suits on us for that meeting too, but I doubt they made much difference to Matty, truth be told.

Later that summer, on the back of further international coverage of our work in Canada, personnel from the Irish army came to us with an offer to test our system for its suitability in the military theatre. They thought it had potential applications here, and we did too. But the continuing problem was cash flow. With no financial cushion under us at all, we had to keep moving. We had a distributor in the UK, we had a distributor in Ireland, we'd now have to cast the net further afield. So towards the end of 2011 we made a strategic decision to set up an operation in Canada. On St Patrick's Day 2012, Ger flew out to Montreal.

Ger:

> We had shipped a container-load from Germany and it was on its way when I landed in Montreal. We had no order to meet that consignment. It was a bit of a gamble but we figured we'd need to have product on the ground. The first thing I needed was a warehouse to hold the consignment. Eventually, through a series of contacts I was put in touch with a company called Vitesse Transport, and we went into an alliance with them. We set up a Canadian company, got it registered, and then Shane came out for three months to start growing the business.

Our next breakthrough came in October 2012, when the NGO Concern placed a small order with us to deploy the Big Bag Defence System in Afghanistan. They would use it primarily in flood crises, acting as a barrier against mudslides or for river diversion and general flood defences. The money involved wasn't major, about €30,000, but it was huge for our credibility. It was validation from a highly reputable international organization. It meant we were proven in the field.

The Irish army's engineering corps meanwhile had tested our product meticulously. Their reports recommended that it could be used to erect solid defensive barriers outside a camp perimeter, chicanes, bunkers, and walls for military fortification. Because our cells would be filled with sand, they were a viable alternative to the more traditional steel walls which can generate significant shrapnel damage in any bomb blast. Word of mouth went round the military community and the European Union Training Mission (EUTM) got in touch with us. When they heard that Concern were already using the Big Bag, they became very interested. They invited us to tender for defence walls, blast walls and bunker management at their base in Somalia. We successfully tendered for a contract worth around $400,000, the company's biggest contract at the time. We would supply nearly 5,000 metres of product to the EUTM, and they wanted us out there to see how best it could be deployed. And we wanted to visit there anyway because it was our first big military contract, and we needed to see how it worked on the ground, what the army's needs were, and how it could be improved.

In the summer of 2013 we attended a UN business seminar, in conjunction with Enterprise Ireland, in New York. This was the second UN business seminar I'd attended with EI in New York, and both were very valuable networking opportunities. It resulted in our company being listed on the UN's official vendors website and allowed us to tender for upcoming contracts. Enterprise Ireland in our experience are a superb resource for Irish companies looking to penetrate international markets. They have a network of relationships around the world, their knowledge of the international scene is invaluable. Evelyn Smith of EI was particularly helpful to us in opening up a pathway into the United Nations. We will always be grateful to Evelyn and all the support staff at Enterprise Ireland for their commitment to us.

About ten days later we flew to Uganda, where we met up with the EUTM officers who would accompany us into Somalia. After a few days in Uganda we flew from Entebbe airport, Kampala, to Mogadishu International Airport (MIA). The latter airport is hard by the sea. As you approach the runway you actually think you're going to end up in the water, all you can see is water. Then suddenly you're on the runway and grinding to a halt.

Somalia is a country struggling for even a semblance of political and economic stability. It is a tragically poor and dangerous place. It is torn by conflict and crime. International agencies like the UN and the EUTM are trying to preserve a modicum of security. Their priority is to keep MIA open and secure. Without it, one of Somalia's last lifelines to the outside world would be shut down. The threat

from terrorism and general anarchy is real and ever-present. The city
of Mogadishu itself is a no-go area for visitors; we were told that a
white person alone on the street will survive for about fifteen minutes there before being kidnapped or robbed or murdered.

A bus was waiting on the runway to take us to the terminal. We
got off the bus to be greeted by the sight of five policemen flailing
away at a young man on the ground with their batons. He had his
hands around his head, trying to protect himself. It was a fairly unset-
tling first impression. Inside the terminal our security detail was
waiting for us. Elsewhere the atmosphere was thick with tension;
you could feel it hanging in the air. We were escorted under armed
guard to airport security check. The security officer glared at me cold
and hard, like I was a terrorist, or an alien from outer space.

There was nobody at passport control; the booths where you
would expect to find immigration officers checking your passport
were empty. Our security detail consisted of two Irish officers from
the Army Rangers, and three European army officers who were also
part of the EUTM. They were all armed. One of them collected our
passports. He went away to get them stamped, but when he came
back two of the passports were missing. We stood around for twenty
minutes while the matter was sorted. We'd only brought hand lug-
gage with us, but one of the EUTM fellas had checked a bag in the
hold. There was no carousel to collect it from, so we went back outside to try and find it. One of our security detail who knew the lie of
the land stopped a passing airport worker and asked him to find the
bag. This young fella disappeared and came back a few minutes later,
saying there was no sign of it. And the officer just stared him down
and ordered him to 'Get the bag.'

The fella came back a second time empty-handed and shook his
head: 'No bag.' He was apparently looking for some financial incentive before the bag could be located.

At this point our officer suddenly turned very serious. He frightened the shit outta this young fella with just his body language and
the look of pure anger in his face. He told the lad that if he didn't
come back with the bag, he'd be in a whole world of trouble.

The fella scurried off and came back a few minutes later with the bag. He didn't get any tip for his troubles.

We were rushed into waiting armoured vehicles, which took us the short journey to the MIA camp. This was the military base protecting the airport and other vital infrastructure such as the hospital and the EUTM HQ. We were issued with security passes and military clothing before passing inside.

The MIA camp is a massive operation. There's a separate UN camp and NATO camp and EUTM camp, but they're all beside each other, functioning as part of the same gigantic campus. Our accommodation was a twenty-foot commercial steel container converted into a living quarters with a toilet and shower, bunk beds made out of plywood and four-by-twos, and a few hooks to hang your clothes. She was a fairly basic billet: rusty and dingy and hot as the hammers of hell. This was to be our home for the next four weeks. When we arrived, there were a couple of Somalis up on the roof packing down sand. We were wondering what they were doing up there. Turned out they were proofing the roof with dry-packed sand to protect it from incoming mortars. I'd slept in a few rough joints in my time, but never a gaff like this. There was also a small hospital on the campus and an overground bunker; you were told to make a dash for that bunker if the camp came under enemy fire.

The main enemy was the Al-Shabaab jihadi brigade. They had a bloody history of destruction and mayhem in Somalia. Just two months later, some of these lunatics would launch the attack on a Nairobi shopping mall that left over sixty people dead. Everyone was on high alert in the MIA camp because two or three nights previously they'd received intelligence that an assault was imminent. They were particularly concerned about an attack from the sea that bordered the camp on one side. If militants got to the beach, they could easily launch rockets and mortars from there. The resident soldiers had dug a dyke into the beach, a trench covered with stacks of razor wire. Then they'd erected a long wall with our bags and filled them with sand to form the next barrier. And outside the perimeter of the camp was a stone wall, also topped with razor wire. Inside the camp you had soldiers on permanent patrol from a couple of towers overlooking the whole surrounding area. Any people seen attempting to cross the barriers outside would be shot. We were also strictly instructed to inform the fellas in the towers whenever we were leaving the camp, otherwise we'd be shot too; it was as simple as that.

Our job there was to help the army engineers conduct surveys of the terrain and come up with the best deployment strategy for our product. Ger liaised closely with them. We were outside the camp practically every day, conducting surveys and designing various configurations for deployment.

There was a refugee camp under UN protection about five or six miles away. They were using the BBDS too, and so we had to travel there a number of times. The trip made everyone nervous. We were issued with helmets and military fatigues and bulletproof vests that were padded front and back with steel plates. They were heavy to wear, and when you were cooped up inside the armoured car you felt like you were sitting in a furnace. Within minutes we were drowning in sweat. No one looked forward to these trips; no one spoke, once the engines started.

You had the driver and the fella sitting beside him in the front seat, you had the gunners manning their machine guns, and you had special forces troops sitting behind me and Ger. They were a mixture of European military: Irish, French, Italian, Dutch, German, Swedish. The Irish Army Rangers we met were very impressive people: capable, articulate, serious operators. Their presence among us was comforting. As civilians we were pretty much helpless in this environment. When you got into that armoured car, you were totally in their hands.

The armoured cars could withstand landmines and various improvised explosive devices. When the convoy left camp it didn't hang around. The drivers hit top gear and travelled at high speeds across the bumpy terrain. There was almost no suspension in these vehicles, they felt absolutely rigid, and if you didn't hold on to something you'd be tossed around inside like a rag doll. Without the helmet you'd have picked up a nasty head wound pretty quick. The noise inside the belly of the vehicle was deafening.

The army surveyors had identified a particular stretch of ground between the two camps that was most vulnerable to an enemy attack. It seemingly offered the best terrain from which to launch mortars and rockets. This stretch of ground, maybe no more than 400 metres, was known as the Kill Zone. If one of the vehicles got hit, at least one more would be there to offer rescue and support. If the front vehicle was hit and immobilized, the rear vehicle would push it out of the Kill Zone, and vice versa.

The refugee camp was a truly shocking experience. The stench of human sickness and destitution was everywhere. The poverty was beyond abject. This was a country not just racked by war, but famine too. It was a hell on earth. Everywhere there were warlords and fanatics who didn't think twice about murdering men, women and children. And here in the middle of it all were people trying to offer some hope and some protection. Ger and I were proud, as a young company, to be playing a small part in helping to protect the refugees. We were proud to see our own invention, our wall of sand-filled systems, deployed in a long, symmetrical line around the perimeter of the camp. It was an impressive sight, if I may say so.

There was a bar in the MIA camp, but there was no big social scene. It was a place to relax for a few hours over a couple of cold beers before retiring for the night. Pretty much everybody was in bed by nine o'clock and up at five or six the next morning. At night I found it impossible to sleep. Back in the container, on the top bunk bed, I'd spend hours staring up at the ceiling. The heat was unbearable, my nerves were on edge and my mind was racing with what I'd seen and heard and smelled. I'd find myself lying awake, pining for my wife and kids back in the safety of home.

I was thinking too of my first ever job, some thirty years earlier, doing the milk round with John Leonard. Looking back, it felt like such a sweet and innocent time. And in hindsight too I could see that doing that job, and loving the doing of it, was maybe the first stirrings of whatever entrepreneurial spirit I had. And it was that same spirit, I suppose, that had taken me eventually to this strange world where everything I'd assumed about the norms of society and the rules of civilization had been turned upside down. I couldn't help but reflect on how far I'd come, in every sense.

I was filled with admiration for the soldiers, civilian personnel, charity workers and all the people who were out here, far from their homes too, trying to help the suffering citizens of this wretched place. These people were putting their lives on the line and living in harsh conditions to do the best they could in awful circumstances. And because I was on the ground I felt I could truly appreciate the calibre of the Irish military staff we worked with out there; they are outstanding ambassadors for our country.

Back at the airport for our flight home, passports went missing again and the atmosphere was as tense as ever. We didn't really feel safe until the plane had taken off because you had this abiding sense that anything could happen at any given time. Coming out of Dublin airport I was grateful for the wind and rain on my face. I headed west for the green fields of Roscommon – and a championship showdown with the mighty St Faithleachs of Ballyleague.

Epilogue

As I write this in August 2014 I've just come back from a week-long business trip to New York.

Ger and I have seen a lot of airports in the four years since we set up Global Flood Solutions. North America, Europe, Africa, the UK and the Middle East have all been part of our itinerary. Ireland has been the least welcoming destination for our product, but it was never going to be big enough anyway to sustain the model we had in mind. From day one we knew we had to go global, and it's been a constant source of encouragement that international markets have been very open to us. It has made us realize one fundamental truth about our business: we have a good product and people want it.

The challenge has been to break into the industries and organizations that are a good fit for our system. Naturally enough, we've had to go to them and make them aware of its existence. This is where all the travelling has come into it. Any new company is a very fragile entity, and we knew we had to keep moving and continue meeting people if ours was going to survive. We had no safety net, we couldn't afford to stand still. We had to learn a huge amount about these industries and organizations in a short space of time. We were complete strangers to the vast military and humanitarian complex; to the oil and gas industry; to the field of environmental protection; to government organizations, foreign municipalities and international NGOs. All these different sectors have their own protocols and procedures, and we had to do a great deal of planning and research in order to start making inroads. We were doing it from scratch. It was a steep learning curve and a non-stop, seven-day-a-week commitment.

We are still a very young company. But we managed to survive the difficult earliest days – the time when the vast majority of start-ups go under – sometimes by the skin of our teeth, and now we're a stable entity on solid ground. If I was to describe it in phases, I'd say we're coming out of the start-up phase and moving into the growth phase.

A lot of our growth is coming through partnerships with international engineering companies, particularly in the mining, oil and gas industries. These are multinational companies and they see a lot of potential applications for our product in water containment, water management, or environmental issues around water. For example, security around tailings ponds is a major priority for such companies: they need to be able to stop breaches in a tailings pond quickly and at short notice; likewise they need to be able to build up levees quickly if they have to pump in extra sludge or water. We feel our company and products have a big role to play in that sector worldwide.

International organizations with a humanitarian mission are starting to use our system for protection against flooding, for water diversion and security fortification. It happens to be quite a bureaucratic sector, so any negotiations take a long time to come to fruition. We believe we are very close now to sealing a major deal in this sector.

We have plans also to set up a manufacturing base in Roscommon. Our German partners will continue to make the cells because they have the management, the industry certification and the quality controls in place. We don't want to tamper with that in any shape or form. But we feel the assembling, packaging and exporting can be done from Roscommon. After all, it's where we're from, it's where we live, and we want to give something back. We would be proud to be able to create jobs in our home place. The neglected towns and villages of Ireland need jobs, people and access to the knowledge economy. We hope to play our part in this. I realize it's going against the trend of the last thirty years that have seen vast swathes of the worldwide manufacturing economy migrate to the Far East. And, of course, the costs are a lot lower there. But I think too that Western economies and their political leaders are beginning to find out how much this is costing them in terms of employment and social capital. And some of them are starting to rediscover the value of self-sufficiency.

It's all very much a work in progress for us, but it's only when we look back over the last four years that we can see how far we've come and how much we've learned. In that time we've managed to consolidate, to put the company on a stable footing and prepare it for major expansion. We are confident and hopeful that this is going to happen in the next few years.

On the football front, I had a bit of a forlorn moment on 24 November 2013. It was on the pitch in Dr Hyde Park. We had just lost our Connacht title in an epic match against the Mayo champions, Castlebar Mitchels. I was hobbling off the field after watching the Castlebar lads lift the cup. I'd wrenched my calf badly, early in extra time, and the shot of pain that came with it was lacerating. But obviously losing the title hurt a lot more. I was now forty-two, going on forty-three. And I remember distinctly looking back towards the goalmouth at the Hospital end and wondering to myself, 'Is that the last time I'm going to stand in those goals?'

All of a sudden I was getting a bit nostalgic, like a lad who was about to say goodbye to it all. But I suppose, typical enough, that mood didn't last long. Back in the dressing room I was togging in when I found myself saying to myself, 'Nah, fuckit, I'll give it another year.' And there and then the crisis was over!

If I wasn't playing on such a good team, I think I'd have packed it in a long time ago. But when you're surrounded by talented and highly motivated players who want to keep on winning, it's easy to continue. People were wondering whether we'd have the appetite to go back to the slog of training after winning the All-Ireland, but it doesn't feel like a slog when you know there's more silverware waiting on the horizon. We came down from the high of St Patrick's Day after about a month of celebrating and got back to business. We more or less breezed through Roscommon and Connacht again until Castlebar put a halt to our gallop.

But once the year turned we set new goals again, and our goal for 2014 is to win a fifth county title in a row and reclaim our provincial title. If we're lucky enough to do that, there'll be no thoughts of retirement until the spring of 2015. But whenever our season ends, I'll probably call it quits after that. *Probably*.

But I will definitely remain in the game. I'll take a coaching role, maybe with our young goalkeepers, with a view to coaching and managing teams further down the line. The club is at the centre of my life and there's no way I'll walk away from it all. I wouldn't want to, and it's just not possible anyway. Lauren and Abby are playing their football there and I look forward to following their progress in the years to come. Lauren is on the Roscommon County Under 14 team this year, and Abby is going to be a county player in time as well. They both have the talent, and they love playing the game. So the cycle of sport continues, the cycle of life continues, and the club is where it all begins and ends.

As long as I'm playing, I can't afford to think of the day when I won't be playing. As always, it's about the here and now. It's about the training and planning and playing the next game. I know that the exit door is beckoning but I'm not quite ready yet to take my leave of the dressing room.

For I have loved this world. I have loved living in this bubble. Serious sport is a form of escapism from real life, and the dressing room is the bolthole to which you escape; it's your sanctuary and your retreat from the outside world. You can say things and do things there that you wouldn't get away with in civilian society. There's a freedom to be found there. And part of the joy for me is that it is a man's world. I say that without apology or reservation. It's a place where men are men and you can be true to that side of your nature.

I don't think there's ever been a day when I felt I didn't belong in that environment. I was confident and happy in a dressing room from the first day I entered one. I knew I was never going to be good in school but I sensed that I could be good in here. I might even get to be the top dog. One way or another I knew it was the place for me. I could express myself in here, and out there, on the football field, in front of an audience. I joined that secret society as a gosson and I've never wanted to be anywhere else, I've never wanted to inhabit a different world.

I've lost count of the number of players I've shared that world with. And I would have to say that I can count very few of them among my close friends. The relationships in there are transient and superficial, by and large. You can have the most intense experiences of your life with some of those lads, but it doesn't really last beyond those four walls and beyond the four lines of the football pitch. It doesn't really survive in the outside world, because the bonds that are forged in there are manufactured, essentially. You are brought together by a shared goal, by the possibility of achievement, and when we no longer have that in common, the bonds just wither and fade. Life takes over: your family, your work, your day-to-day reality. We go our separate ways. You may have had the best times of your life with them and we might still meet up for a couple of pints or a game of golf. And soon as you do, the old banter and crack starts up automatically all over again.

But beyond that, we resume our different lives on civvy street. Like a certain type of hothouse flower, I suppose, the friendships forged in that dressing room don't really survive the transplant to the world beyond it.

Is that a source of regret? No. It's just how it is, it's just how it works. We've had our time together. We were the animals in the zoo, the prisoners in the jail, the zombies in the institution. We'll always have that, and it's plenty, more than enough.

And I can honestly say with hand on heart that I don't regret a day of the thirty-five years I spent in that place. I had the most fantastic times and the best education I could ever have wanted. I was blessed and lucky to wring so much out of it, to win the medals I did, and to compile such a catalogue of memories and stories.

And I'm so glad to be able to say that I didn't waste the talent I discovered as a child in Castlerea. I didn't throw it away. I put it to good use, I extracted the maximum from it. A regret like that would be unbearable. But, thanks be to God, I don't have to carry it. I think I honoured whatever talent I inherited.

The will to win, to succeed and to achieve has been with me since childhood, and I am forever grateful to my parents Tommy and Pauline for the great foundation they gave me. I have tried to carry these traits into every part of my life.

I hope to be in this world for many years to come, but the day I have to leave it, I will have no regrets. I will have given life my best shot. I'll have had my ups and downs – but it is impossible to keep a man down who keeps getting up. When you think positively and surround yourself with positive people, as I have tried to do in my life, every day is a fantastic day.

Acknowledgements

I have so many people to thank for the good fortune and many blessings that have come my way in life. But first and foremost it started with my wonderful parents, Tommy and Pauline, who gave me all the love and support you could wish for. A big thanks also to my brothers, Jason and Evan, and to my brother-in-law Jonathan and my sisters-in-law, Liz and Catherine. I owe a debt of gratitude to all my extended family in Castlerea and beyond. A special mention to my deceased aunt Peggy, and to my deceased uncle Johnny, who was both my biggest critic and my number one fan. The countless hours spent in uncle Johnny and auntie Kathleen's house, arguing over football, is one of my most treasured memories of growing up in Castlerea. Thanks for the memories. Sharon's parents, John and Rosie, have been great to me; they've also been kind and caring grandparents to Lauren and Abby. I have a lot of friends with whom I've shared great craic, among them Paddy Downey, Declan Kelly, Paddy and Carmel Harrison, Ronnie and Ann Byrne, Seamie and Brenda Gallagher, and Martin Curran. I send my warmest gratitude to all my other friends and acquaintances, too numerous to mention here.

My working life has been enriched by the many colleagues and employers over the years who in time became friends as well. To my two business partners in GFS, Ger Brennan and Frank McNamara, a sincere thanks. They have made a huge contribution in developing the business internationally, and their loyalty and dedication in the face of adversity have been admirable. They are entrepreneurs to the core. Thanks also to their wives, Lisa and Eileen.

We have been helped at crucial junctures by people who were generous with their time and expertise when it was much needed. Special thanks to Brigadier General Gerald Aherne (retired), Tom Purcell, Gerry Mongey, trade commissioner at the Embassy of Canada in

Dublin, Paraic McGrath of ESB International and Evelyn Smith at Enterprise Ireland. In Germany we were so lucky to find partners who shared our vision: Ulrich Dworznik and Elisabeth Harbeck have been unstinting in their efforts to make our idea become a sustainable business, and they have become great friends. All my respect and gratitude to Ulrich and Elisabeth. In Canada, Claude Dauphin and Jean-François Cloutier have done invaluable work for us, as have Murray Smith at Hatch Engineering and Randy Clarke and Darryl Olson at Crosswind Resources. Matty Walsh of MW Hire in Kilkenny has given us staunch support. Many thanks, too, to Roscommon County Council, to Louise Ward and Anne Browne at Roscommon Enterprise Board, to Pearse Gately and Jimmy Darcy, and to our accountants Michael Cuddy & Co.

In my sporting life I can only thank from the bottom of my heart all the coaches, mentors and managers who played their part in helping me along the way. They gave their time and knowledge to me, man and boy, and quite simply I wouldn't have had the career I enjoyed without them. To every player I ever shared a dressing room with, many thanks for the laughs, the medals and the memories. St Brigid's has become a big part of my life, and many in the club have been very supportive over the years. Particular thanks to Sean Kilbride, P. J. Martin and Danny Murray, to name but a few. To the management team – Kevin McStay, Benny O'Brien and Liam McHale – thanks for the opportunity. To Pat Regan, the team physio, thanks for keeping me intact physically and mentally – not an easy job. I must also acknowledge the kind help I have received from Dr Martin Daly and Dr Damien Tiernan over the years in assessing and controlling my injuries. To my Brigid's teammates one and all, too many to mention individually, my sincerest thanks for your commitment to excellence and for delivering our greatest honour. Thanks to the tea ladies who made numerous cups for me over the years, to Noel Murray for his encouragement, and to Conor and Aine Martin for the slagging. And a special acknowledgement to Eamon O'Rourke: it would not have been possible to win the All-Ireland without you.

This book wouldn't have happened without the foresight and enthusiasm of Michael McLoughlin at Penguin Ireland. Also at

Penguin, Brendan Barrington has been a superb editor of the raw – sometimes very raw – material. Tommy Conlon of the *Sunday Independent* dragged the material out of me and turned it into the words you see on the page. We had some fun doing it. I think he captured my voice; I thank him for his work. The book needed quite a bit of research, and much of it was spent in the offices of the *Roscommon Herald* and *Westmeath Independent*. A big thank you to Christina McHugh and Ian Cooney at the *Herald*, and to Kieran Galvin and Tadhg Carey at the *Independent*, for giving us their time and opening up their archives. Thanks also to Anna Barrett for transcribing dozens of hours of recorded interviews under the pressure of an unforgiving deadline.

So many people have helped me in so many aspects of my life that it would be impossible to mention them all here. But let me take this opportunity to acknowledge their support and to express my heartfelt gratitude.

Finally, and most importantly, thanks to the three people who have the most unfortunate of jobs, that of sharing a house with me. The proudest moment of my life was marrying Sharon. We have two gorgeous girls who thankfully take after their mother. Lauren and Abby are our most valuable treasures. As a dad and husband I am extremely proud of you all and grateful for all your love and support.

Shane Curran
Cam
August 2014

Index